Antonin Artaud and the Healing Practices of Language

Antonin Artaud and the Healing Practices of Language

How Life Matters in Artaud's Later Writings

Joeri Visser

BLOOMSBURY ACADEMIC
NEW YORK · LONDON · OXFORD · NEW DELHI · SYDNEY

BLOOMSBURY ACADEMIC
Bloomsbury Publishing Inc
1385 Broadway, New York, NY 10018, USA
50 Bedford Square, London, WC1B 3DP, UK
29 Earlsfort Terrace, Dublin 2, Ireland

BLOOMSBURY, BLOOMSBURY ACADEMIC and the Diana logo are trademarks
of Bloomsbury Publishing Plc

First published in the United States of America 2021
This paperback edition published 2023

Copyright © Joeri Visser, 2021

Cover design by Eleanor Rose
Cover image @ Getty Images

All rights reserved. No part of this publication may be reproduced or transmitted in any form or by any means, electronic or mechanical, including photocopying, recording, or any information storage or retrieval system, without prior permission in writing from the publishers.

Bloomsbury Publishing Inc does not have any control over, or responsibility for, any third-party websites referred to or in this book. All internet addresses given in this book were correct at the time of going to press. The author and publisher regret any inconvenience caused if addresses have changed or sites have ceased to exist, but can accept no responsibility for any such changes.

Whilst every effort has been made to locate copyright holders the publishers would be grateful to hear from any person(s) not here acknowledged.

Library of Congress Control Number: 2021935679

ISBN: HB: 978-1-5013-7232-2
PB: 978-1-5013-7236-0
ePDF: 978-1-5013-7234-6
eBook: 978-1-5013-7233-9

Typeset by Integra Software Services Pvt. Ltd.

To find out more about our authors and books visit www.bloomsbury.com and sign up for our newsletters.

[T]here is life to live
that is all
[…]
I want to live
I will never
again, under
any pretext
whatsoever
pretend
to live
I do not want to
simulate a feeling
I want to live it.[1]
—Antonin Artaud, Notebook 287, CI,
p. 794

Life is not a
stationary state—
it is only worthy
to the extent
that it changes[2]
—Antonin Artaud Notebook 326, CI,
p. 1433

"When I use a word," Humpty Dumpty said in rather a scornful tone, "it means just what I choose it to mean—neither more nor less."
"The question is," said Alice, "whether you can make words mean different things."
"The question is," said Humpty Dumpty, "which is to be master—that's all."[3]
—Lewis Carroll, Through the Looking Glass, *p. 223*

Contents

Notes on the Translation and the Abbreviations		x
Avant-Propos: Writing for a People to Come. Or, Looking for an Intercessor		xv
Introduction: Artaud—A Life in Language. Or What Comes with Language?		1
The Enchantment of Marseille		1
A Violent Loss of Life		3
Reading the Writings of a Madman		8
Still Relevant Forces at Work		11
1	The Healing Practices of Language: On Flesh, Mind, and Expression	15
	Do We Know What the Body Can Do?	15
	Articulating the Flexional Singularity of the Body	16
	To Believe in This World	18
	The Dance of the Flesh	21
	The Articulation of a Vital Body	22
	The Exploration of the Infra-Sense of the Body	25
	The Vitality of the Flesh	26
	A Commitment to Life	29
	The Healing Powers of the Flesh	31
	In Praise of a Madman	34
	An Enterprise of Health	37
2	A Zoology of Language: On the Disorder of Language and Artaud's Poetics	45
	The Outside of Language	45
	A Cynical Reading of Spinoza	47
	Spinoza's Confusion	48
	The Forces of Zoe	50
	Destratification and the Art of Caution	51
	To Believe in Grammar	53
	A Zoology of Language	54

	Untranslatable Forces	56
	To Have Done with Mythomania	57
	Artaud Poetics: The Creation of Animated Words	60
	A New Human Agony	62
	"Only the Madman Is Really Calm"	64
3	A Magical and Materialist Theosophy: On the Development of Artaud's Later Works	67
	The Man Crucified on Golgotha	67
	"I Have to Laugh When You Talk about His Message"	69
	Artaud in the Land of the Tarahumaras	71
	Our Advanced Civilization and the Search of an Organic Culture	74
	Expressing the Mexican Discoveries	75
	Violating the Art of Caution	77
	A Sense of Persecution and Megalomania	81
	A New Religion	84
	The Healing Powers of Magic	87
	A Magical and Materialist Theosophy	89
	"Man Will Find Nothing in Artaud's Work"	90
4	The Writing of Cruelty: On the Art of Crescive Writing	97
	Artaud's Return to Paris	97
	"I Ended Up Hanging/a Door in Language"	100
	The Theater of Cruelty and Language	103
	An Impossible Theater	105
	Cruelty as Necessity and Life	107
	Cruelty as a Healing Practice	109
	A Concrete and Physical Language	111
	The Writing of Cruelty I: From a Mechanized Anatomy to a Machinic Anatomy	114
	The Writing of Cruelty II: The True Story of Jesus Christ	120
	The Writing of Cruelty III: The Laboratory of Life	123
	Practices of Creative Writing	126
	Practices of Performative Writing	128
	Practices of Asemic Writing	131
	The Art of Crescive Writing	132
	"[Life] Is Only Worthy/to the Extent/That It Changes"	134

Conclusion: Toward a Postsecular Religion of Language. Or, etc., etc.	145
A Treatment of Auto-Detoxification	145
The Contract with Nature	150
To Believe in the Flesh	152
A Postsecular Society of Immanence	155
A Postsecular Religion of Language	157
Postscriptum: Reading Artaud Today. Or, a Plea for a Language in Movement	163
References	166
Index	177

Notes on the Translation and the Abbreviations

There is a growing interest in the works of Antonin Artaud that is manifested by different exhibitions of his drawings and manuscripts and an expansion of the publications, monographs, and translations that are undertaken. Only a small part of Artaud's writings, however, has yet been translated into English. The quality of these available writings differs and I have, therefore, if appropriate or necessary, modified one or two words in these translations. To enable the reader to compare the two, the French originals are reproduced in the endnotes. For this book, I have nevertheless decided to use the available English translations for two reasons: firstly, to show the reader the availability and location of the English translations of a part of Artaud's works (along with the French original) and secondly, to critically reconsider and discuss some of these translations. In the text, we use the following abbreviations in reference to these translations:

AN *Artaud Anthology*. Trans. Daisy Aldan, David Rattray and others. Ed. Jack Hirschman. San Francisco: City Lights Books, 1965.
CW *Collected Works*. Trans. Victor Corti. vol. 1. Parchment: River Run Press, 1968.
SW *Selected Writings*. Trans. Helen Weaver. Ed. Susan Sontag. California, University of California Press, 1976.
TD *The Theatre and Its Double*. Trans. Mary Caroline Richards. New York: Grove Press, 1958.
WRS *Watchfiends and Rack Screams: Works from the Final Period*. Trans. Clayton Eshleman. Boston: Exact Change, 1995.

Many texts by Artaud, and mainly his later works, have not yet been translated into English. For the original French texts that I have translated for this book, I have used the *Œuvres complètes*, published by Gallimard, which was edited by Paule Thévenin. Ranging from tome I (published in 1956) to tome XXVI (published in 1994), Thévenin edited the first fourteen tomes, which are mostly and more or less thematically ordered, together with Artaud (who reread and corrected the texts) and ordered and corrected the other tomes, which consisted mainly of the many notebooks from Rodez herself. Because of her death in 1993 and the ongoing polemics around Artaud's inheritance, Thévenin's intended last six tomes (the *Œuvres complètes* should have ranged to tome XXXII) have never been published. Apart from these works, I have used the well-structured and annotated selection of Artaud's works by Évelyn Grossman that was published in a chronological overview as *Œuvres*, published by Quarto, in 2004. Because Thévenin's edition is unfinished, I have used different sources for Artaud's later writings. The translations of these texts, along with the other French sources that have not been translated in English, are mine. Especially Artaud's later notebooks are written in a hastened but decided manner. Whenever possible, I have also translated the mistakes, grammatical errors or deviances, and cross-outs in these writings. Translating Artaud is not an easy task and is always open to discussion. To fully account for the constitutive play with words in Artaud's writings and to facilitate a critical reconsideration of these translations, I have reproduced the French originals in the endnotes. For the French original texts, I use the following abbreviations:

OCI* *Tome I. Volume 1. Préambule—Adresse au Pape—Adresse au Dalaï-Lama—Correspondance avec Jacques Rivière—L'Ombilic des Limbes—Le Pèse-nerfs suivi des Fragments d'un Journal d'Enfer—L'Art et la mort—Premiers Poèmes (1913-1923)—Premières Proses—Tric Trac du Ciel—Bilboquet—Poèmes (1924-1935) Textes Surréalistes.* Ed. Paule Thévenin. Paris: Gallimard, 1976.

OCI** *Tome I. Volume 2. Lettres. Appendice.* Ed. Paule Thévenin. Paris: Gallimard, 1970.

OCII *Tome II. Théâtre Alfred Jarry—Une Pantomime—Un Argument pour la Scène—Deux Projets de Mise en Scène—Notes sur "les Tricheurs" de Steve Passeur—Comptes Rendus—À Propos d'une Pièce Perdue—À Propos de la Littérature et des Arts Plastiques.* Ed. Paule Thévenin. Paris: Gallimard, 1961.

OCIII *Tome III. Scenarii—À Propos du Cinéma—Lettres—Interviews.* Ed. Paule Thévenin. Paris: Gallimard, 1961.

OCIV *Tome IV. Le Théâtre et son Double—Le Théâtre de Séraphin—Les Cenci.* Ed. Paule Thévenin. Paris: Gallimard, 1964.

OCV *Tome V. Autour du Théâtre et son Double et des Cenci.* Ed. Paule Thévenin. Paris: Gallimard, 1964.

OCVI   Tome VI. *Le Moine de Lewis raconté par Antonin Artaud*. Ed. Paule Thévenin. Paris: Gallimard, 1966.

OCVII   Tome VII. *Héliogabale ou l'Anarchiste Couronné. Les Nouvelles Révélations de l'Être*. Ed. Paule Thévenin. Paris: Gallimard, 1982.

OCVIII Tome VIII. *De Quelques Problèmes D'Actualité aux Messages Révolutionnaires. Lettres de Mexique*. Ed. Paule Thévenin. Paris: Gallimard, 1971.

OCIX   Tome IX. *Les Tarahumaras—Lettres de Rodez*. Ed. Paule Thévenin. Paris: Gallimard, 1979.

OCX   Tome X. *Lettres écrites de Rodez (1943–1944)*. Ed. Paule Thévenin. Paris: Gallimard, 1974.

OCXI   Tome XI. *Lettres écrites de Rodez (1945–1946)*. Ed. Paule Thévenin. Paris: Gallimard, 1974.

OCXII   Tome XII. *Artaud le Mômo. Ci-gît précédé de la Culture Indienne*. Ed. Paule Thévenin. Paris: Gallimard, 1971.

OCXIII Tome XIII. *Van Gogh le Suicidé de la Société. Pour en Finir avec le Jugement de Dieu suivi de Le Théâtre de la Cruauté. Lettres à Propos de Pour en Finir avec le Jugement de Dieu*. Ed. Paule Thévenin. Paris: Gallimard, 1974.

OCXIV* Tome XIV. Volume 1. *Suppôts et Suppliciations*. Ed. Paule Thévenin. Paris: Gallimard, 1978.

OCXIV** Tome XIV. Volume 2. *Suppôts et Suppliciations*. Ed. Paule Thévenin. Paris: Gallimard, 1978.

OCXV   Tome XV. *Cahiers de Rodez (Février–Avril 1945)*. Ed. Paule Thévenin. Paris: Gallimard, 1981.

OCXVI   Tome XVI. *Cahiers de Rodez (Mai–Juin 1945)*. Ed. Paule Thévenin. Paris: Gallimard, 1981.

OCXVII Tome XVII. *Cahiers de Rodez (Juillet–Août 1945)*. Ed. Paule Thévenin. Paris: Gallimard, 1982.

OCXVIII Tome XVIII. *Cahiers de Rodez (Septembre–Novembre 1945)*. Ed. Paule Thévenin. Paris: Gallimard, 1983.

OCXIX   Tome XIX. *Cahiers de Rodez (Décembre 1945–Janvier 1946)*. Ed. Paule Thévenin. Paris: Gallimard, 1984.

OCXX   Tome XX. *Cahiers de Rodez (Février–Mars 1946)*. Ed. Paule Thévenin. Paris: Gallimard, 1984.

OCXXI   Tome XXI. *Cahiers de Rodez (Avril–25 Mai 1946)*. Ed. Paule Thévenin. Paris: Gallimard, 1985.

OCXXII	*Tome XXII. Cahiers du Retour à Paris (26 Mai–Août 1946).* Ed. Paule Thévenin. Paris: Gallimard, 1986.
OCXXIII	*Tome XXIII. Cahiers du Retour à Paris (Août–Septembre 1946).* Ed. Paule Thévenin. Paris: Gallimard, 1987.
OCXXIV	*Tome XXIV. Cahiers du Retour à Paris (Octobre–Novembre 1946).* Ed. Paule Thévenin. Paris: Gallimard, 1988.
OCXXV	*Tome XXV. Cahiers du Retour à Paris (Décembre 1946–Janvier 1947).* Ed. Paule Thévenin. Paris: Gallimard, 1990.
OCXXVI	*Tome XXVI. Histoire Vécue d'Artaud-Mômo. Tête à Tête.* Ed. Paule Thévenin. Paris: Gallimard, 1994.
CI	*Cahiers d'Ivry (Février 1947–Mars 1948).* Ed. Évelyne Grossman. Paris: Gallimard, 2011.
DM	*50 Dessins pour Assassiner la Magie.* Paris: Gallimard, 2004.
ER	*Nouveaux Écrits de Rodez. Lettres au Docteur Ferdière 1943–1946 et autres Textes Inédits.* Paris: Gallimard, 1977.
GA	*Lettres à Génica Athanasiou.* Paris: Gallimard, 1969.
LET	*Lettres. 1937–1943.* Ed. Serge Malausséna. Paris: Gallimard, 2015.
O	*Œuvres.* Ed. Évelyne Grossman. Paris: Quarto, 2004.

The works of Gilles Deleuze and Félix Guattari play an important role in my reading and understanding of Artaud. For the references to their works, I have also decided to use abbreviations. I think that an abbreviation more effectively locates Deleuze's (and Guattari's) texts instead of a year of publishing. The translations of his works are easily available and are generally good. I have nevertheless compared these English translations with the French originals and sometimes commented on the problems of certain words in the translation. For the references to the English translations of Deleuze (and Guattari), we use the following abbreviations:

C2	Deleuze, Gilles. *The Time-Image.* Trans. Hugh Tomlinson and Robert Galeta. London: Continuum, 1989.
CC	Deleuze, Gilles. *Essays Critical and Clinical.* Trans. Daniel Smith and Michael Greco. London: Verso, 1998.
D	Deleuze, Gilles and Claire Parnet. *Dialogues II.* 1987. Trans. Hugh Tomlinson and Barbara Habberjam. New York: CUP, 2007.
FB	Deleuze, Gilles. *Francis Bacon: The Logic of Sensation.* Trans. Daniel Smith. London: Continuum, 2003.

K	Deleuze, Gilles and Félix Guattari. *Kafka. Toward a Minor Literature*. Trans. Dana Polan. Minneapolis: UMP, 1986.
LS	Deleuze, Gilles. *The Logic of Sense*. Trans. Mark Lester. London: Continuum, 1990.
N	Deleuze, Gilles. *Negotiations. 1972–1990*. Trans. Martin Joughin. New York: Columbia University Press, 1995.
PI	Deleuze, Gilles. *Pure Immanence: Essays on a Life*. Trans. Anne Boyman. New York: Urzone, 2001.
S	Deleuze, Gilles. *Spinoza: Practical Philosophy*. Trans. Robert Hurley. San Francisco: City Light Books, 1988.
TP	Deleuze, Gilles and Félix Guattari. *A Thousand Plateaus*. 1987. Trans. Brian Massumi. London: Continuum, 1988.
WP	Deleuze, Gilles and Félix Guattari. *What Is Philosophy?* Trans. Graham Burchell and Hugh Tomlinson. London: Verso, 1994.

Notes to Epigraphs

1 "il y a de la vie à vivre / c est tout / […] je veux vivre / je ne veux plus / jamais sous / quelque pretexte / que ce soit / faire semblant / de vivre / je ne veux plus / simuler un sentiment / je veux le vivre" [my translation].

2 "La vie n est pas un / etat stationnaire – / elle ne vaut que / dans la mesure / où elle change" [my translation].

3 "il y a de la vie à vivre / c est tout" [my translation].

Avant-Propos:
Writing for a People to Come.
Or, Looking for an Intercessor

In his entertaining analysis of the appearance of reality in the theater, filmmaker Andy Jones writes that "[t]he first time you experience them, frankly it's creepy. Artaud Acolytes. They're the ones who think every last thing Antonin Artaud ever said or penned is a true work of genius. He's not a theater practitioner to them. He's not a nutter who also happened to understand the deep inner-workings of all successful performance. He's basically a messiah. Or at least a prophet. This makes him a scary subject to study" (67). Jones's observation is right: Antonin Artaud (Marseille, September 4, 1896–Ivry-sur-Seine, March 4, 1948) does have indeed a lot of admirers among readers and scholars and yet also literary and academic adversaries who eschew his writings. Not only nowadays but also during his lifetime, Artaud had a lot of devoted friends and yet also enemies who wanted to prevent him from reentering society after his stay in various psychiatric hospitals. Speaking generally, Artaud is considered to be the avant-gardist playwright who has turned, after the thirties, into a visionary, a madman, or, at least, an extremely complex personality, suffering from serious psychological instability, whose life, language, and writings are somewhat derailed. While writing these introductory words after several years of research on especially the most controversial part of Artaud's works—that means, his later writings—I think that I at least, not only as a scholar but also personally, have become an Artaud Acolyte.

In this book, we are not so much interested in Artaud as the challenging playwright but rather in Artaud as the creative and struggling writer whose later works in particular give the reader an experience that ranges from disgust to admiration, from fear to audacity, and from indifference to sympathy. Similar to these experiences, the qualifications and critiques of Artaud's works—and mainly his later writings—give way to different responses: from divergent linguistic readings in French literature to a more psychological or philosophical reading of the later writings (if these works are not almost completely neglected) in Anglo-Saxon literature. These different appreciations of his writings have, without any doubt, several causes, but one of them might well be that Artaud is indeed not an easy object or, as Jones asserts, a scary subject to study. Especially because of these different appreciations and the discrepancy in the many qualifications and critiques of his writings, this book focuses on the period after the 1930s in which Artaud wrote his most contested works. If we want to understand the healing practices of language that, as this book argues, are at work in Artaud's later writings, we also need to reread the earlier writings in which words, ideas, and concepts are articulated that will bloom after the 1930s.

We are living in an age where depressions flourish, where the categorizations of personality disorders increase a sense of normativity, and where any dysfunctionality—be it physically (pain and suffering) or mentally (gloomy feelings or autistic behavior)—is remedied as quickly as possible. It is in our Western world that we see symptoms of overmedicalization along with an increased codification and overcodification of the subject that is more and more caught in a web of normativity and productivity through different forms of control—one is immediately tempted to think about institutions and governments, but control is also, in a more diluted way, exercised by technological progresses and social media that turn its users principally into subjugated products instead of autonomous users. However beneficial the developments within the field of medical health care or the progresses of capitalism have been, it is a good thing to critically consider the symptoms of the world in which we live and to ask ourselves if we still fit or want to fit in this prestructured world. Do my feelings of pain, suffering, and gloomy thoughts still have their proper place in this world? Are the various remedies along with the sense of normativity and productivity genuinely beneficial to my mental ecology? Or do they disvalue the still unexplored potentialities, which are the vital forces, the impulsive energy, and the initial intensities of my body and *this* life? This book focuses on the healing practices of language that we see at work in the writings of Artaud. As will be discussed, we contend that there is a crisis of the subject and that we live in a contradictory age where man is detached from the vitality of *this* life, that the link between man and *this* world is broken, that he feels indifferent about it, and that he outsources many potentials that are left unused and unexplored through the structures by which our Western society is organized. In order to heal this detachment, we argue that language can play an important role because language essentially restricts, regulates, and controls the way in which we see, understand, and experience our world. And yet a creative play with this language can also broaden, deepen, and enrich this world.

In many of Artaud's works, language plays an important role, but it is especially in his later writings that language happens to play a key role. It is in these writings that Artaud, as a creative writer—or, what I call in this book a "*crescive* writer" since the word "crescive" (etymologically derived from the word "crescere" meaning "growing" or "swelling") highlights the spontaneous, generative, and open-ended development within and through Artaud's writings—engages with the materiality of language and thus sustainably brings into being another possibility of life that is as healthy as the imposed standard of a good health that medical health care postulates and as happy as the conception of true happiness that capitalism wants us to believe in.

In the essay "The Intercessors,"[i] Gilles Deleuze, whose reading and understanding of literature, life, and creation are an important philosophical and methodological framework for this book, argues that "[c]reation's all about [intercessors]. [...] Whether they're fictive or real, animated or inanimate, you have to form your [intercessors]. [...] I need my [intercessors] to express myself, and they'd never express themselves without me: you're always working in a group, even when you seem to be on your own" (N, 125). An intercessor allows us to think beyond the standard of common sense and beyond ourselves. As Deleuze puts it concisely: "These powers of the false to produce truth, that is what [intercessors] are about" (N, 126). In the search for a detoxification of the subjugating structures of our world and of the age in which we live, we need to look for our intercessors. We need the ruptures, the cracks, and the falseness to produce the truth and life; we need another, that is, an initial, fragile, or deviated health to acquire a greater health; and we need a productive delirium to find another possibility of life. It is in this sense that literature, following Deleuze, "appears as an enterprise of health: not that the writer would necessarily be in good health [...], but he possesses an irresistible and delicate health that stems from what he has seen and heard of things too big for him, while nonetheless giving him the becomings that a dominant and substantial health would render impossible" (CC, 3). If literature is thus about the creation of an affirmative and generative delirium, "[t]he ultimate aim of literature is to set free, in the delirium, this creation of a health or this invention of a people, that is, a possibility of

---

[i] Martin Joughin has poorly translated the French word "intercesseur" by the more neutral term "mediator." In order to preserve the religious connotation of the word "intercessor"—an important connotation that refers to the necessity to *believe* in this world (we will come back to this discussion in Chapter 1) and that heals us from the detachment from this world—I will replace the word "mediator" by "intercessor."

life. To write for this people who are missing … ('for' means less 'in the place of' than 'for the benefit of')" (CC, 4). It is precisely with these people that are missing, or these people whose lives are marginalized, rendered invisible or even impossible, that literature, and art in general, is engaged.

Together with Félix Guattari, Deleuze asserts that "[t]he writer uses words, but by creating a syntax that makes them pass into sensation that makes the standard language stammer, tremble, cry, or even sing: this is the style, the 'tone,' the language of sensations, or the foreign language within language that summons forth a people to come" (WP, 176). In this book, we focus on Artaud as a writer who creatively struggles with language in order to articulate this foreign, vital, and healing language. Intercessors can assist us in the creation of healing practices and they can even offer us their healing practices of auto-immunization as examples. In this book, we consider Artaud as an intercessor because his "crescive writings" are still relevant, important, and necessary healing practices that are written for the people of his time, for us, and for a people to come. If these words sound like the words of an Artaud Acolyte, make sure you do not get caught in that trap too.

Introduction:
Artaud—A Life in Language. Or What Comes with Language?

Life seems to us in a state of violent loss.[1]
—Antonin Artaud, "The Theater and the Gods," OC VIII, p. 198

The Enchantment of Marseille

On the northside of the Rue des Trois Frères Carasso in the Marseille of today, there is a pharmacy surrounded by small restaurants. Walking southward, one can see this street ends at a striking tattoo shop that is called "Under my skin." Without probably noticing, the wanderer has also crossed the classic, stately but gray building on number 15, where Antonin Artaud was born on Friday, September 4, 1896, as Antoine Marie Joseph Paul Artaud. Describing the cosmopolitan harbor city of Marseille, Olivier Penot-Lacassagne concludes that the young Artaud "discovers other worlds within himself, other meanings and other forms of life. Artaud wanders to the limit of reality" (2007, 25). Instead of living in these real and imaginary worlds that he feels and discovers under the skin, he is, however, more and more drawn to the world of pharmacies and hospitals. At the age of five, he suffers from a meningitis syndrome; at the age of six, he almost drowns; and at the age of seven, he suffers from scarlet fever (see Danchin and Roumieux, 30–41; O, 1707–13 and Penot-Lacassagne 2007, 25–8). In spite of, or maybe because of, his fragile health and the constant moving of his parents—they will move several times within Marseille—Artaud starts to write poems but throws them all away at the age of eighteen, when he suffers from depressions. At the age of twenty, Artaud is declared healthy enough—in spite of the neurasthenia with which he was diagnosed by doctor Joseph Grasset in 1915—to serve in the French army that is at war with the Germans during the First World War. He is stationed in Digne-les-Bains but is already declared unfit for military service eleven days later. Until his move to Paris, he would have stayed in various nursing homes and clinics to be treated for his neurasthenia.

Living in Villejuif, a southern suburb of Paris (bordering on Ivry-sur-Seine where he would die twenty-eight years later), Artaud becomes interested in the Dada and the Surrealist movements and engages with the experiments that take place within the theater. Participating in *The Atelier*—a newly founded school for actors by Charles Dullin—Artaud meets Génica Athanasiou with whom he falls in love (see O, 1707–13 and Penot-Lacassagne 2007, 25–8). His letters bear witness to his unlimited feelings of love, but after a year, they also reveal his physical suffering. In a letter from July 1923, Artaud laments that "when I touch myself, I do not have the feeling of touching MY self but rather of encountering a conscious obstacle; I give myself the sensation of being a skeleton without skin or flesh, or rather a living void"[2] (GA, 89). In February 1924, he dramatizes his suffering even more by asserting that he feels dumbfounded and that "[m]y sorrow surrounds me *physically*. I feel that my head dulled as if it has been beaten with a truncheon. [...] In a disease like mine, a similar sorrow is terrible. I feel I will not bear it"[3] (GA, 141, emphasis in original). Because of the many treatments and cures—since his doctor Grasset thinks that Artaud's neurasthenia comes from a hereditary syphilis, he also undergoes anti-syphilis treatments— Artaud also uses a lot of opium to which he gets addicted. Penot-Lacassagne thus concludes, following the development of Artaud's early writings, that "he must therefore, in addition to the care of which he ascertains the desperate ineffectiveness, seek to understand 'the true nature of evil' overwhelming him. To bring back by words its least manifestations, write it reach it, describe it to cure it" (2007, 31).

Something has indeed happened, because twenty-three years after his lamentations to Génica Athanasiou, Artaud, without any recourse to the pity of his reader, stately declares in a poem that "I have been sick all my life and I ask only that it continue"[4] (AN, 191). It seems that the forces of life, in all their joyous *and* terrible manifestations, have finally been accepted and have even been welcomed by Artaud. Walking from north to south on the Rue des Trois Frères Carasso in the Marseille of today, one not only passes Artaud's birthplace but also traverses Artaud's life and writings. It is a walk that starts with a pharmacy and ends with a tattoo shop that is called "Under my skin." This walk also raises some questions: What is this "true nature of evil" that Artaud discovered? How did his attitude toward his suffering and his sickness develop and eventually change, and in what way did his writings participate in this process? And, finally, what can we, in an age of overmedicalization and in a world of advanced capitalism, learn from these writings that eventually praise the forces of life in all their manifestations?

A Violent Loss of Life

Artaud's engagement with the forces of his suffering has everything to do with language and writing. Already in *The Nerve-Meter*, he claims that "[a]ll writing is garbage"[5] (SW, 85). What then follows is an enlisting of blames to those "bearded critics"[6] (SW, 86) who hold to the fixity of thinking and a mastering of language. He asserts that those people "for whom certain words have meaning, and certain modes of being, those who are so precise, [...] those who believe in an orientation of the mind, those who follow paths, who drop names, who recommended books,—these are the worst pigs of all"[7] (SW, 85). Instead of clinging to a teleological discourse that is reigned by a transcendental understanding of the world, of life and of matter, Artaud pleads for a dedication to absolute immanence, which means "no works, no language, no works, no mind, nothing. / Nothing but a fine Nerve Meter. / A kind of incomprehensible stopping place in the mind, right in the middle of everything"[8] (SW, 86). The Nerve Meter, with which the "bearded asses, pertinent pigs, masters of the false word, [and] serial writers"[9] (SW, 86) have never engaged, makes one forget the "I" and hence engages with singularity and genuine thinking—Évelyn Grossman notices that the French word "pèse-nerf" (translated as "nerve meter") is also a "quasi anagram for 'thinking' ['penser']" (2003a, 83)—that thinks the untranslatable, ungraspable, and unthinkable forces of life that "are never named, these eminent positions of the soul, ah, these intermissions of the mind"[10] (SW, 86). In other words, dedicating ourselves to absolute immanence essentially means engaging with genuine thinking, that is, engaging with the hitherto unexplored forces of life that traverse our bodies. The play that is inherent to the French word "pèse-nerf" already shows the difficult task in translating Artaud's texts—the word "Nerve Meter" only captures the alleged semantic meaning of the word—but also reveals that its meaning can be generated, by means of an anagram, that is from a material play with language. Artaud contends that the Nerve Meter contests the words that he has always used and that have not advanced his thinking. It is in this contestation that the Nerve Meter is, following Grossman, "the writing of the open flaw which suspends the sense and maintains this trembling between two words, two meanings; it is this vibration of a language in suspense in the equilibrium of two terms" (2003a, 86). The writing of the Nerve Metter is an impossible writing since it engages with the ungraspable and unthinkable forces of the body that escape from the fixity of words and that can only be hinted at in a vibrating language. This essentially means that the Nerve Meter can only be articulated through a creative language and perceived along with a close reading that focuses on both the form (the morphology of the words) and the content (the etymology of the words) of this creative language.

These untranslatable and unthinkable forces are healing in a way, because, as Artaud would ten years later contend in the article "The Theater and the Gods," which he wrote for *El Nacional*, "[i]n the body of the French youth an epidemic of the mind buds, which must not be taken for an illness but which is a terrible demand"[11] (OCVIII, 196). In other words, there are forces at work among the French youth that must not be combatted but that rigidly urge for an engagement and an inevitable submission to them. Artaud writes his article in a tumultuous time in which he hopes to realize his ideas around what he terms the "theater of cruelty"—we analyze the conceptualization and eventual flourishing of this theater more extensively in Chapter 4—but that failed with the staging of *The Cenci* in 1935. *The Cenci* was a reworking of Shelley's drama of the same name, staged violence, and incest and was accompanied by concrete music.[i] Artaud's attempt to realize the "theater of cruelty" turned out to be a failure—*The Cenci* was only staged seventeen times—because, in the words of Jannarone, "the reviewers of *The Cenci* were largely unanimous in their response: the text was awful, the acting incomprehensible, and the production as a whole disastrously ineffectual" (166).

After his failed project, Artaud concentrates again on his travel plan for Mexico, where he hopes to find—as he writes in a letter to Jean Paulhan on July 19, 1935—"a civilization with Metaphysical bases which express themselves in religion and in acts by a kind of active totemism"[12] (OCVIII, 334). Asserting that the theater has left him materially impoverished and socially marginalized, the healing forces that he hopes to find with the Indians in Mexico make him feel that he is "at an important crossroads of my existence"[13] (OCVIII, 336). His journey to Mexico and his experiences with the Tarahumaras Indians, which we discuss

---

[i] See Chalosse (2002) for a discussion of the sounds and music that Artaud envisioned in his staging of *The Cenci*.

in Chapter 2, indeed turn out to be an important crossroads. It is from these experiences that Artaud discovers a still living practice of an "organic culture" that he describes as "a culture based on the mind in relation to the organs, and the mind bathing in all the organs, and responding at the same time"[14] (OCVIII, 201). In other words, the organic culture that he discovered during his stay in Mexico is a practice in which one engages with the forces of the body and hence a culture where the mind is intricately related to this body. This organic culture seems to be forgotten by the Western world, because, following Artaud, "[a]gainst the culture of Europe, which holds to written texts and makes us believe that culture is lost if the texts are destroyed, I say that there is another culture on which other times have lived and this lost culture is based on a materialist idea of the mind"[15] (OCVIII, 200). Clinging to the rusted words that do not advance or engage with our thinking, Artaud contends that we have lost the contact with the earth and with the forces that traverse matter, life, and the body.

It is because of this loss that he asserts that "Europe is in a state of advanced civilization: I mean that she is very ill. It is in the spirit of the youth of France to react against this state of advanced civilization"[16] (OCVIII, 198). This advanced civilization makes people cynical, passive, and ill, because it presents false ideas of reality—false ideas that the theater contests by staging genuine reality—and hence "[l]ife seems to us in a state of violent loss"[17] (OCVIII, 198). The forces of life that he wanted to stage with *The Cenci* could not heal and cure the illness of society, and Artaud attributes this failure to a tendency to "separate the theater from everything that is not space, and to return the language of the text to the books from which it should not have come out. And this language of space, in turn, acts on the nervous sensibility"[18] (OCVIII, 203). During his stay in Mexico, Artaud has discovered that the Mexican Gods were, first and foremost, found in this space and that these Gods, who, following Artaud, "are not satisfied with their simple human stature"[19] (OCVIII, 206), hence adopting an inhuman form, create zigzagging lines to fathom space. Putting it differently, the Mexican Gods keep on creating new lines of existence that occupy the space in which they manifest themselves. For the theater, this consequently means that "a line is a noise, a movement is a music, and the gesture that emerges from a noise is like a clear word in a sentence"[20] (OCVIII, 206). Artaud's theater thus searches for these clear and concrete words that are the vibrating and singular materializations emerging from the lines that we trace in space. This theater stages reality and the forces of life that the spectator must affirm in both its joyous *and* terrible manifestations. It is in this sense that the playwright is in an intercessor who plunges its spectators into a yet unexplored reality and therewith stimulates them to create their own possibilities of life.

Artaud's Mexican experiences are not only a crossroads for a new conceptualization of the "theater of cruelty" but they also give way to new experimentations within the articulation of the organic culture that he discovered and eventually a harsh derailment during his voyage to Ireland in 1937 after which he would have been interned in various psychiatric hospitals until 1946. Looking at one of his last notebooks—Artaud wrote more than four hundred notebooks from 1945 until his death in 1948—from February, one perceives a different, more hastened, violent, and yet vital writing style that nevertheless elaborates on the same themes, ideas, and concepts that he touched upon during his voyage to Mexico. In a notebook from February 1947, Artaud writes that

> the beings have only the signs
> and manifestations
> of a reality
> of which they have never
> suspected the nature
> and which have always
> sufficed them
> the alphabet of a ~~poetry~~ poem
> whose source
> is forever unknown to them
> and of which they mumble
> the litanies
> without understanding
> the destination.[21] (CI, 145–6)

Artaud thus reproaches the advanced civilization that it has never questioned the nature of the reality that was voiced and expressed in a language that only makes them mumble litanies—the word "litany" does refer to both a liturgical prayer and a monotonous repetition—whose destination it does not understand. In other words, the advanced civilization keeps on clinging to the same monotonous and liturgical words—we come back to this point in Chapters 2 and 3—that it ritualistically mumbles in order to sustain a certain reality in which the forces, energy, and intensities of life are neutralized or emptied out. As we discuss more elaborately in Chapter 3, this reality, and hence this language, enabled Artaud's various internments, treatments, and cures in order to heal him from all the physical and mental illnesses with which he was diagnosed.[ii] Changing and combatting this reality thus also mean changing, twisting, and playing with the language that facilitates its functioning in order to cure the illness of an advanced civilization. It essentially means affirming and engaging with the forces of life, with which the advanced civilization loses contact, and creating a language of space that is a vibrating materialization of language. In other words, changing this reality essentially necessitates a dedication to absolute immanence that is an engagement with the reality of *this* world.

In this process that mainly develops after the failure of *The Cenci*, Artaud is sometimes difficult to follow, to grasp, and to understand (which could well be a particularity of this new language). In another notebook from February 1947, Artaud therefore speaks as a martyr because it is

> as being me
> this unique body,
> from which anything
> even god had
> gone out,
> that I was violated for life,
> insulted, offended, sullied,
> ~~polluted~~, dirtied,
> messed,
> day and night,
> ever since I lived;
> no man at the end
> of his scroll
> who can not find
> in artaud
> something to make
> a living again,
> that I was everywhere
> martyred,
> […]
> murdered, poisoned,
> beaten to death, electrocuted,
> and to prevent me from

[ii] See Danchin and Roumieux, 95–198, for an extensive discussion of the various diagnoses and treatments that Artaud underwent during his internments.

> regaining consciousness
> and the knowledge of my
> capacities and of my forces
> and from defending myself
> against my persecutors;
> for god of his true name
> is called Artaud.²² (CI, 50-1)

Contending that he has a unique body, that is a singular and authentic body, Artaud, as a genuine intercessor, claims to be the god from whom even the wisest man can learn. Persecuted by an advanced civilization, Artaud did not have the chance to defend himself and to genuinely engage with these forces "with which to/remake oneself in reality, and/make a reality"²³ (CI, 52). These forces with which a more healthier and happier reality can be created might well be the forces of the "true nature of evil" that, in an affirmative engagement, also give rise to an inevitable submission to the joyous *and* terrible forces of *this* life and *this* body.

Reading the Writings of a Madman

After his journey to Mexico, Artaud's writings develop from messianistic, occult, and Kabbalistic texts to more mystical and religious texts that are traversed by dramatized complaints of his various internments—"[t]o treat me in a delirium is to deny the poetic value of suffering"²⁴ (ER, 96)—demands for drugs—"[cocaine] must become / like bread / and replace it"²⁵ (CI, 149), and critiques to our advanced civilization—"[s]ociety has against us the strength"²⁶ (OCXI, 273). Although there is a growing interest in the philosophical implications of Artaud's later works, there seemed to be an underestimation of the language of these later writings in the Anglo-Saxon literature that was mainly interested in Artaud's early writings on the cinema and the theater. In this literature, Artaud was mainly considered to be the French playwright who was once the key figure in revolutionizing the practices of formal theaters. The hundreds of notebooks that are nowadays regaining in popularity (partly due to their growing availability in translation), were almost as good as neglected in the view that the Anglo-Saxon literature had developed on Artaud. The reasons for this underestimation can be numerous, but we comment on two possibilities for this neglecting. Firstly, Artaud's later writings are difficult to read in their original language and are not easy to translate into English and thus demand a good understanding of the French language in order to more fully grasp the creative play with language along with the enormous richness and (etymological) depths of the words, which are often also neologisms that Artaud uses. A critical textual analysis of Artaud's writings necessitates, I think, a close reading that pays attention to both the form and the content of his creative play with the French language. It can well be that this restrains some scholars from reading the writings of Artaud. Secondly, it could also well be that a defense of a madman—Artaud is often considered to have become mad, and hence illegible and thus irrelevant, after his voyage to Mexico and his career as a playwright—is perceived to be irrelevant or immoral. Artaud's later writings are then too marginal, too minoritarian, or even too dangerous for serious scholars to consider. As we have already asserted, during his stay in various psychiatric hospitals, Artaud indeed turns into a madman or, at least, a complex personality, suffering from serious psychological instability; he, as a writer, produces works that are difficult to read but that nevertheless merit our attention because there is something at work in the struggle and play with language of these writings that is still relevant for the reader of today.

In the French literature on Artaud, on the contrary, various literary theorists, philosophers, and linguists valued his later works differently and appreciated his material, phonetic, and semantic play with language and his conceptualizations of the body. In their close readings (see for example Bouthors-Paillart, Grossman 2003a or Tomiche 2002) and their material approaches to Artaud's bodily practices of language (see for example Derrida 1967/1978), this literature considers Artaud, besides the important playwright that he was in the thirties, as the poet or writer who creatively engaged with a bodily practice of language. Through a critical textual analysis, based on a close reading of his later writings in particular (the most contested part of his works that, as mentioned above, give way to many different appreciations), the aim of this book is to contribute to the growing interest of the Anglo-Saxon field of scholarly research on Artaud by setting up dialogues with the French approach (of, for instance, close readings that particularly focus on the performances of language or the material approaches to Artaud's bodily practices of language) and by studying in what way Artaud's later writings (that is, despite the increasing interest, a still understudied part of his works in the Anglo-Saxon literature) are telling us something relevant and important about the role and use of language, about the role of literature in our lives and our society and of course, in the first place, how his later writings do something different with language. In doing so, my reading of Artaud does not intend to analyze solely the use of language, but rather wants to consider what politics (of life) is at work in his writings through a critical textual analysis of his language; it is the text that does the work.

In doing so, this book wants to offer, what Gilles Deleuze and Félix Guattari would call, a *schizoanalysis* of Artaud's later writings in particular. The term "schizoanalysis" is used by them to differentiate between analyses that only focus on given frameworks or that repeat already given structures. A schizoanalyst, or a nomadologist (see TP, 43), will, following Guattari, "never limit itself to an interpretation of 'gives facts'; it will be interested, much more fundamentally, in the 'giving' to assemblages that promote the concatenation of affects of meaning and pragmatic affects" (2009b, 208). Guattari consequently asserts that "there will not be any normalized schizoanalytic protocol, but a new fundamental rule, an 'anti-rule rule' will impose a constant putting into question of analyzer assemblages" (2009b, 208). In other words, a schizoanalysis of literature is not interested in a reiteration of what is already given (categorizations of style or a mere description of what is factually written), but rather focuses on the ruptures and the cracks within language that bring about something new. Focusing on language, Guattari therefore similarly claims that, for a schizoanalyst, "it will be inevitable to reexamine a certain traditional conception *of the unity and autonomy of language* as a plane of expression as well as a social entity. [...] The unity of language is always inseparable from the constitution of a power formation" (2011, 27, emphasis in original). In other words, the schizoanalyst is not interested in language as a formalized system of signs, but rather in the creative engagement with language (we will come back to language as the constitution of a power formation in Chapter 2). It is in this creative play with language that something new can emerge.

My claim is that especially in Artaud's later writings, the ruptures and the cracks within language (as, for instance, the neologisms, the puns and plays on words, the etymological depths of words) play a crucial role, because in a notebook from February 1947, he writes, "I am Artaud / who fabricates the signified / as well as the <u>signifier</u>"[27] (CI, 160) and, some days later, he writes in another notebook from February 1947 that all the great initiated are engaged in the creation of "the signifier / contain[ing] the signified"[28] (CI, 204). Fabricating the signified as well as the signifier, or creating the container that *contains* the contained, indeed implies a different, and far more immanent, approach to language. It suggests the enlarging of a reconsideration of what entails genuine expression and the revaluation of the constitutive materiality of language. In other words, an immanent approach to language revalues the generation of meaning through the materiality of language.

A schizoanalytic reading of Artaud's writings focuses therefore on the agential materiality of his language, and his related bodily approach to it, by looking at the ruptures, the cracks, and the forces that are expressed in its play with not only morphology but also phonetics, semantics, and etymology. In this schizoanalytic reading, the fixity of language is questioned in order to investigate its unfolded potential. In her article "Posthumanist Performativity," Barad criticizes the power that is granted to language by claiming that "performativity" "is not an invitation to turn everything (including material bodies) into words; on the contrary, performativity is precisely a contestation of the excessive power granted to language to define what is real" (802). Considering meaning as an effect that does not only emanate from words, our schizoanalytic reading will therefore also focus on the medium, the sketches, and the drawings in Artaud's later writings that also participate in his creation of a language in space. In investigating this language, we will also briefly introduce, whenever necessary, the developments in Artaud's life that often run parallel to the developments in his writings (if his writings are essentially engaged with life, it is also interesting to focus, if appropriate, on their interaction). His changed attitude toward his suffering and his sickness, for example, does also issue from a different way of writing. In a way, and we will come back to this point in Chapter 2 and 4, Artaud's writings are practices of auto-detoxification that participate in a process of auto-immunization. Putting it differently, they defend themselves against the various (mental) illnesses that our advanced civilization and the current developments within mental health care tend to impose. In this sense, the body that is traversed by great and yet unthinkable forces participates in the articulation of a new language. In our materialist or schizoanalytic reading, we thus also rethink what writing is and what writing can do.

Still Relevant Forces at Work

In this book, we mainly focus upon the constitutive and mattering role that language plays in Artaud's later writings. Language plays an important role in the subjectification, subjugation, and overcodification of its speaker; it is at the same time through a creative play with this dominant language that one genuinely reengages with the vitality of the expression of matter and hence the reappropriation of the singularity of our body, expression, and desire. This reengagement consequently participates in the combat against our current state that is largely caused by the developments of advanced capitalism, indifference, passivity, and cynicism that is essentially a state of loss of a vital life. A revaluation of Artaud's later writings can therefore be considered as a healing practice and a molecular resistance where relevant forces (of life) are at work.

In this book, we discuss these vital forces with which Artaud's language engages, the form of this language, and the significance of this language. Before doing so, we first investigate the relatedness of language to the flesh, understood as the vitality of the body, and the mind that is expressed by it. It is already in his earlier works that Artaud suggested the constitutive role of language within the articulation of healthier body. Focusing rather on the cinema, the theater, and eventually participating in ancient rituals that would reveal a more earthly approach to the sick body, Artaud's attempts to heal his sick body fail and he is finally interned for more than nine years in various psychiatric hospitals in France. It is finally in the psychiatric hospital of Rodez, where Artaud is interned for three years, that Artaud seriously starts to write again. It is during this period that Artaud more consciously writes with, through, and within language, because, as this book discusses, it is only through and within language, essentially understood as a bodily practice, that a healthier body and happier life can be articulated. From this later period, I will formulate, elaborating on ideas and concepts from his earlier works that eventually flourish in his later writings, Artaud's poetics that we read on a formal and a more philosophical, or, better, a theological level. We can contend that where Artaud's performative realization of the theater of cruelty in his earlier works failed, he finally suggests a language of cruelty in his later writings that more sustainably articulates a healthier body and a happier life.

Artaud's later writings engage with the ungraspable and joyous as well as terrible forces of life that we can only accept as an inevitable submission to their necessity. This life is modeled, subjugated, and codified by a language that permits communication from which the functioning of society is regulated. At the same time, this language also restricts the infinite capabilities of the singularities of our bodies, expressions, and desires. Following Artaud's later writings, the reader perceives how life matters in writing through a creative play with and within language through which we can eventually reengage sustainably with the joyous *and* terrible forces of life.

Notes

1. "La vie nous semble dans un état de déperdition violente" [my translation].
2. "et que lorsque je me touche, je n'aie pas le sentiment de ME toucher moi-même mais de rencontrer un obstacle conscient, que je me fasse la sensation d'être un squelette sans peau ni chair, ou plutôt un vide vivant" [my translation].
3. "Mon chagrin m'entoure *physiquement*. Je sens toute ma tête engourdie comme si on l'avait frappée à coups de matraque. […] Dans une maladie comme la mienne un chagrin pareil est terrible. Je sens que je ne vais pas le supporter" [my translation].
4. "J'ai été malade toute ma vie et je ne demande qu'à continuer" (OCXXII, 67).
5. "Toute l'écriture est de la cochonnerie" (OCI*, 100).
6. "critiques barbus" (OCI*, 100).
7. "pour qui certains mots ont un sens, et certaines manières d'être, ceux qui font si bien des façons, […] ceux qui croient encore à une orientation de l'esprit, ceux qui suivent des voies, qui agitent des noms, qui font crier les pages des livres,—ceux-là sont les pires cochons" (OCI*, 100).
8. "pas d'œuvres, pas de langue, pas de parole, pas d'esprit, rien. Rien, sinon un beau Pèse-Nerfs. Une sorte de station incompréhensible et toute droite au milieu de tout dans l'esprit" (OCI*, 100).
9. "barbes d'ânes, cochons pertinents, maîtres du faux verbe […] feuilletonistes" (OCI*, 101).
10. "ces états qu'on ne nomme jamais, ces situations éminentes d'âme, ah ces intervalles d'esprit" (OCI*, 101).
11. "Dans le corps de la jeunesse française une épidémie de l'esprit bourgeonne, qu'il ne faut pas prendre pour une maladie, mais qui est une terrible exigence" [my translation].
12. "une civilisation à bases Métaphysiques qui s'expriment dans la religion et dans les actes par une sorte de totémisme actif" [my translation].
13. "à un carrefour important de mon existence" [my translation].
14. "une culture basée sur l'esprit en relation avec les organes, et l'esprit baignant dans tous les organes, et se répandant en même temps." [my translation].
15. "En face de la culture de l'Europe qui tient dans des textes écrits et fait croire que la culture est perdue si les textes sont détruits, je dis qu'il y a une autre culture sur laquelle d'autres temps ont vécu et cette culture perdue se base sur une idée matérialiste de l'esprit" [my translation].
16. "L'Europe est dans un état de civilisation avancée: je veux dire qu'elle est très malade. L'esprit de la jeunesse en France est de réagir contre cet état de civilisation avancée" [my translation].

17 "La vie nous semble dans un état de déperdition violente" [my translation].
18 "séparer le théâtre d'avec tout ce qui n'est pas l'espace, et pour renvoyer le langage du texte dans les livres d'où il n'aurait pas dû sortir. Et ce langage de l'espace à son tour agit sur la sensibilité nerveuse" [my translation].
19 "ne se contentent pas de leur simple stature d'homme" [my translation].
20 "une ligne est un bruit, un mouvement est une musique, et le geste qui émerge d'un bruit est comme un mot clair dans une phrase" [my translation].
21 "les êtres n ont que les signes / et manifestations / d une realité / dont ils n ont jamais / soupçonné la nature / et qui leur ont toujours / suffi / l alphabet d un ~~poesie~~/poème / dont la source / leur est à jamais inconnue / et dont il marmonnent/ les litanies / sans en comprendre / la destination" [my translation].
22 "etant, moi, / ce corps unique, / d'où tout / même dieu fut / sorti, / que j'ai été viole à vie, / insulte, offense, sali, / ~~pollué~~, crotté, / salopé, / jour et nuit, / depuis que je vis; / pas d homme au bout / de son rouleau / qui ne sache trouver / dans artaud de / quoi se refaire / une existence, / que j ai été un peu partout / martyrise, / [...] assassiné, empoisonne, frappé a mort, electrocute, / et afin de m empêcher de / retrouver la conscience / et la science de mes / capacites et de mes forces / et de me defendre / contre mes / persecuteurs; / car dieu de son vrai nom / s appelle Artaud" [my translation].
23 "de quoi se / refaire en realite, et / se faire une realite" [my translation].
24 "Me traiter en délirant c'est nier la valeur poétique de la souffrance" [my translation].
25 "elle [= cocaïne] doit devenir / comme du pain / et le remplacer" [my translation].
26 "La société a contre nous la force" [my translation].
27 "je suis Artaud / qui fabrique le contenu / aussi bien que je <u>contenant</u>" [my translation].
28 "le contenant/contient le contenu" [my translation].

1

The Healing Practices of Language: On Flesh, Mind, and Expression

I surrender to the fever of dreams, but only in order to derive from them new laws.[1]

—Antonin Artaud, "Manifesto In Clear Language," SW, p. 109

Do We Know What the Body Can Do?

The question if we know what our bodies can do is raised by Spinoza (see E3P2Schol) and is reiterated by Deleuze and Guattari, who claim that "[w]e know nothing about a body until we know what it can do, in other words, what its affects are, how they can or cannot enter into composition with other affects" (TP, 284). In his rereading of Spinoza's question, Deleuze is interested in the forces, the energy, and the intensities that are inherent to matter and therewith constitute a philosophy of immanence. This book is also concerned with the question of Spinoza and is therefore interested in the Deleuzian philosophy of immanence. Claiming that language is also a body of forces, energy, and intensities of which we do not yet know what it can do, this book reinvestigates Spinoza's question and similarly perceives language in its agential materiality.

The negligence of Spinoza's question is reflected in the still ongoing developments within mental health care: focusing upon what a body *is* rather than on what it *can do*, mental health care imposes a falsely appropriated image of the body and therewith reduces the forces, energy, and intensities of the body and thus restricts the vitality of what a body can do. In this chapter, we focus on the impulsiveness of matter and the healing powers of a body with which one immanently reengages. Claiming that language only differs from the body in degree, this chapter mainly focuses upon the healing practices of an affirmative language—a language understood in its agential materiality—in the reengagement with our bodies. It is through this creative play with language that another remedy is proposed as a healthy, sustainable, and critical alternative for the current developments within mental health care.

Articulating the Flexional Singularity of the Body

In his reading of the use of language in the writings of Pierre Klossowski, Deleuze contends that language loses its denoting function because of its expressive or expressionist use (LS, 299). Discussing this alternative use of language, Deleuze concludes that

> [e]voked (expressed) are the singular and complicated spirits, which do not possess a body without multiplying it inside the system of reflections, and which do not inspire language without projecting it into the intensive system of resonances. Revoked (denounced) are corporeal unicity, personal identity, and the false simplicity of language insofar as it is supposed to denote bodies and to manifest a self. (LS, 299)

Considering language as a formalized system of signs that falsely appropriates the singularities of bodies, Klossowski's novels would disclose the ground that makes both thinking and speaking possible. In his literary and critical works, Klossowski is interested in the tension, preoccupying so many writers and poets, between the expression of the forces, the energy, and the intensities of the body and the limitations of the formalized system of signs.

In exploring and reflecting on ways to express the linguistic inexpressibility of flexion, that is the vitality, singularity, and intensity of a body, Klossowski is therewith constantly confronted with language as a formalized system of signs and language in its agential materiality or, following his words, with the tension between a pure language that evokes an impure silence and an impure language that articulates a pure silence. It is in this tension that we can similarly raise the question: do we know what language can do? Reading Deleuze and Guattari's materialist linguistic model, DeLanda rightly summarizes that "the sounds, words, and grammatical patterns of a language are materials that accumulate or sediment historically, then they are consolidated by another process, like the standardization of a dialect by a Royal Academy and its official dictionaries, grammars, and rules of pronunciation" (qtd. in Dolphijn and Van der Tuin 2012, 39). It is through this process of consolidation, which paves the way for a transcendentalized and formalized system of signs (that thus neglects the agential materiality of language), that we lose sight of what language *can do* and that we are caught up in a system that structures our ways of acting and thinking or, in the words of Rahimy, "[b]eing into language suggests that we are willing to speak, willing to relate and communicate while knowing that we cannot communicate fully and clearly" (156). Making a minor use of this consolidated language means that one should speak differently and creatively engage with the formalized patterns. Again following Rahimy's nomadic take on language, we must "speak poorly [which] is philosophy on a diet, a philosophy that is not slaved by its past, but uses its age to enter in different ways" (157). A cure of detoxification or a treatment of auto-immunization through language thus means that one arms oneself against the toxic, weakening, and passive forces that act upon the body through a consolidated language.

Following again Klossowski's play with body and language, Deleuze argues that "[t]he body is language because it is essentially 'flexion.' In reflection, the corporeal flexion seems to be divided, split in two, opposed to itself and reflected in itself; it appears finally for itself, liberated from everything that ordinarily conceals it" (LS, 286). In other words, it is only through the repetition, that is, reflection, that we can perceive the initial difference—the flexional singularity of both body and language. There is thus only flexion through reflection. This flexional singularity of the body can be conceived, hence inevitably reflected, as a field of forces that are empowering or weakening or, putting it differently, leading to actions or passions or, considering Artaud's life, mere happiness, or suffering.

This field of forces in which the body is immersed ultimately shows what the body is capable of in its potency to affect or to be affected by these forces. Although reflection precedes flexion in a certain sense, Deleuze considers its effectuations and violations improper or, to use a word that is closer to Klossowski's writings, obscene. Deleuze therefore notes that

> the obscene is not the intrusion of bodies into language, but rather their mutual reflection and the act of language which fabricates a body for the mind. This is the act by which language transcends itself as it reflects a body. "There is nothing more verbal than the excesses of the flesh … The reiterated description of the carnal act not only reviews the transgression, it is itself a transgression of language by language." (LS, 281)

These last sentences from Klossowski's essay on Georges Bataille in *Such a Deathly Desire* are interesting since they notice the transgressive nature of a description of carnal excess, but Klossowski similarly indicates the transgression of language through the act of description. The excesses of the flesh are events that cannot simply be reproduced by a pure language which he considers to be a too limited formalized system of sings, and must thus consequently be reiterated in a description of the carnal act that finds its articulation in an impure language. In line with Klossowski's reasoning, Deleuze therefore considers flexion as a double "transgression"; "of language by the flesh and of the flesh by language" (LS, 286–7). Putting it differently, whereas flexion disrupts both flesh and language, reflection creates bodies for the mind and an obscenely doubled language. It is in this obscenely doubled language that mental health care in an age of advanced capitalism can prosper since it neutralizes the flexional singularity that essentially resists reflection. It is important to notice for our further analysis, which Deleuze differentiates between "body" ("corps") and "flesh" ("chair"). As discussed earlier, Deleuze concludes that whereas flesh is flexion, the body must be seen as a product of reflection. But in what way, then, does the flesh relate to the body? And if expression becomes intelligible, or linguistically expressible, within a formalized system of signs, how can language ever adequately and intelligibly denote this flesh? And how, finally, might we then ever touch upon these vital powers of flexion?

To Believe in This World

Revaluating and reengaging with the vital powers of flexion, the intensity of the flesh, and the singularity of expression is difficult and a seemingly insignificant task in an age of advanced capitalism that Deleuze characterizes with symptoms such as sickness, sluggishness, and burnouts—an age where we, following Spinoza, still don't know what the body is capable of. Looking at the increasing popularity of social media—which undeniably have an enormous political potential that should be cherished—one perceives the development of a virtual reality in which a false simplicity, a fixed identity, and a determined unicity that tend to restrict and control the yet unexplored forces of the body are postulated. This outsourced potential stimulates the rise of depressions,[i] the emergence of a whole new range of various personality disorders, and an ever

---

[i] Belhaj Kacem characterizes our age as a time of "depressionism," because we are constantly trying to encapsulate the present (see 2005, 147).

increased feeling of cynicism, indifference of passiveness which is essentially the outcome of a detachment from this world; one does not experience the capability to act in *this* world. Along with the developments within mental health care—which overmedicalizes the body and tends to neutralize, normalize, and cure any caprice—our age reactively longs for what Protevi rightly, following Deleuze and Guattari, calls an experimentation with "bio-social-technical body relations in diachronic transversally emergent assemblages" (2009, 112). Ascertaining that we keep holding on to a paranoid and narcotizing fixity within body that is the idea of a definable and healthy organism; mind that is the transcendentally formalized spirit of man; and language, understood as an overcodifying, subjectifying, and subjugating system of signs, Deleuze sets his hope on the "creation of a health [...], that is, a possibility of life" (CC, 4). As a genuine physician, he diagnoses our age of advanced capitalism as a time where the vital and healthy link between man and his body is broken and where we have stopped *believing* in this world—*this world*, a world of immanence that is not predetermined; that escapes determination, interpretation, and definition; and that is consequently full of potency, vitality, and still unexplored creative forces. In *The Time-Image*, Deleuze consequently contends that "[t]he modern fact is that we no longer believe in this world. We do not even believe in the events which happen to us, love, death, as if they only half concerned us" (C2, 166). No longer believing in *this* world essentially means that we scientifically understand the world reflectively, that is, selecting and transcendentalizing singular actions into a realm of normalization. In this process, the modern fact cynically stimulates the developments within mental health care and advanced capitalism, because *this* world, that is this world of absolute immanence that is traversed by inexplicable and untranslatable forces, no longer seems a healthy or valuable possibility of life. In a more healthier society, we are assisted by intercessors who enable us to engage with the vitality of flexion, explore the intensity of the flesh, and reappropriate the singularity of expression and are thus in *this* world through a vital link. This vital link finds its articulation in an act of flexional singularity and can thus not be known, thought, or represented, and Deleuze consequently asserts that we must *believe* in this impossible but vital link. It is thus not believing in a different world or a world beyond this world, but believing in *this* world. To believe in *this* world therefore means that man reengages with hitherto unexplored forces of *this* life, *this* body and *this* world. The link between man and *this* world is broken because man seems to have lost the power and force to genuinely think and therewith believe in the vital forces. The detachment from this world makes man megalomaniac and specular but also passive, indifferent, and cynical.

If we want to heal—in its etymological sense of "curing" and "making whole"—this broken but vital link between man and his body, we must dare thinking the unthinkable and, from there, *believe*—we must keep in mind that a belief is something different than a knowledge or a science—in the vital forces of *this* world, *this* life, and *this* body. Intercessors can assist us in this conversion and stimulate us through their artworks or writings that plunge us into a hitherto unexplored reality, to express a more healthy and happy singular flexionality in which we can only believe. Deleuze specifies that to believe "is simply believing in the body. It is giving discourse to the body, and, for this purpose, reaching the body before discourses, before words, before things are named [...]. Artaud said the same thing, believe in the *flesh* [...]. Give words back to the body, to the flesh" (C2, 167, emphasis in original). Alluding to Artaud as a genuine initiator, pioneer, and physician in the process of healing and reconverting man to a belief in this world, Deleuze contends that "[w]e need an ethic or a faith, which makes fools laugh; it is not a need to believe in something else, but a need to believe in this world, of which fools are a part" (C2, 167). A belief in *this* body and *this* world is thus essentially a commitment and a conversion to absolute immanence in which a reading of Artaud's writings, as Deleuze rightly suggests, is relevant. This commitment or conversion to absolute immanence essentially implies a process of dis-identification and disordering. In an interview for the monograph *New Materialism*, Braidotti rightly points at the dangers of this commitment, because "[d]is-identification involves the loss of cherished habits of thought and representation, a move that can also produce fear and a sense of insecurity and nostalgia" (35). These fears and counterforces should be taken into account and are worth a more thorough and critical discussion.

In this chapter, we discuss the immanent conversion that Deleuze prescribes as a remedy for the broken link between man and his body. I think that Artaud's writings can function as intercessors because they unfold still relevant healing practices of language in a process of auto-immunization that is articulated as a critical cure of detoxification of the modern fact. In doing so, we look at an early work of Artaud—in which he describes the forces of matter that are the "true nature of evil," which eventually leads to a revelation of both the joys and miseries of what he calls "flesh"—after which we analyze the poem "The Patients and the Doctors" in which he radically affirms his suffering and the forces besieging him. Before doing so, we firstly select the concepts for our analysis by discussing

Deleuze's differentiation between body and flesh. The interrelatedness of body, flesh, mind, expression, and language will be further developed in the analysis of the two works by Artaud that describe, evoke, and perform the vitality and the impulsiveness of the materiality of language.

The Dance of the Flesh

Before reading Artaud's works, we discuss some concepts that were introduced by Deleuze and that will help us in our analysis of the commitment to immanence that we see at work in these writings. In *The Logic of Sense*, Deleuze does not extensively elaborate or exemplify the distinction between body and flesh, which are interesting but also necessary concepts with which we, in a rereading of these concepts, understand the distinction between language as a formalized system of signs and a more vital language that is understood in its agential materiality. In order to understand these terms thus more clearly, we read these two concepts along with Deleuze's *Francis Bacon: The Logic of Sensation* in which he usefully distinguishes between body, flesh, meat, bones, and spirit. A clear differentiation and understanding of these concepts is necessary before we can consider the constitutive role of the healing practices of language.

In his discussion of a large number of paintings by the Irish painter Francis Bacon—that Eckersley rightly considers as a schizoanalysis of his paintings (cf. 206-7)—Deleuze substantiates the logic of sensation that creates a consistency or rhythm while remaining catastrophically chaotic in order to recreate an initial unity of the senses (FB, 30). The differentiation between body ("corps"), flesh ("chair"), and meat ("viande") will be both useful in understanding the logic of sensation, the task, and difficulties of expression and in grasping the distinction that Deleuze makes between body and flesh in *The Logic of Sense*. Already at one of the first pages of his analysis, Deleuze opposes the figurative against what he calls the "Figure." Whereas the figurative narrativizes and merely represents, this Figure breaks with narration and representation through isolation[ii]— "Isolation is thus the simplest means, necessary though not sufficient, to break with representation, to disrupt narration, to escape illustration, to liberate the

---

[ii] Deleuze insists that the articulation of the Figure is not the only way to escape from the figurative, the narrative, and the illustrative because one can also look for a pure and "factual" form through abstraction.

Figure: to stick to the fact" (FB, 2). The strategy of the Figure is to break with the conventional relation between image and object and therewith articulates a disorganized whole that resists representation. In this sense, the Figure is a mode of sensation that is, as Deleuze contends, "master of deformations, the agent of bodily deformations" (FB, 26). The hierarchized, formalized, and organized body—one could, of course, also read "language" instead of "body"—is thus the material for the Figure that isolates it and therewith disrupts its former figurative, narrative, and illustrative characteristics.

The Figure must however not be reduced to a clumpy piece of meat, an unreasoned brushstroke or an incorrect sentence, because "[i]t is a spirit which is body, corporeal and vital breath, an animal spirit; it is the animal spirit of man" (FB, 15). In other words, the Figure and its nonstructured bodily material pervert the imposed organization in order to articulate the corporeal and vital breath that is the animal spirit of man. This corporeal vitality is important since it essentially opens up to the infinity of potentialities that life can offer. In this sense, the animal spirit is a disorganized body and a mesmerizing cry that Deleuze, borrowing the concept from Artaud's *To Have Done with the Judgment of God*, calls the body without organs (BwO). Deleuze situates this BwO "[b]eyond the organism, but also at the limit of the lived body" (FB, 32). The BwO therewith transcends the phenomenological concept of the lived experience, because this BwO dwells beyond or under the organism where the organized body becomes exhausted and subject to impossible and inconceivable forces. Deleuze insists that the BwO is rather opposed to the organization of the organs instead of the organs as such. Whereas the sick-making disciplined body is an organized, normative, or stratified whole that is dominated and bridled by the judgment of God, the BwO is "an intense and intensive body. It is traversed by a wave that traces levels or thresholds in the body according to the variations of its amplitude" (FB, 32). The BwO is thus a nonhierarchized body that, liberated from all its (terminological) determinations, operates on the plane of consistency that is the realm of absolute immanence.

The Articulation of a Vital Body

The concept of the BwO cannot be pinpointed to one exclusive definition and therewith already performs the instability, the energy, and the creativity to which it alludes. At the best, it can only be described, evoked, or suggested. Related to the body, flesh, and meat, Deleuze asserts that "the Figure is the body without organs (dismantle the organism in favor of the body [...]); the body without organs is flesh and nerve" (FB, 33). The flesh that Deleuze equates with the Figure and the BwO must be understood as a vital substance from which genuine thinking emerges. Before drawing such a radical conclusion, it is useful to look at the specific relation between the body and the flesh. Like the body, flesh equally contributes to the articulation of the Figure but only in the sense that it is a powerful nonhuman and organic life that disrupts and subverts any form of supposed fixity. The intense and vital body, the BwO, is thus only articulated when the flesh dances again inside out. Putting it differently, and following the words of Braidotti, this vital body is made up of "a folding-in of external influences and a simultaneous unfolding outwards of affects" (qtd. in Dolphijn and Van der Tuin 2012, 19). The vital body, thus understood as a generative and open-ended subject, is committed to the forces of life from which it, at the same time, contests any formalized and organized subjectification. Before we can understand the role of language and the way in which language articulates the flesh—Klossowski's idea of a perfect silence in an imperfect language—we must pay attention to the role of bones and meat in Deleuze's reading of Bacon's paintings.

Deleuze considers the bones to be the framework within which the flesh can play its tricks, because "the bones are like a trapeze apparatus (the carcass) upon which the flesh is the acrobat. The athleticism of the body is naturally prolonged in this acrobatics of the flesh" (FB, 17). The body is thus exactly the corporeal extension of the interplay between flesh and bones. But what if the acrobat falls from one of his gymnastic apparatuses? What if the flesh loses its grip from the bones? Deleuze considers meat as precisely this state of the body where "flesh and bone confront each other locally rather than being composed structurally. [...] In meat, the flesh seems to *descend* from the bones, while the bones rise up from the flesh" (FB, 16, emphasis in original). We must however take care not to equate meat with lifeless flesh, because meat "retains all the sufferings and assumes all the colors of living flesh" (FB, 17). Whereas Deleuze contends that meat must not be confused with dead flesh, I think on the contrary that meat must be understood as dead flesh, but not as lifeless. The difference between "dead" and "lifeless" is subtle, but in order to clearly differentiate between body and flesh, it will be useful to consider meat as dead but not lifeless flesh. The meat that emerges from the confrontation between the bones and the flesh—the emergence of the skeleton from which the flesh has dropped off—constitutes what Deleuze calls "the common zone of man and the beast, their zone of indiscernibility; it is a 'fact'" (FB, 17). Meat thus creates this "fact"—the undecidable form of the Figure—and therewith constitutes a double becoming. Deleuze asserts that within this zone of the indiscernible "[m]an becomes animal, but he does not become so without the animal simultaneously becoming spirit, the spirit of man, the physical spirit of man presented in the mirror as Eumenides or fate" (FB, 16). Being confronted with meat, we simultaneously see, feel, and perceive how this meat affects us through its becoming of the physical spirit of man or, as Arsalan Memon concisely summarizes, "[t]he human becomes the animal, while the animal becomes the animal-spirit of the human. Flesh becomes meat and concomitantly, meat becomes spirit" (16).

Deleuze insists that this mutual becoming is not the combining of a determined form of man and that of animal; they reveal, on the contrary, "rather a common fact: the common fact of man and animal" (FB, 16). The common fact between man and animal is thus meat that becomes the physical spirit of man when it emerges in front of our eyes. And when the meat becomes the physical spirit of man, thus provoking the vital body or the enfleshed subject, our flesh dances again around the bones. This dance differs however from the organized dance, because it is an animal dance or, better, a dance in which the difference between man and animal becomes undecidable. The flesh makes the body think, reason, and speak, and it is in this dance that a healthy possibility of life can be done justice because the body can only acquire a great health when it becomes dysfunctional. Deleuze's revaluation of the flesh is thus first and foremost a cult of the meat, because the intense body, the BwO, and the vital powers of flesh are essentially unrepresentable and incommunicable. Taking the work of the Irish painter as a point of departure, Deleuze creates a logic of sensation that he substantiates with Bacon's approach to meat. Because of the way in which Bacon produces affects with meat, Deleuze consequently concludes that "[t]he painter is certainly a butcher, but he goes to the butcher's shop as if it were a church, with the meat as the crucified victim"[iii] (FB, 17). Deleuze does not consider Bacon to be Christian painter, but rather as a religious painter or, better, an intercessor that tries to recreate the broken link between man and *this* body, *this* life, and *this* world. Meat has the potency to revitalize our flesh: genuine life is thus to be found among the dead.

[iii] In the English translation, the direct association with Christ—the Crucified (Deleuze uses the word "Crucifié" written with a majuscule)—gets lost in order to generalize *the* crucified written with a minuscule.

The Exploration of the Infra-Sense of the Body

The concept of the BwO was first used by Deleuze in *The Logic of Sense* in which he associated the term with the active nonsense that generates what Artaud termed as "cruelty." Reading Deleuze's take on literature, Bogue similarly contends that "Artaud not only dissolves language but also articulates its inarticulable passions and actions, converting cry-words and breath-words into a theater of cruelty" (2003b, 29)—we will discuss the role of language and writing within the theater of cruelty more thoroughly in Chapter 4. Focusing on formalist linguistics, Deleuze finds their logic that merely focuses on the surface of language insufficient. Their logic should not concern the problem of sense and nonsense, but, on the contrary, the critical and clinical problems of language. Whereas the first set of problems focuses on "the determination of differential levels at which nonsense changes shape, the portmanteau word undergoes a change of nature, and the entire language changes dimension" (LS, 96), a clinical approach concerns "a problem of sliding from one organization to another, or a problem of the formation of a progressive and creative disorganization" (LS, 96). Following these definitions, the BwO is a clinical practice of creative disorganization of both body and language—in his discussion of Artaud's writings, Éric Alliez rightly describes the BwO as "a pure language-affect" instead of "the effect of language" (101)—that opens up to a productive nonsense.

In *The Logic of Sense*, Deleuze considers Artaud as the main pioneer in this creative destruction, because "Artaud is alone in having been an absolute depth in literature, and in having discovered a vital body and the prodigious language of this body. As he says, he discovered them through suffering. He explored the infra-sense, which is still unknown today" (LS, 105). The term "infra-sense" is interesting since it positively subverts the negative connotation of the word "nonsense"—maybe it would thus be more fruitful to speak in terms of sense and infra-sense. Whereas "nonsense" inflicts a torsion[iv] on words by perverting the stability of the formalized system of signs, the "infra-sense" is a vacuole[v] in which

---

[iv] By using, following Grossman (see 2003a, 49), the physical term "torsion," I also want to highlight, following Artaud in a letter from September 22, 1945, to Henri Parisot (see OCIX, 169–72), the inherent energy of words themselves.

[v] A vacuole is a botanical term that designates an organelle—the functional unit within any cell—which functions quite similar to a mammalian kidney or a liver. The vacuole is indispensable to a plant, because besides water, it also contains "stored food, salts, pigments, and metabolic wastes" (Solomon, 84). A vacuole is thus an organelle of becoming, a unit of non-fixity and a site of creation.

we are confronted with the vibration of words and the stuttering of the system of signs. This vacuole is an important site in the enterprise of auto-immunization since it essentially collaborates in the healing practices of language. Participating in the cure of detoxification of the modern fact, Bogue rightly, following Deleuze, concludes that "to write is to trace a line of flight and thereby engage the line of an anorganic life, a line-between toward health and new possibilities for living" (2003b, 192). It is in this sense that the writing of a generative language itself is a remedy against the modern fact that is the broken link between man and *this* world. In *Dissemination*, Derrida rereads Plato's *Phaedrus* and equates writing with the Greek word "pharmakon" understood as remedy. Continuing his reading of Plato, Derrida argues that writing as "pharmakon" can also be translated as "poison" (see Derrida 1981, 98). In fact, writing understood as "pharmakon," that is as well a joyous *and* a terrible force, can be both a beneficial medicine and a suicidal drug. If we speak about writing as a healing practice or eventually a "pharmakon," we should thus remind ourselves of the dangers that can be involved within writing. We will come back to this point in Chapter 2.

Returning to language and the therewith related body, we understand the functioning of the formalized and organized body in the same way as Deleuze understands "sense"—in its opposition to the nonsense of formalist linguistics. The BwO should then be understood not as the opposite of the body, but rather as the infinite depths of the body that is the vital and healthy power that constantly haunts the sick-making stratified body. The vibrating and vital body is engaged with a virtual multiplicity of potentialities: the infra-body is life. But how can this infra-body be suggested, evoked, or folded out within an intelligible language? How can language ever attain the vital flexion of the infra-body? And in what way is the mind folded in this interrelatedness?

The Vitality of the Flesh

In December 1925, Artaud publishes his article "Situation of the Flesh" in *La Nouvelle Revue Française*. His article starts off with an absolute engagement: "I reflect on life"[2] (AN, 58). After his commitment to life, Artaud continues by throwing a dark glance over his beginning—"All the systems I may erect never will match these cries of a man engaged in remaking his life" (AN, 58). In other words, the cries that engage with life can never be expressed within any system of thought or expression. Despite this impossibility, Artaud imagines a system in which "all of man would be involved, with his physical [flesh[vi]] and its heights, the intellectual projection of his mind" (AN, 58). In two rich and eloquent sentences, Artaud defines what he calls flesh: "One day my reason must surely honor the undefined forces besieging me—so that they replace higher thought—those forces which, exteriorly, have the form of a cry. There are intellectual cries, cries which proceed from the *delicacy* of the marrow" (AN, 58). Undefined forces, forces from the outside and the delicacy of the marrow, thus create intellectual cries—cries that are incommunicable forces if they are articulated within the conventions of the formalized languages—that must, sooner or later, be welcomed by the "higher" thoughts. Artaud insists that these thoughts must not be separated from life and he therewith suggests an intricate relationship between flesh and what we habitually call consciousness. Grossman consequently defines the Artaudian flesh as "the complete body, this not yet broken body-thinking *continuum* [...]. The flesh is an inseparable double from matter and mind, from merged organic and spiritual features" (2003a, 76, emphasis in original). Body and thinking are thus different modes of the same vital substance and it is within this flesh that body and thinking form a continuum. It is in his short article "Situation of the Flesh" that Artaud linguistically explores ways in which he can articulate and express this continuum: the flesh.

It is only by a deprivation of life—life is understood as the incessant flow of undefined forces or, in Artaud's words, "man's incomprehensible magnetism" (AN, 58)—that we can see to what extent "the Sensibility ['Sens'] and Science of every thought is hidden in the nervous vitality of the marrow" (AN, 58). This awareness shows how intelligence and intellectuality are deceptive since sensibility, sense, and science—on a phonetic level the mutual implication of these terms is already suggested—ultimately come from the flesh. In revaluating all old-fashioned values, Artaud states that he has lost his life—without any doubt, he also has his suffering and his sickness in mind. In his search of the vital substance that he calls life, he considers himself "[i]n a way [...] the Excitator[vii] of my own vitality: a vitality more precious to me than my conscience, for what to others is only the means for being a Man is for me the whole Reason" (AN, 59). Artaud thus wants to live his life in accordance with this vitality and

---

[vi] In the English translation, the French word "chair" has wrongly been translated as "body." Remaining faithful to Artaud's logic, I have replaced the word "body" by the more appropriate word "flesh."

[vii] The French word "excitateur" has a religious and technical connotation. Whereas Weaver translates the word by "Generator" (SW, 110) and Aldan by "Animator" (AN, 59), I have chosen to preserve the religious connotation by using the word "excitator."

not escape the chaos of the flesh through a misleading use of reason. Genuinely living therewith implies and even necessitates the downgrading (or, depending on the perspective one takes, upgrading) of reason to the vitality of the flesh. Artaud warns however that one has to look for this vitality slowly and cautiously, especially "if you have lost *understanding of words*. It is an indescribable science which explodes by slow thrusts" (AN, 59, emphasis in original). On a textual level, it is only through a slow, close, and almost recitative reading, which is a materialist reading of the French original, that we perceive the analogy between "connaissance des mots" and "science indescriptible" in order to touch upon the vitality and undefined forces of the words, that is, the Figure.

Language thus seems to operate along the same axes as the flesh, and Artaud illustrates this implication when he describes the significance of the flesh:

> For when I say Flesh I say, above all, *apprehension* ["*appréhension*"], hair standing on end ["hérissé"], flesh naked with all the intellectual deepening ["approfondissement"] of this spectacle of pure flesh, and all the consequences ["conséquences"] in the senses ["sens"], that is, in feeling ["sentiments"]. And whoever says feeling ["sentiment'] says intuition ["pressentiment"], that is, direct knowledge ["connaissance"], communication turned inside out to its source to be clarified interiorly. (AN, 58)

Both on the level of sense and the level of phonetics, we perceive the vitality of the nerves which function as undefined but intense forces. By exemplifying "appréhension" with "poil hérissé," Artaud linguistically generates an intimate relationship between hair standing up—an expression that is mostly used for animals—and apprehension. The established assemblage, derived from a close reading, goes on to extend itself and breaks up through its connection with "approfondissement intellectuel de ce spectacle de la chair pure." Intellectual deepening is thus not to be found in a critique of pure reason, but rather in a critique of pure flesh. Apprehension, hair standing up, and intellectual deepening are overlapping, if not implying or even generating one another, on the level of sense, sonority, and materiality. Artaud therewith shows how the sonority of the words produces a spiritual unity that is essentially material or, better, carnal. The formalized system of signs thus loses its predetermined organization and its original denoting function because the significance and meaning of words are generated from a creative play with them: meaning is thus a process of creation. In other words, the subtle and creative play with the sound, form, and restricted meaning of linguistic units makes words vibrate, the system of signs stutter, and language perform its initial instability.

The words that generate and imply each other thus reveal that "[t]here's a mind in the flesh but a mind quick as lightening" (AN, 59). The same flashing spirit that emanates from the vitality of the flesh—the delicacy of the marrow—is created when Artaud equates feeling—"sentiment"—with presentiment or intuition— "pressentiment." Artaud already embedded "feeling" in the consequences of the intellectual deepening of the naked flesh. In other words, "feeling" is a consequence of the "flesh." Reasoning the other way round, this "feeling" is equated with "intuition" that is in turn characterized as direct knowledge, communication that turns from the inside to the outside. In other words, sense and mind are effects of the vitality and undefined forces of the flesh or, to use Artaud's words: "the perturbation of the flesh partakes of the high substance of the mind" (AN, 58). Artaud finishes his article, in which the performativity of words is crucial, by claiming the uniqueness of the flesh. Flesh is interrelated with sensibility—one should note the beautiful connection that "sensibilité" makes with "sentiment," "pressentiment," "connaissance," etcetera—and sensibility must be understood as "an intimate, secret, profound assimilation, absolute in relation to my own suffering, and consequently a solitary and unique consciousness of this suffering" (AN, 58). However vital and energetic Artaud started off, he thus sadly ends his article by noticing that the flesh also creates a solitary and unique consciousness around his suffering—without any doubt, he also has in mind Génica Athanasiou's half-hearted reactions toward his suffering. This sadness is however only relative if we take into account that Artaud has nevertheless managed to articulate the unique consciousness of his suffering. Combatting the system of signs that has not ceased to submit, subjugate, and domesticate in vain the vitality of his flesh, Artaud has formulated a body-language (an impure language, as Klossowski would have it)—a biopolitical intervention of language—that serves as a vacuole against the paranoid and narcotizing fixity within body, mind, and language that Artaud called the judgments of God and to which we sickly and cynically keep holding on to today.

A Commitment to Life

Artaud's short article opened up with a commitment to life. This life turns out to be a capricious, but healthy and vital life that is inseparable from the delicacy of the marrow from which it emerges. In this sense, life is, following Braidotti, "the site of birth and emergence of the new" (2011a, 306). This means that life knows no predetermined structures; life is essentially productive and creative and is traversed by joyous as well as terrible forces that we can only accept in an inevitable submission to their necessity. Engaging with this life and subtly sacrificing words in order to suggest the corporeal ground from which they emerge is the strategy of Artaud's writing that fathoms the depths and the vitality of language. In doing so, Artaud clearly substantiates the intricate relationship between flesh, mind, and expression—he both describes and performs how the mind is an expression of the flesh—and illustrates how meat, bones, and flesh are related to words, grammar, and sense (in a way that is similar to how Francis Bacon made paintings in which a relationship was created between meat, bones, and flesh). In "Situation of the Flesh," Artaud therewith shows how reflection can attain the singular flexion and how the repetition of a transcendent order-word assemblage can suggest the initial difference through the subtle articulation of the infra-sense of language. Artaud calls his corporeal writing a "nerve-meter" that he describes as "[a] kind of incomprehensible stopping place in the mind, right in the middle of everything"[3] (SW, 86). The incomprehensible station of the "nerve-meter" thinks the unthinkable forces of the flesh that incite us to think and makes them vibrate within words. Deleuze equates this incomprehensible station with a hysteria which gives way to "a very peculiar feeling that arises from within the body, precisely because the body is felt *under* the body, the transitory organs are felt under the organization of the fixed organs" (FB, 35, emphasis in original). Deleuze relates the vital powers of the BwO to the sensual writings of the "nerve-meter" that is thus a creative and non-organized, non-stratified and undefined force of becoming. The "nerve-meter" is therewith the Figure that disrupts representation and the conventional sense of words in order to articulate the ground where body, thinking, and language meet.

In an article devoted to Deleuze's analysis of Bacon's paintings, O'Sullivan concisely summarizes that it is the task of art to voice "the production of worlds (the figural) that sit between that which is known (the figurative) and that which is unknown (chaos)" (255–6). In a similar way, writing should alienate language to itself through a subtle and creative play with the chaos that this intelligible language excludes (see also Bogue 2003b, 102). The vital language of the "nerve-meter," the expression of the flesh, and the suggestion of the infra-body will then give us reasons to believe in *this* world since these creative vacuoles evoke the flexional singularity from which body, mind, and language emerge, which is the expression of matter. It is, in other words, in this agential materiality of language that the modern fact of indifference, cynicism, and passivity can be eluded and that we can, healthily and happily, explore what language can *do*. The writings of Artaud, in which meaning is generated through a creative play with the materiality of language, can therewith be considered as intercessors because they give the readers a key that disrupts the formalized system of signs and that opens the door to another possibility of life. Following Deleuze and Guattari, the thus evoked possibility of life "is evaluated through itself in the movements it lays out and the intensities it creates on a plane of immanence: what is not laid out or created is rejected" (WP, 74). It is in this sense, and in conclusion from this schizoanalytic reading, that Artaud's writings subtly play with language in its agential materiality by creating new possibilities of life on the realm of absolute immanence.

The Healing Powers of the Flesh

The commitment to immanence has enormous implications for our conception of health and sickness. On June 7, 1946, Artaud writes his poem "The Patients and the Doctors,"[4] which he records in a radio show by Jean Tardieu the next day. This poem from Artaud's later writings more concretely demonstrates and substantiates the necessity of his project to revitalize language into healing practices in order to reengage with the impulsiveness of matter. It therewith also shows how his attitude toward his suffering and his sickness changed from an initial lamentation and a difficult and painful understanding of his suffering to an affirmative resignation and a creative engagement with this suffering.

Artaud begins his poem with the neutral observation that health and sickness are two distinct states. In what follows, this state of affairs is perverted in order to revalue the fruitfulness of sickness in relation to health. "Lousier" than sickness, Artaud asserts that he finds the state of health "meaner and pettier" (AN, 191). Health is protective, conservative, and prescriptive and therewith more restrictive, narrow-minded, and bridling than sickness. From this assertion, Artaud states in an affirmative resignation: "I have been sick all my life and I ask only that it continue" (AN, 191). With a certain pride and wisdom, he explains that "[f]or the states of / privation in life have always told me a great deal more about the plethora of my / powers than the middleclass drawing – / AS LONG AS YOU'VE GOT YOUR HEALTH" (AN, 192). If we do not know what a body is capable of, it is in a state of suffering and sickness that we discover the abundant powers of the nervous system, the delicacy of the marrow, and the vitality of our flesh. The use of the word "plethora" is significant in this sentence, because it designates, on the one hand, the infinite potentialities of our bodies, while, on the other hand, the word also medically connotes an abundance of blood. "Plethora" and "my powers" are linked in such a way that the poem generates a direct relationship between the body and the power to act within the virtual multiplicity of life. The health of the petty middle-class bourgeoisie shall therefore be insufficient or inadequate if we want to attain or effectuate the vital and disorganized BwO.

After a praise of his hideous, dreadful, and feverish being and after having expressed his aversion against those who want to heal the sick—"Curing a sickness is a crime" (AN, 192)—the poem establishes a triad relationship between love, sickness, and the effects of drugs. Artaud evokes this Trinity by italicizing interrelated words: "But, *sick*, one doesn't get [*high by opium*],[viii] by cocaine, or by morphine. / It's the dread of the fevers / you got to *love*, / the jaundice and the perfidy, / much more than all euphoria" (AN, 192, emphasis in original). When the patient learns to love the caprices of his suffering and sickness, the use of drugs becomes redundant, because these stimulating medicines will sooner or later emanate from the sick body itself. Affirming suffering and sickness is therewith believing in the vital powers, the infinite potentialities, and the yet still unknown capabilities of *this* body: a reengagement with absolute immanence. Focusing on pain, Braidotti similarly praises the fruitfulness of suffering that "forces one to think about the actual material conditions of being interconnected and thus being in the world. It frees one from the stupidity of a perfect health, and the full-blown sense of existential entitlement that comes with it" (2011a, 317). A few lines after his praise of sickness, Artaud wishes therefore that his sickness shall be his administered drugs because he asserts that "cocaine is a bone, / and heroin a superman in the bones" (AN, 192). Heroin—the French word "heroïne" also interestingly means heroine—as a kind of Übermensch[ix] reveals the inhuman forces that are too great to conceive. The following glossolalias are perhaps the most adequate expressions of these vital forces that are located in the flesh and the marrow of our bones. Grossman

---

[viii] In the French poem, the word "dopé" is also put in italics. In the English translation, only "sick"("malade") and "love" ("aimer") are italicized so that the interrelatedness between love, sickness, and the effects and drugs gets lost. For this reason, "high" or "high by opium" should also have been put in italics.

[ix] Because of the many mediocre and often vulgarizing or trivializing English translations (of which "superman" is one of them), I will use the original German term "Übermensch," which Nietzsche firstly coined in *Thus Spoke Zarathustra*.

argues that this "primitive language" of the body is a specific strategy of writing in which Artaud plays with anagrams, graphic derivations, and the etymology of words (Grossman and Rogozinski, 81). Apart from the play with French words, Artaud also spoke Greek—the language of his mother who originally came from Smyrna (that is now renamed to Izmir)—and Italian, which he learned from the nursemaid—languages that also echo in his glossolalia. Artaud continues by stating that his flesh thus dopes his sick body with an incomprehensible and yet singular language which expresses the "con-science of sickness" (AN, 193). This thinking that moves by shocks and constantly disrupts and perverts any fixation emerges from the vitality of the flesh. Consciousness—the French word "conscience" contains the prefix (which is linguistically not considered to be a prefix) "con" or "cunt" so that consciousness could well designate the "science of the cunt"—thus already linguistically generates the corporeal, material, and fertile ground from which this carnal thinking emerges. Like a phoenix that rises from its ashes—"this excremation of an old kid" (AN, 193)—the vitality of the flesh that sensually dances around the bones frees the body, thinking, and therewith language from its limitations in order to experience inhuman forces (spiritual silences and vital cries) that are too great to conceive but that bear witness to a great health.

Ironically expressing his will to "cure all doctors,—born doctors by lack of sickness" (AN, 193), Artaud accuses the doctors of being ignorant of the valuable experiences of their patients. Before they "impose their insulintherapy on me" (AN, 193)—a therapy that does not cure but rather makes the patient dependent on insulin—Artaud therefore asserts that doctors should learn about "my dreadful states of sickness" (AN, 193). Their normative, disciplinary, and torturing therapies—Artaud especially complained about the severity of the electroshock therapy that he underwent in 1943 and 1944 during his internment in the psychiatric hospital of Rodez[x]—slowly consolidate themselves—"opium of the father and shame, / shame on you for going from father to son" (AN, 193). The French words "fi," translated as "shame on you," and "fils" ("son") share a phonetic and material proximity that directly suggests the easily transmittable

---

[x] The Lettrist poet Isidore Isou would later even claim that Artaud has been interned because of such fundamental misunderstandings. He boldly accuses the electroshock therapy, used by psychiatrist Ferdière, and claims that "the frightening misunderstanding between the great creator and his 'doctor' derived from the fact that the first was a genius, who based himself on a traditionalist, Kabbalistic, mystical and alchemical doctrine of the world, extended in a form of expression derived from mechanical, surreal writing; and that the second, the 'scholar,' was a reactionary nullity, based on a dementia; a super-Nazi" (55–6).

terror of these therapies. The son incarnates therewith the detestabilities of the father—the son is caught in the formalized system of signs—and thus constitutes a regime of health that is "meaner and pettier" compared to the state of sickness.

Alluding to the powers of heroin, Artaud asserts that "now you must get [powder][xi] back at you" (AN, 193). This powder should cure all doctors by unfolding the vitality of the flesh, the infinite capabilities of the body, and thus the importance of sickness through which they will renounce the normative, restrictive, and cynic, hence "middleclass" idea of a good health. Putting it differently, by showing how the body and its interrelated thinking (its mind) and language (its expression) go off the rails and therewith reveal inhuman forces that have hitherto been unknown, we can escape the terrible regimes of judgments and thus create a possibility of life that reengages with the vitality of the expression of our body. Artaud therefore ends his poem by qualifying insulintherapy as a "health / for a worn out / world" (AN, 193)—a world where the vital link between man and *this* world, *this* body and *this* life is broken. These final lines of the poem "The Patients and the Doctors" clearly suggest that Artaud resigned to his suffering and his sickness. From a revolt against and a lamentation of his suffering to a reflection of the forces—that is the "true nature evil"—that were revealed through his suffering and his sickness, Artaud ends up accepting his fate by affirmatively living the caprices to which this fate gives way. This attitude is reminiscent of a Stoic attitude of "amor fati" that, in the words of Braidotti, is "a way of accepting vital processes and the expressive intensity of a Life we share with multiple other, here and now" (2013, 190). This turn to Stoicism is an important attitude in eluding the modern fact—it is essentially a critical attitude toward the ongoing developments within medical health care—because it reengages affirmatively with the forces traversing matter, *this* world and *this* life.

In Praise of a Madman

In a discussion with Grossman on Deleuze's reading of Artaud, Rogozinski asserts that

---

[xi] The French word "poudre" designates both the power of gunpowder but also connotes heroin. By translating the word "poudre" with the neutral—maybe more religious—word "dust," Rattray omits the fruitful connotation of gunpowder (that physically serves similar to the carnally inherent heroin). For this reason, I will use the more effective and powerful word "powder."

> Deleuze deviates from Artaud's experience on two critical points: because of his *praise of folly* considered as a resource for writing and because of his apology of the *destruction of the ego*. [...] Artaud's experience of madness fits well with a desubjectification, in which his personal identity seems to disappear and by which he can no longer sign his own name. But this is first and foremost a proof of a *disaster*: Artaud was not that genius of a poet *because* he was mad, but *because he has been mad*. (79, emphasis in original)

However right his statement might be, Grossman nevertheless contends that Deleuze does not misread Artaud, because "I do not think that there is a praise of folly in Deleuze's thinking, but a praise of delirium, which is something very different. He understands the word in its well-known etymological sense: what goes out of the furrow, the straight line. A praise of curves, swirls, those forces that make the discourse deviate from its common law to an outside that overflows it" (79). Grossman's reading of Artaud rightly summarizes what this chapter is about, because Artaud indeed creatively destructs the formalized sense of words in order to suggest and explore a more profound sense or infra-sense that can be found by making words delirious—by making them go off the rails without completely throwing them into a destructive psychosis, fathoming the depths of language and filling the interstices with a deafening but productive hum. If we understand writing as "pharmakon," the practice of writing can be both a remedy and a poison. Following Grossman's remark, we should keep in mind that Deleuze does not praise Artaud's destructive moments of folly, psychosis, or severe illness (see, e.g., TP, 161 or Bogue 2003b, 191) but rather his creative moments of madness, delirium, and constitutive suffering. From these moments Artaud's writings are important healing practices of language (a "pharmakon" understood as remedy), because they expose its reader to yet unknown forces of the body. These biopolitical interventions of language therewith suggest that another health is to be found in the vitality of the flesh, an intense life and affectively vibrating words: flexion and matter. Diagnosing Artaud as a schizophrenic—a rather philosophical concept, as a creative counterpart to his clinical diagnosis of schizophrenia in 1937, that insists on the destructive and yet creative split, the ex-centricity, within his writings—Deleuze considers his writings to be healing practices or, better, intercessors, because they make the system of signs stutter, make words vibrate, and thus create vacuoles that affectively stimulate a healing process of the broken link between man and *this* world and *this* body.

In *The Logic of Sense*, Deleuze contends that every alimentary word—a word that is supposed to have an intrinsic meaning—that is scattered and decomposed directly affects and acts upon the body since these words are essentially physical. Deleuze therefore asserts that Artaud "means to activate, insufflate, palatalize, and set the word aflame so that the word becomes the action of a body without parts, instead of being the passion of a fragmented organism" (LS, 102). Turning the word into a vital body—the action of an intense body—is essentially what Artaud aims at in his positioning of the flesh: the productive infra-sense of language emanates from a creative play with words—a mind emanates from, between, and within the ruins of these order-words—like the powers and powders of the flesh that appear from its dance around the bones—dead but not lifeless meat gives way to an animal spirit that revitalizes the yet still unknown potency of the nervous system, the delicacy of the marrow, and the vitality of the flesh. In this sense, Deleuze does not praise Artaud's folly—or better: his moments of severe physical sickness or mental illness—but rather celebrates his capacity to make body, thinking, and language unstable, delirious, and, from there, creative and full of potency.

Submitting himself to the joyous *and* terrible manifestations of life, Artaud adopts the same Stoic attitude that Deleuze sees at work in the writings of Joë Bousquet. Focusing on the submission to the forces of life that are essentially wounds and events, Deleuze characterizes Stoic as "a concrete or poetic way of life" (LS, 148) that is an immanent and creative approach to life which, again, is a reason to believe in *this* world. Bousquet, following Deleuze, engaged with the wound that he bore in his body—paralyzed during the First World War, Bousquet was bedridden until his death in 1950—and apprehended it as an event. Commenting on these unbearable and unthinkable forces of life that are too great to conceive, Deleuze contends that "events are actualized in us, they wait for us and invite us in. They signal us: 'My wound existed before me, I was born to embody it.' It is a question of attaining this will that the event creates in us; of becoming the quasi-cause of what is produced in us" (LS, 148). Embodying the wound does not mean, as we have already discussed, praising and celebrating moments of severe pain and sickness; it is rather an invitation to genuinely engage with the forces that traverse the body[xii]—the forces that intricately relate flesh to mind and language. Again referring to Stoic virtues, Deleuze comments that "[i]t is in this sense that the *Amor fati* is one with the struggle of free men. My misfortune is present in all events, but also a splendor

---

[xii] This invitation is open to anyone, because, as Bousquet contends, "I owe to my wound having learned that all men are wounded, like me" (183).

and brightness which dry up misfortune and which bring about that the event, once willed, is actualized on its most contracted point" (LS, 149). Submission thus means eternally engaging with the joyous *and* terrible forces of the wound that constantly invites us to embody it. Accepting the invitation of the wound to embody it is about taking risks and yet also about endurance and cautiousness. It is in this sense that Deleuze asserts that

> [t]he eternal truth of the event is grasped only if the event is also inscribed in the flesh. But each time we must double this painful actualization by a counter-actualization which limits, moves, and transfigures it. [...] [T]o double the actualization with a counter-actualization, the identification with a distance [...] is to give to the truth of the event the only chance of not being confused with its inevitable actualization. (LS, 161)

Focusing on Artaud's life, as we will discuss more thoroughly in Chapter 2, we see the dangers of not taking into account the importance of these counter-actualizations. Deleuze's praise of Artaud does therewith not celebrate the psychotic derailments but rather acclaims his Stoic attitude in taking the risk to creatively embody the wound.

An Enterprise of Health

After many treatments and cures, André Roumieux, former psychiatric nurse at the psychiatric hospital of Ville-Évrard, concludes that "[s]ince medicine proves to be inoperative, Antonin Artaud must cohabit with a suffering with unexplained causes. But thanks to his writing, his suffering is no longer limited to itself: being a source of literary expression, it also becomes a source of revolt, of struggle and of a justification of existence. Thirsting for the absolute and for love, flayed alive, more and more shut up in difficulties and pain, having discovered, on the one hand, the power of laudanum and, on the other, that of writing, Artaud will live his life; his completely singular life" (Danchin and Roumieux, 41–2). It is in this observation that one perceives the concrete functioning of writing as a medicine, a healing practice, or a concrete tool in a process of auto-immunization, because already at a young age, Artaud is confronted with suffering, pain, and sickness, and while investigating and exploring the forces that are too great to conceive, besieging him, his writing becomes indeed an ally in combatting, coming to terms, and eventually articulating these forces. In his correspondence with

Jacques Rivière—a correspondence that started after Rivière's refusal to publish Artaud's early poems in *La Nouvelle Revue Française*—Artaud explains in a letter on June 5, 1923, that he suffers from a sickness of his mind that uproots his thinking and disturbs his search in finding the right words and forms to express his suffering. Thus commenting on the quality of his refused poems, he claims that "as soon as *I can grasp a form*, however imperfect, I pin it down, for fear of losing the whole thought"[5] (SW, 31, emphasis in original). In other words, Artaud seeks a language that expresses the forces of his suffering and that thus reconnects him with his thinking. Reflecting on these forces, he perceives that these flexional forces, this "true nature of evil" that is the field of both joyous and terrible forces, traverse his body and are expressed from the flesh as a mind, or a thought, that is as quick as lightening. Positioning this flesh in the center of our concerns means committing ourselves to this physical spirit that is the vital breath and the infra-body that can be explored by an absolute engagement with the forces of *this* body.

In his short article on the vitality of the flesh, Artaud also explored the intricate relationship between flesh, mind, and expression. In doing so, the reader perceives that this language that is essentially a minor—which is thus neglected, underestimated, or undervalued—expression of the body, is a healing practice that operates along the same axes as the flesh, because it exposes us to a greater health that frees us from the normative idea of good health. This great health makes us averse from pharmacies and (psychiatric) hospitals, insofar as these institutes try to impose their ideas and ideals of a good health on us and explore the practices that operate under the skin—the practices that reengage with the forces of the flesh. Creatively engaging with the flesh that is believing in, or submitting oneself affirmatively to, the vital fluxes that traverse and emanate from it, is also a practice of writing in which an open-ended and far more creative language is generated that gives a form to these vital forces. Deleuze therefore concludes that

> the writer as such is not a patient but rather a physician, the physician of himself and of the world. [...] Literature then appears as an enterprise of health: not that the writer would necessarily be in good health [...], but he possesses an irresistible and delicate health that stems from what he has seen and heard of things too big for him, too strong for him, [...] while nonetheless giving him the becomings that a dominant and substantial health would render impossible. (CC, 3)

It is in this sense that writing, understood as an enterprise of auto-immunization and a healing practice of language, might have changed Artaud's attitude—from cynicism to Stoicism—toward his suffering and his sickness.

Diving into the formalized system of signs to fathom its depths and from there performing its instability disorganizes language and evokes how the flexional vitality of the flesh, or the Figure (following Deleuze's analysis of Bacon's paintings), is the ground of what we might have thought to be just some bones of a carcass. Artaud's revaluation and creative reengagement with the vibrating and flexional cries, sounds, and words of the flesh combat the paranoid and narcotizing fixity within body, mind, and language. Evoking, suggesting, and celebrating a triad relationship of flesh, mind, and expression, Artaud's writings support his devotion to the impulsiveness of matter and the generation of the BwO: the evocation of an infra-body. His perpetually unstable and vibrating writings in an impure and schizophrenic language have the potency to cure the broken link between man and the vitality of *this* world, the creative forces of *this* life, and the unexplored but infinitely potential and healthy powers of *this* body. It is in this sense that they work as intercessors that plunge us into yet unexplored realms of forces, energies, and intensities and that thus enable us to breathe or create new possibilities of life. As a medically affective therapy and a healing practice to cure the sickness of our modern age—that is the overmedicalization of our body and the ever-growing codification, subjectification, and subjugation from the structures of advanced capitalism—this language creates vacuoles that interrupt, pervert, and break the sensory-motor circuits of the formalized system of signs by deterritorializing language in order to make a minor use of it that is subject to a constant becoming. Although this vacuole is the unstable product of an impersonal life and a flexional singularity, it nevertheless destabilizes and perverts the formalized system of signs that has collaborated in the breaking of the vital and healthy link between man and the infinite possibilities of *this* world.

In this chapter, we have seen that the formalized system of signs, which is the consolidation of the various patterns of language, is potentially a sick-making burden that gives way to the still pertinent modern fact that concerns the detachment from man with *this world*, but language also has the potency, as we have seen, to reengage with absolute immanence and to heal the broken link between man and his body if we make it creatively delirious, delicately imperfect, and subtly unstable. This more generative language, with which many of Artaud's writings engage, participates in a cure of detoxification of the modern fact. Before analyzing more closely this potency of language that is the creative play with its phonetics, semantics, and materiality that is an enterprise of health, it is useful to discuss the burden of language. In what sense is language a burden to its speakers? How does language participate in the modern fact that is the broken link between man and *this* world?

Notes

1. "Je me livre à la fièvre des rêves, mais c'est pour en retirer de nouvelles lois" (OCI**, 53).
2. We quote Artaud's article (AN, 58–9) in its entirety to fully account for the performative play with words in the French original: "Je pense à la vie. Tous les systèmes que je pourrai édifier n'égaleront jamais mes cris d'homme occupé à refaire sa vie. J'imagine un système où tout homme participerait, l'homme avec sa chair physique et les hauteurs, la projection intellectuelle de son esprit.

    Il faut compter pour moi, avant tout, avec le magnétisme incompréhensible de l'homme, avec ce que, faute d'expression plus perçante, je suis bien obligé d'appeler sa force de vie.

    Ces forces informulées qui m'assiègent, il faudra bien un jour que ma raison les accueille, qu'elles s'installent à la place de la haute pensée, ces forces qui du dehors ont la forme d'un cri. Il y a des cris intellectuels, des cris qui proviennent de la *finesse* des moelles. C'est cela, moi, que j'appelle la Chair. Je ne sépare pas ma pensée dans ma chair.

    Il faut avoir été privé de la vie, de l'irradiation nerveuse de l'existence, de la complétude consciente du nerf pour se rendre compte à quel point le Sens et la Science de toute pensée est caché dans la vitalité nerveuse des moelles et combien ils se trompent ceux qui font un sort à l'Intelligence ou à l'absolue Intellectualité. Il y a par-dessus tout la complétude du nerf. Complétude qui tient toute la conscience, et les chemins occultes de l'esprit dans la chair.

    Mais que suis-je au milieu de cette théorie de la Chair ou pour mieux dire de l'Existence ? Je suis un homme qui a perdu sa vie et qui cherche par tous les moyens à lui faire reprendre sa place. Je suis en quelque sorte l'Excitateur de ma propre vitalité: vitalité qui m'est plus précieuse que la conscience, car ce qui chez les autres hommes n'est que le moyen d'être un Homme est chez moi toute la Raison. Dans le cours de cette recherche enfouie dans les limbes de ma conscience, j'ai cru sentir des éclatements, comme le heurt de pierres occultes ou la pétrification soudaine de feux. Des feux qui seraient comme des vérités insensibles et par miracle vitalisées.

Mais il faut aller à pas lents sur la route des pierres mortes, surtout pour qui a perdu la *connaissance des mots*. C'est une science indescriptible et qui explose par poussées lentes. Et qui la possède ne la connaît pas. Mais les Anges aussi ne connaissent pas, car toute vraie connaissance est *obscure*. L'Esprit clair appartient à la matière. Je veux dire l'Esprit, à un moment donné, clair.
Mais il faut que j'inspecte ce sens de la chair qui doit me donner une métaphysique de l'Être, et la connaissance définitive de la Vie.
Pour moi qui dit Chair dit avant tout *appréhension*, poil hérissé, chair à nu avec tout l'approfondissement intellectuel de ce spectacle de la chair pure et toutes ses conséquences dans les sens, c'est-à-dire dans le sentiments.
Et qui dit sentiment dit pressentiment, c'est-à-dire connaissance directe, communication retournée et qui s'éclaire de l'intérieur. Il y a un esprit dans la chair, mais un esprit prompt comme la foudre. Et toutefois l'ébranlement de la chair participe de la substance haute de l'esprit.
Et toutefois qui dit chair dit aussi sensibilité. Sensibilité, c'est-à-dire appropriation, mais appropriation intime, secrète, profonde, absolue de ma douleur à moi-même, et par conséquent connaissance solitaire et unique de cette douleur" (OCI*, 50–1).

3 "Une sorte de station incompréhensible et toute droite au milieu de tout dans l'esprit" (OCI*, 100).
4 We quote this poem (AN, 191–3), again, in its entirety to show the performative play with words in the French original:
"La maladie est un état.
La santé n'en est qu'un autre,
plus moche.
Je veux dire plus lâche et plus mesquin.
Pas de malade qui n'ait grandi.
Pas de bien portant qui n'ait un jour trahi, pour n'avoir pas voulu être malade, comme tels médecins que j'ai subis.

J'ai été malade toute ma vie et je ne demande qu'à continuer. Car les états de privations de la vie m'ont toujours renseigné beaucoup mieux sur la pléthore de ma puissance que les crédences petites-bourgeoises de:
LA BONNE SANTÉ SUFFIT.

Car mon être est beau mais affreux. Et il n'est beau que parce qu'il est affreux.
Affreux, affre, construit d'affreux.
Guérir une maladie est un crime.
C'est écraser la tête d'un môme beaucoup moins chiche que la vie.
Le laid con-sonne. Le beau pourrit.

Mais, *malade*, on n'est pas *dopé* d'opium, de cocaïne et de morphine.
Et il faut *aimer* l'affre
      des fièvres,
la jaunisse et sa perfidie
beaucoup plus que toute euphorie.

Alors la fièvre,
la fièvre chaude de ma tête,
– car je suis en état de fièvre chaude depuis cinquante ans que je suis en vie, –
me donnera
mon opium,
– cet être, –
celui,
tête chaude que je serai,
opium de la tête aux pieds.
Car,
la cocaïne est un os,
l'héroïne, un sur-homme en os,
      ca i tra la sara
      ca fena
      ca i tra la sara
      cafa
et l'opium est cette cave,
cette momification de sang cave,
cette raclure
de sperme en cave,
cette excrémation d'un vieux môme,
cette désintégration d'un vieux trou,
cette excrémentation d'un môme, petit môme d'anus enfoui,
dont le nom est:
      merde,
        pipi,
con-science des maladies.

Et, opium de père en fi,

fi donc qui va de père en fils, –
il faut qu'il t'en revienne la poudre,
quand tu auras bien souffert sans lit.

C'est ainsi que je considère
que c'est à moi,
sempiternel malade,
à guérir tous les médecins,
– nés médecins par insuffisance de maladie, –
et non à des médecins ignorants de mes états affreux de malade,
à m'imposer leur insulinothérapie,
santé
d'un monde
d'avachis" (OCXXII, 67–9).

5 "Lors donc que *je peux saisir une forme*, si imparfaite soit-elle, je la fixe, dans la crainte de perdre toute la pensée" (OCI*, 20).

2

A Zoology of Language: On the Disorder of Language and Artaud's Poetics

The truth of life lies in the impulsiveness of matter. The mind of man has been poisoned by concepts.[1]
—Antonin Artaud, "Manifesto In Clear Language," SW, p. 108

The Outside of Language

In the previous chapter, we have already touched upon a discussion of language understood as a transcendentalized, consolidated, and formalized system of signs and thus concluded that language should rather be considered and approached in its agential materiality and as a living force. In this chapter, we more thoroughly discuss the functioning of language understood as a formalized system of signs and we will consider Artaud's specific use of language in his later writings that we will eventually characterize as a zoology of language.

Our language is similar to the ambiguity that surrounds Pandora: the all-endowed who, at the same time, disturbs balance. Language is a theological burden—Pandora was a gift from the king of the gods—which, at the same time, brings salvation. Language is, following Artaud, a sick-making treason to this world of immanence that, at the same time, can be turned into a healing practice. In his "Manifesto in Clear Language," Artaud already asserted that "[m]y mind, exhausted by discursive reason, wants to be caught up in the wheels of a new, an absolute gravitation. For me it is like a supreme reorganization in which only the laws of Illogic participate, and in which there triumphs the discovery of a new Meaning"[2] (SW, 108). A new meaning, that is, a new language that is not structured by reason but by the illogic is the breath of an absolute gravitation and the "realm of pure flesh"[3] that is "my flesh irrigated by nerves"[4] (SW, 108).

In other words, this new meaning is generated by the forces that traverse and emerge from the flesh that is the expression of matter.

Literature—or better, following Deleuze, "[t]hese powers of the false to produce truth" (N, 126)—is the muscle that allows the formalized system of signs to be moved, pushed, and twisted. If language, understood as the formalized system of signs, selects matter and slips it into the realm of transcendence where it is hierarchically coded and overcoded by means of oppositions, the ultimate goal of literature is, following Deleuze, "to release this creation of a health or this invention of a people—that is, a possibility of life" (CC, 4). It is up to literature and writing that are essentially enterprises of auto-immunization and healing practices of language to twist, combat, and play with the formalized system of signs that constitutes our daily language. Deleuze subsequently asserts that "[w]e can see more clearly the effect of literature on language: as Proust says, it opens up a kind of foreign language within language, which is neither another language nor a rediscovered patois but a becoming-other of language, a 'minorization' of this major language, a delirium that carries it off, a witch's line that escapes the dominant system" (CC, 5). This delirium is a "pharmakon" or writing understood as a beneficial medicine that is essentially a creative cure of detoxification of the modern fact. Deleuze distinguishes three aspects within the practice of literature that hollows out, articulates, and opens up to another language within and through the dominant language. The first two aspects are that literature decomposes or even destroys language but also creates and reorganizes a new language within language through the creation of a new syntax. The third aspect is more complex and pushes language to its limits since it suggests and articulates "veritable Ideas that the writer sees and hears in the interstices of language [...]. They are not outside language, but the outside of language. The writer as seer and hearer, the aim of literature: it is the passage of life within language that constitutes Ideas" (CC, 5). This third aspect is the most complex and ungraspable force of literature because it articulates what the dominant language excludes from its organization; it touches upon the Figure, the flesh, the nerves, the marrow, and the vitality and potency of *this* body, *this* world, and *this* life. More concisely, Bogue rightly concludes that in this third aspect of literature where visions and auditions are articulated, "writers make sensible the limits of language, the nonlinguistic painting and music that language alone can produce" (2003b, 186). Deleuze asserts that "[t]hese three aspects, which are in perpetual movement, can be seen clearly in Artaud"

(CC, 5). If Artaud's writings articulate the outside of language, it is useful to consider in what sense language is a burden to its speakers. It goes without saying that any language imposes limitations to the possibilities of expression of its speaker, but what are the implications or consequences of these limits?

In this chapter, we take a closer look at the ambiguity of language and Artaud's specific use of language by focusing upon the three aspects, distinguished by Deleuze, under which literature operates. In doing so, we read Spinoza's and Nietzsche's writings on language in order to see how language is at the basis of confusion and illness. In order to understand the healing practices of language, I think that these two thinkers have stirred some interesting discussions on the sick-making functioning and structuring of language understood as a formalized system of signs. We finally analyze Artaud's problem with language—that is, as we've already seen, also related to the body and thinking—after which we discuss Artaud's articulation of a foreign language or his becoming-other of language, which I will call his "zoology of language."

A Cynical Reading of Spinoza

Before discussing Spinoza's thoughts on language, it is interesting to consider Artaud's notebook—Artaud wrote more than four hundred notebooks from 1945 until his death in 1948—from June 1947, written in Paris, that starts with an extensive letter to Albert Camus in which he, among others, claims that "[o]ur world, mister Albert Camus, is very ill, and it has been dying of something for a long time, and very precisely of what so many geniuses have died, and because, when they wished to speak, we would not believe them. I also speak but one does not want to believe me"[5] (O, 1609). Repeating the argument that he made in *Van Gogh, the Man Suicided by Society*, in which he claimed that the collective consciousness of society provoked the deaths of geniuses, in his letter to Camus, the notebook ends with a small commentary on Spinoza in which he asserts that "I have never seen a man more bestially devoted/to his principles, that are as unverified as they are unverifiable, than Spinoza"[6] (CI, 861). These unverifiable principles give Artaud an idea of unrest and incertitude because he even sees the return "of the head of the gentleman whose existence we / did not know and / who is called, it seems, mister God"[7] (CI, 861). While writing, Artaud perceives that he is victim to the same principles of which Spinoza writes, because "the words that we / use stick they stick to the / thought that one has like / a miraculous glue"[8] (CI, 860[i]). From this perception that words and thoughts are interrelated, Artaud goes on by claiming that the return of the gentleman—whom he equates with God—"is very good"[9] (CI, 860), but the problem is that Spinoza wanted to *prove* its existence and essence. He then goes on asking why Spinoza would not have come up with other names for this gentleman and why he actually found a need to return to matter and to remember us of the universality of matter— why did he undertake "the operation to start again / what we are going to bury / instead of letting circulate"[10] (CI, 861)? In other words, Artaud reproaches Spinoza that he tries to prove essentially unverifiable principles, therewith reconfirming the essence and existence of God and the universality of matter that our society—at least, this is what *Van Gogh, the Man Suicided by Society* and Artaud's letter to Camus, written in the same notebook, suggest—is actually disputing and burying nowadays. This impossibility in Artaud's later writings, these unverifiable principles, is interesting, because writing, following Artaud, should express something that seems nowadays forgotten or disdained but that is essentially untranslatable. We will come back to this point later in Chapter 4.

Spinoza's Confusion

However cynical a discussion of Spinoza, according to Artaud, might thus be, it is nevertheless useful to discuss his thoughts on language in order to eventually describe Artaud's relation to this confusion of language. In the last proposition from the second part of *The Ethics*, Spinoza states: "There is in the mind no volition or affirmation and negation, save that which an idea, inasmuch as it is an idea, involves" (E2P49). That is to say that the understanding of A can solely exist if one has the idea of A. We can affirm A if it is a true idea. Spinoza's proof to his thirtieth proposition of the first part of *The Ethics* gives a key to what a true idea is, because what "is contained in the intellect in representation must necessarily be granted in nature" (E1P30Dem). A true idea must thus correspond to matter; it must be granted in nature, that is, in life. In an extensive commentary to the last proposition of the second part of *The Ethics*, Spinoza asserts that our understanding is often troubled since we confuse three things: images, words,

---

[i] Zigzaggingly writing, Artaud begins his account of Spinoza on the back on the twenty-first page but then ends it on the front of the twentieth page of his notebook.

and ideas. Our confusion is a burden "both for philosophic purposes and for the wise ordering of life" (E2P49Schol). Images belong to the field of perception or imagination but should not be confused with ideas as this confusion might lead to a denial of ideas of which we cannot form mental pictures. A confusion of words and ideas is rather dangerous, because Spinoza argues that

> those who confuse words with ideas, or with the affirmation which an idea involves, think that they can wish something contrary to what they feel, affirm, or deny. This misconception will easily be laid aside by one, who reflects on the nature of knowledge, and seeing that it in no wise involves the conception of extension, will therefore clearly understand, that an idea (being a mode of thinking) does not consist in the image of anything, nor in words. The essence of words and images is put together by bodily motions, which in no wise involve the conception of thought. (E2P49Schol)

In other words, thinking is a flux that cannot be caught in images or words—images and words are politically and socially useful but philosophically delusive and constrictive nets—but must nonetheless be thought. According to Spinoza, we must thus not confound thinking—ideas are modes of the attribute thought that is in its turn an expression of nature or matter—with images or words since they are modes of extension.

At the end of the extensive note to his proposition, Spinoza sums up the advantages of a state without this confusion.[ii] One of the advantages is that a healthier state is advantageous to our mental ecology, because "[s]uch a doctrine not only completely tranquilizes our spirit, but also shows us where our highest happiness or blessedness is, namely, solely in the knowledge of God, whereby we are led to act only as love and piety shall bid us" (E2P49Schol). Knowledge and understanding of "God or nature" (E4Praef) is beneficial and healing because it keeps reminding and confronting us of the vital potentialities of matter. It is for this reason that the vital body, which is the expression of matter, is devoted to the forces of an immanent understanding of God or nature. Deleuze and Guattari consequently assert in their understanding of Spinoza that "all BwO's pay homage to Spinoza" (TP, 170). A healthier state is also advantageous to our social ecology since "[t]his doctrine raises social life, inasmuch as it teaches us

---

[ii] A state without this confusion is not easily achieved, and David Savan rightly concludes that Spinoza "has shown us a road which is difficult to travel" (225). In combatting the organization of the body and in articulating the BwO (physically, linguistically, or in what other way one creatively explores it), it is important to keep in mind that this is indeed not an easy process. We will come back to this point in Chapter 3.

to hate no man, neither to despise, to deride, to envy, or to be angry with any" (E2P49Schol). However interesting, important, and necessary these advantages to our social ecology (and also environmental ecology) are, in this book, we mainly focus on the benefits of a healthier state for our mental ecology.

The Forces of Zoe

In his *Spinoza: Practical Philosophy*, Deleuze rereads *The Ethics* and states that "Spinoza calls out to us in the way he does: you do not know beforehand what good or bad you are capable of; you do not know beforehand what a body or a mind can do, in a given encounter, a given arrangement, a given combination" (S, 125). Spinoza's theory of understanding God or nature, which involves a clear distinguishing between words, images, and ideas, is a cry (Deleuze uses the word "cri" to characterize Spinoza's *The Ethics*): we can be far more happy and healthy if we manage to stay away from the state of confusion in which we confound words, images, and ideas. A devotion to the vitality of matter, the potencies of this world, and the potentialities of life goes beyond language, because, as Spinoza stated, the essence of words is put together by bodily motions. Language, understood as a formalized system of signs, is therefore a perversion or a crude fetishism of sense that does not adequately represent nature, matter, or life. Following Spinoza, language is a system of rules and conventions ("langue," the French language usefully differentiates between "langue"—the system of signs—and "langage"—the appropriation or the human faculty to use the system of signs) that one appropriates through experience ("langage") but that in no way expresses the vitality of nature which is the domain of thought or silence. True ideas are thus the outside of language and find themselves in a realm of exclusion, repression, and invisibility. These true ideas are excluded from what Braidotti calls "bios"—the "discursive, intelligent, social life" (2011a, 331)—but can be rediscovered within the realm of "zoe" that is the bare and "brutal 'animal life' [that] as generative vitality is a major transversal force that cuts across and connects previously segregated domains" (2011a, 331) or, put differently, the "mindless vitality of Life carrying on independently, regardless of rational control" (2006a, 37). "Zoe" is thus the realm of the forces, which Artaud investigated as the "true nature of evil," that incessantly traverse matter, flesh, and *this* world. True ideas are, following Spinoza, concepts that position life as a generative process.

Destratification and the Art of Caution

In line with this thinking, Deleuze and Guattari draw upon the "Danish Spinozist" (1987, 48) linguist Hjelmslev by asserting that in the beginning there was only nature or matter that they describe as

> the Body without Organs or the destratified Plane of Consistency; the Matter of the Plane, that which occurs on the body or plane (singular, nonsegmented multiplicities composed of intensive continuums, emissions of particles-signs, conjunctions of flows); and the abstract Machine, or abstract Machines, insofar as they construct that body or draw that plane or "diagram" what occurs (lines of flight, or absolute deterritorializations). (TP, 80)

Looking at different processes in nature, what logically and inherently follows is a process of stratification, and Deleuze and Guattari continue that

> [o]n the intensive continuum, the strata fashion forms and form matters into substances. In combined emissions, they make the distinction between expressions and contents, units of expression and units of content, for example, signs and particles. In conjunctions, they separate flows, assigning them relative movements and diverse territorialities, relative deterritorializations and complementary reterritorializations. (TP, 80)

This geological approach to language—a selection, deduction (substance) and structuring (form) make formed matter or content, and a selection (substance) and organization (form) form functional structures or expressions—shows that words arise from matter as strata. Spinoza already stated that the essence of words—the formed matter or substance—is formed by bodily motions, but Hjelmslev doubles these words by relating the essence of words to functional structures or expressions that have their own internal dynamics. This double bind renders destratification, the process to articulate the BwO of language, rather difficult and dangerous (one has to deal with two reciprocally presupposing multiplicities) and gives way easily to a confusion of words and ideas.

Destratification is always an art of caution and involves, as Braidotti claims, the mapping and creating of "thresholds of sustainability" (2012, 190) that she describes as "a portion of forces that is stable enough to sustain and to undergo constant, though non-destructive, fluxes of transformation" (2012, 192). These thresholds of sustainability, or as discussed earlier, these counter-actualizations, are thus the endurance of a delicate health that renders the realization of the greater health always possible. Applied to the becoming-other of language in literature, we could conclude for this moment that the thresholds of sustainability should ensure the possibility of language to be intelligible in order to affect. Even Spinoza was already aware of this caution since his stamp contained his initials "BDS" and a rose—a beautiful flower that, whenever unwarily plucked, has venomous prickles—but also the Latin word "caute" meaning "cautiousness" or "be careful"—the capitalized word "CAVTE" under his stone portrait can also be found on his alleged grave in The Hague.

Deleuze and Guattari are also well aware of the danger of a too rough destratification and instruct their readers to

> [m]imic the strata. You don't reach the BwO, and its plane of consistency, by wildly destratifying. [...] If you free it with too violent an action, if you blow apart the strata without taking precautions, then instead of drawing the plane you will be killed, plunged into a black hole, or even dragged toward catastrophe. Staying stratified—organized, signified, subjected—is not the worst that can happen; the worst that can happen is if you throw the strata into demented or suicidal collapse, which brings them back down on us heavier than ever. (TP, 178)

Looking at Artaud's writings around the years 1936–1943, we perceive that the literarily illegible and hermetic letters along with his megalomaniac, messianic, and asocial behavior have thrown the strata back on him harder than ever during the many years of his internments in various mental hospitals. It is during this period that his writings are a "pharmakon" that can be better understood as a suicidal drug.

The initial negligence of the Anglo-Saxon literature on Artaud's later writings might also be explained from the obscurity of the majority of the works written during this period. In his biography of Artaud, Schafer even contends that the works following these obscure years "lack coherence and inform us more on his ideas on the temporality and superficiality of tangible existence" (14) and then more generally concludes that "[t]he bulk of Artaud's ideas—and their almost seamless vacillation between incoherence and lucidity—developed largely during the second half of his life" (14). Apparently neglecting the importance of the capricious style, the energetic form, and the constitutive materiality of Artaud's later writings, Schafer radically characterizes an important part of his later works as "incoherent ramblings on familiar topics: religion, sexuality, drugs and persecution by demons" (167). These conclusions that can be drawn from a superficial reading instead of a more close reading of Artaud's later writings essentially show that writing too needs to take into account the art of caution if it wants to be a "pharmakon" that is understood as a remedy. The vitality of matter that is at the outside of language is a healing realm that needs a program or, in Braidotti's words, "a sense of limits" (2012, 191), if one wants to attain it. Spinoza already summed up different reasons why a clearing of our confusion and a better understanding of ideas are more advantageous for our mental being and our society, and Deleuze and Guattari, following the Spinozist linguist Hjelmslev, also plea for a healthier engagement with the strata. As we have seen for both Spinoza and Deleuze and Guattari, language creates a state of confusion, disorder, or a state of rusted stratification, subjugation, and organization, but language, if one is well aware of its geological organization, can also be the source of a greater health, liberation, and salvation.

To Believe in Grammar

Ideas are difficult to think if thinking is guided or confused by a discursive language. The form and substance of its possibilities of expression are ideologically, politically, and even theologically structured and therewith affect the form and substance of content. These two reciprocally presupposing assemblages form the basis of a non-neutral organization that is a subjugating and restricting but also suppressing and sick-making language. Following Nietzsche, Azzan Yadin asserts that "[a]s man enters into social life, language must change to accommodate this transition, and as a result, the primordial word, the creative outcome of an irreducibly individual experience must give way to the 'concept'" (182). Language thus needs a preestablished and preexistent structure to organize man's social life. Yadin consequently concludes that what he calls "social language" is "the language of forgetting, of effacing individual difference" (183). Speaking this social language thus means speaking within the limitations of preestablished concepts and hence the alienation from the singularity of the initial flexion of expression. Nietzsche was well aware of this confusing structuring of language. In his *Twilight of the Idols*, Nietzsche returns to the statement that he earlier made in *The Gay Science* about the death of God. Focusing on reason, Nietzsche asserts that "we become involved in a crude fetishism when we make ourselves conscious of the basic premises of the metaphysics of language, in plain words: of *reason*" (1998, 13–14, emphasis in original). Reason, Nietzsche goes on, postulates being, unity, and oppositions, because reason "is what sees doer and deed everywhere: it believes in the will as cause in general; it believes in the 'I,' in the I as Being, in the I as substance, and *projects* the belief in the I-substance onto all things—only then does it *create* the concept 'thing'" (1998, 14, emphasis in original). In other words, language is guided by the prejudice reason, and reason presupposes a range of premises and thus "compels us to establish unity, identity, duration, substance, cause, materiality, Being—we see ourselves to a certain extent tangled up in error" (1998, 13). Nietzsche uses the German word "Dinglichkeit" (here translated as "materiality") that stresses more effectively the defined, determined, organized, and structured "things" or strata that form matter into substances; the word "thingness" thus more adequately covers what reason creates. We might thus well have killed our judging, omnipresent, and transcendent God, but we still speak its language. In *A Thousand Plateaus*, Deleuze and Guattari consequently assert that "[t]o express is always to sing the glory of God" (TP, 49). This contradiction makes Nietzsche disappointedly conclude that "I am afraid we are not getting rid of God because we still believe in grammar" (1998, 14).

Having faith in grammar that is the structural rules governing phrases or words means that our thinking is confused with an already organized, structured, and, following Nietzsche, theological language that is governed by reason. Language is consequently an ideological and political but moreover, as we have discussed above, a biological—understood as the "discourse about social and political life" (Braidotti 2011a, 326)—and theological enterprise since it still sings the glory of a transcendentalized God that posits unity, identity, and thingness. Getting rid of this God means that we should stop believing in grammar and begin believing in the untranslatable, ungraspable, and unthinkable forces within the materiality of language that incite us, although unthinkable, to genuinely think, that is, the human, animal, *and* organic forces of life, that is, the vitality of matter. To stop believing in grammar does not mean that we should stutter or speak in tongues or silence; to stop believing in grammar also involves the art of caution or the creation of thresholds of sustainability, because to stop believing in grammar means that one must hollow out a foreign language in the imposed logic of the dominant politics and discourse that structure our language.

A Zoology of Language

What we must therefore try to articulate, suggest, and create is a language that engages with the unthinkable and untranslatable forces of life that is a zoological language or, better, a language that breaks with the privileging of "Theos" and "bios" over "zoe." This does not mean that this zoological language is an atheist or an a-biological language. On the contrary, respecting the art of caution and the creation of thresholds of sustainability, this zoological language cannot and should not completely go astray from "Theos" and "bios." We must thus rather search for a language that is a theological, a biological, *and* a zoological enterprise: an affirmative language that encompasses "Theos" (the discourse of reason, unity, and opposition), "bios" (the political discourse of human and discursive life), *and* "zoe" (the animal, organic, pre- and nonhuman and vital life); a language that is bios/zoe; a zoology of language. When I speak of the zoology of language or a zoological language, I thus mean the affirmative bios/zoe language that respects the thresholds of sustainability by hollowing out a foreign language *within* the formalized system of signs; the affirmative bios/zoe language thus brings forth a becoming-foreign or a becoming-other of language. This zoology of language has broad implications and consequences, because, in the words of Braidotti,

> [t]he potency of *bios/zoe* [...] displaces the humanistic vision of consciousness, which hinges on the sovereignty of the "I." It can no longer be safely assumed that consciousness coincides with subjectivity [...]. Far from being merely a crisis of values, this situation confronts us with a formidable set of new opportunities. Renewed conceptual creativity and a leap of the social imaginary are needed in order to meet the challenge. (2006a, 42)

In other words, a zoological language is also a reappropriation of the singularity of the flesh and a reengagement with the vital forces traversing it. It is in this sense that a zoological language is also an enterprise of auto-immunization and a cure of detoxification of the modern fact that is the detachment of man from *this* world. Language, understood in its agential materiality and perceived as a vital force, plays a key role in the challenge for a displacement of our rather theological and biological language that causes our confusion, cynicism, and illness.

To heal the disorders created by this theology and biology of language that valorizes, privileges, and recognizes only some aspects of life (and thus restricts and neglects other potentialities of *this* life), one must hollow out another language, which is a zoological language, in this suppressing and sick-making language. This zoological language should also engage with thinking, because as Deleuze asserts in his book *Nietzsche and Philosophy*, "[l]ife would be the active force of thought, but thought would be the affirmative power of life. Both would go in the same direction, carrying each other along, smashing restrictions, matching each other step for step, in a burst of unparalleled creativity. Thinking would then *mean discovering, inventing, new possibilities of life*" (NP, 101, emphasis in original). Our addictive, sensory-motor, and cynic use of a rather theological and biological language that is structured by reason and that therewith posits a discursive, intelligent, and human life or a unity, identity, and thingness excludes genuine thinking since it already structures our thinking. Spinoza claimed that words do not belong to the domain of thinking; a zoological language that does not obey the imposed formalized structures or grammar of the dominant language will therefore play with words in such a way that it enables us to articulate, to suggest, or to evoke the realm of ideas, the vitality of matter, and the potentialities of this life. This foreign language is the language of literature that enables us to genuinely think the unthinkable fluxes traversing matter and to create new possibilities of life. As Deleuze almost mathematically demonstrates in his book on Nietzsche's philosophy: "'we the artists' = 'we the seekers after knowledge or truth' = 'we the inventors of new possibilities of life'" (NP, 103). The artists, writers, and poets are therefore the healthy and happy seekers who are devoted to immanence, life, and nature or, as Spinoza would say, God.

Untranslatable Forces

In his earlier writings, Artaud is already confronted with the limits and confusion and yet also the potency and vitality of language. In his search for the expression of his suffering and his sickness, he muses that the forces besieging him and that incite him to think are untranslatable in our daily language. In his "Further Letter about Myself" that is addressed to a masculine but anonymous reader, Artaud writes that "[m]y mind is open through the belly and from below it piles up dark, inexpressible knowledge full of subterranean tides, concave blocks, and frozen turbulence. Do not mistake this for imagery. It cries out to take shape as loathsome understanding. I crave only silence from whoever has any regard for me, but if I may venture to say, intellectual silence, like my waiting, on edge"[11] (CW, 187–8). A mind stems from the flesh, a corporeal and material thinking that is untranslatable (Artaud uses the word "intraduisible"; the word "inexpressible" that is used in the quoted translation by Victor Corti echoes fatalism since "untranslatable" does not necessarily imply that it is inexpressible) because it can be caught in neither images nor words. Full of underground tides, concave buildings, and frozen agitations or turbulence—these three paradoxes that challenge reason are the form of a loathsome knowledge, a knowledge of which Artaud wishes to silence, a silence that is like a tense waiting or expectation. But silence does not thwart the language that renders this knowledge untranslatable. In *The Writing of the Disaster*, Maurice Blanchot therefore asserts that "[p]*reserving* silence: that is what, all unknowing, we all want to do, writing" (122, emphasis in original). It is from this silence and these untranslatable forces, which make him love but also suffer, that Artaud wants to articulate a new language. As we have already seen, Artaud's attitude toward the forces besieging him finally develops into an affirmative or Stoic resignation and a creative engagement with this suffering. It is mainly in his later writings that he explores and investigates the intricate relationship between flesh, mind, and expression. These later writings seek for the expression of a new corporeal and material language that is the articulation of a zoological language breaking through the restrictions and ordering structures of our daily language in order to engage with the untranslatable forces that traverse the vitality of matter.

To Have Done with Mythomania

During his interment in the psychiatric hospital of Rodez from February 1943 to May 1946, Artaud starts to write poems, unfinished and unsent letters, and short articles and thoughts in small notebooks. Asking Artaud to write a commentary to Ronsard's poem "The Hymn to Demons," the doctor and psychiatrist Ferdière manages to improve his living conditions by, among others, making him write again.[iii] Around February or March 1946, a few months before his return to Paris, Artaud writes an important text on language that shortly summarizes his problems with language understood as a formalized system of signs. His text begins by claiming: "I think that Mythomania is at the base of every language that has entered history and that is grammatically organized"[12] (OCXX, 14). The word "Mythomania" is interesting because it is used by psychiatrists to diagnose

---

[iii] In an interview with Jean-Claude Fosse, Ferdière contends that "[h]e had stopped writing for years. When I took Artaud on hand, one can admit that he had not written for four or five years" (in Danchin and Roumieux, 684).

patients who seek their refuge in lies in order to escape from reality—a disorder with which Artaud has never been diagnosed but that might well apply to some of his later works (*Heliogabalus*, for example), letters (mainly the letters that he wrote during his internments in Ville-Évrard and Rodez and where he begins changing his name and claims to be Jesus Christ), and behavior (his violent, megalomaniac, and mythomaniac behavior in Dublin, for example). Artaud asserts that every grammatically organized and historical language—that is thus any language that disposes a dictionary—suffers from pathological lying. What then follows is a grammatically incorrect or, better, an unorganized, paralyzing, and delirious sentence that I quote, for a more comprehensive analysis, in its original entirety.

> Non pas le goût des dramatiques symboles où par je ne sais quelle volonté utérine de l'âme, quelle charité intra-utérine de l'âme, l'anus de l'être s'est projeté et encarté, mais cette espèce d'ossification mesquine, ce cri d'ossements prématurés, où dans le Mythe au lieu de la douleur et de sa conscience, au lieu de cet affre œgipan qui est le nom non pas d'un oiseau mais d'une âme, et cette âme enfantée criant, l'esprit ne voit plus la parole naissante, le sang fœtus qui en être dramatiquement s'ouvrira comme le tronc de l'arbre feuilles sort des charbons carbonisés, pour éclater de conscience, faire éclater ces jamais nés qu'on appelle des consciences, mais s'attarde à l'idée engendreuse au lieu d'aimer l'homme engendré, et au lieu d'aimer cet enfant jamais né qui appelle sa conscience et l'invite à commencer à l'aimer, pense sans fin à son accouchement sans pitié pour l'être accouché, mais toujours pesant sur la mère pour lui demander de toujours accoucher sans égard pour l'âme accouchée (OCXX, 215)

In this dense sentence, Artaud elaborates on his preceding assertion that every cultivated language is not inspired by the dramatic and theatrical preference of symbols that is the dynamics of unformed matter. By an inexplicable will—a womb-will that, as this neologism suggests, has the ability to create new life—of the soul, the anus of being has projected itself on language. Filled with indignation, Artaud even ironically speaks of an intra-wombish charity of the soul. In other words, the anus of being—in contrast to the womb, the anus only produces death, repetition (the French word "caca" literally evokes this repetition[iv]), and decay—has replaced not only the soul but also the faculty of creativity and potency that is inherent to the womb of the soul. Possibly referring

---

[iv] See Tomiche (2002, 144, 2012, 344–52), or Murray, 18, for an interesting reading and interpretation of the word "caca."

to Christian charity workers, Artaud suggests that pathological lying has infected the soul that is now even involved in charity work. Our cultivated language is thus not inspired by the creativity, vitality, and hitherto unknown possibilities of the mind (that, as seen above, stems from the impulsiveness of the flesh), but by the petty ossification and the cry of premature bones—a corpse that has not had the possibility to live life at its fullest, a corpse that has never been able to create different possibilities of life. This process of ossification or stratification of language, where the anus of being reigns, is the myth, or lie, that is not inspired by pain and consciousness[v] or "Aegipanlike" (i.e., the goat-footed God of the animal instinct) physical and intellectual torments. In other words, this process of consolidation is not inspired by, what he calls, the soul, that is the shouting soul of the flesh. Because of the myth, the mind—Artaud distinguishes between mind ("esprit") and soul ("âme")—does not see the nascent words and the fetus blood, the potent energy, from which consciousness bursts, and these never-borns from which a plurality of consciousnesses springs. Under the influence, burden, and confusion of the myth, the soul lingers at the fathered or caused idea that is already created instead of the caused man or the never-born child. Because of the myth the mind incessantly thinks of his childbirth without pity for having been given birth to his consciousness. He nevertheless always weighs on his mother and asks her to always mercilessly give birth to this born soul. Language thus turns the soul into a product that was never destined to be born, a rusted being that suffers from a petty ossification. Putting it simply, language, in conclusion from a close reading of Artaud's words, turns its speakers into pathological liars and alienates them from the forces traversing vital matter.

Artaud goes on by reasoning that myths—the pathological lies—come from beings that have been tormented by life and whose cries, fears, and revolts have been turned into things. The Mythomaniac—the pathological liar—is thus the "voyeur of sleep where consciousness rests and where he gives birth to already born children; who cannot be sufficient to live and that his vice has resurrected from the side where they were aborted"[13] (OCXX, 216). Playing with the myth of Lazarus, the Mythomaniac is resurrecting children, who were already born and who are not worth living, at the side where they were aborted: the soul. The basis

---

[v] In Chapter 1, we have already discussed the poem "The Patients and the Doctors" in which he plays with the word "conscience" by putting a hyphen between "con" and "science" and therewith turning "con" into a perverted prefix. Artaud thus thwarts the word "conscience" by writing "con-science" (the science of the cunt); this neologism reveals that consciousness finds its origin in the flesh and in matter. For this passage, we also read "conscience" as "con-science."

of every organized and Mythomaniac language thus ossifies and stratifies our initial cries—the screaming fluxes and streaming forces—and imposes already-born children that are not ours. Focusing on the necessity of grammar for this Mythomania, Artaud asserts that "grammar in any country where one speaks organized languages is only the typification of necessities that are not taken from the direct hideousness of an *experienced* life but from I do not know what stylistic necessities of myths that are only the larval outcome of an inorganic unconsciousness that we want to organize"[14] (OCXX, 216, emphasis in original). Grammar does thus not follow the direct torments of an experimented life; a life that is not subjected to preestablished rules, organizations, and structures; a life that is a generative and open-ended project that invites man to live it, discover it, and experience it. The grammar of organized languages—languages that are subjected to formal rules—is a stylistic necessity of myths that are only the larval outcome of an inorganic unconsciousness. Myths are thus the stratified seeds, the larva that were not granted a life, of an inorganic unconsciousness that man wanted to organize. Following Artaud, we should search for this "non-verbal but animated man"[15] (OCXX, 216), this man that is immerged within Ciguri (the peyote—a hallucinogenic drug—god that Artaud experienced during his visit to the Tarahumaras Indians in Mexico; we come back to these experiences in Chapter 3), this man that dedicates his life to the void which animates him, this man that believes not in grammar but in *this* world and *this* life. This nonverbal man lives, reasons, and acts in a spirit of absolute immanence, because he has done with Mythomania that, following Artaud's reasoning, arrests and restricts the potentialities of life.

Artaud Poetics: The Creation of Animated Words

In an unfinished and unsent letter to Georges Le Breton from March 1946, Artaud speaks with admiration of the work of Gérard de Nerval—during his last years in Ivry-sur-Seine, Artaud even thinks that he slept in the same room as De Nerval once did. Focusing on De Nerval's poetry, Artaud asserts that "there is in these poems a drama of the mind, of consciousness and of the heart that is brought forward by the strangest consonances not of sound, not of the auditory register, but *animated*"[16] (OCXI, 192, emphasis in original). The French word "animé" ("animated") is interesting, because the verb "animer" is derived from the Latin verb "animare," which means "to fill with breath or air," "to revive" or "to refresh," "to transforme into a living being," or "to give or bring life." The word "animé" succinctly summarizes what literature or poetry—the word "poetry" itself is derived from the Greek word "ποιέω," which means "I make" or "I create"—following Artaud, should do, bringing breath, oxygen, and hence life to language. The artist, writer, or poet should make grammar delirious in creating vital, affective, and animated words that bring about life, understood as the vital forces of "zoe." Reengaging with the vital forces of life in the agential materiality of language therewith foregrounds writing as "pharmakon" understood as a remedy and a cure of detoxification of the modern fact. Diving into the hitherto unexplored potentialities and possibilities of language is then essentially a healing practice because it creatively reconnects us with the vitality and the impulsiveness of the agential materiality of language. It is in this reappropriation of our singularity that we can revitalize the broken link between man and *this* world.

Artaud's poetics consists of creating foreign but animated words that do not obey the rules of grammatically organized and structured languages. These words are filled with breath because their meaning engages with the dynamics of matter. This affirmative, animated, and generative language bears and brings about the vitality of life and is an appropriate response to Nietzsche's statement that we have not gotten rid of God. A zoology of language, that, as defined earlier, is an affirmative language that encompasses the discourses of "Theos," "bios," *and* "zoe" and is a language that creates a field where the forces traversing flesh, *this* life, and *this* world are perpetually vibrating, streaming, and flowing. This zoology of language enables the reappropriation of singularities in creating foreign but animated words that articulate the animal spirit of man, the Figure, or the infra-body and that thus participates in the creation of a greater health. Getting rid of God thus means getting rid of the humanly imposed judgment of God insofar as it restricts, orders, and neutralizes the forces of the perpetual movements, both joyous and terrible, within the realm of "zoe." Having done with this God means challenging and disordering our rather theological and biological language that inhibits the unfolding of creation and thus the expression of matter and that therewith causes confusion (for Spinoza), cynic believers (for Nietzsche), and Mythomaniacs (for Artaud).

With these concepts in mind, the enterprise of Artaud's later writings becomes clearer: if we dare to abandon our belief in grammar, our belief in the preestablished logic of reason, and if we dare to look beyond our daily sensory-motor circuits, then we open ourselves up to the creative musicality, the vital forces, and the infinite potency of the materiality of words. In *The Logic of Sense*, Deleuze asserts that Artaud explored the infra-sense, which is the language of a vital body, through suffering (see LS, 105). It is in the affirmative or Stoic resignation and the creative engagement with suffering, these forces that traverse the flesh, that he explored an infra-sense, articulated beyond the superficial opposition of sense and nonsense, that opens up to the vitality of words, matter, and life. The articulation or expression of this infra-sense is essential to the zoological enterprise of Artaud's poetics and participates in what Braidotti calls the "generalized 'becoming infrahuman' of bios" (2006a, 38) in which one looks for new connections with the forces of the nonhuman.

A New Human Agony

In a letter from October 26, 1947, to Arthur Adamov, the playwright who was one of the most important figures in getting Artaud to Paris in 1946 and who played an important role in the organization of the fund-raising performances during the benefit at the Sarah Bernhardt Theater, Artaud laments that no one, not even Adamov himself, has understood his works, because "it is around this point X that turns the Nerve-Meter which is a book written in a void and on a void, but that nobody, spectacularly speaking, not even you [...] has been able to detect of what kind of villainous and absolutely (can we say *inane*) void *it is about*"[17] (O, 1630, emphasis in original). No one has thus understood or detected this low, petty, empty, and senseless void that constituted his suffering, from which his writings stem, but Artaud continues his letter in order to be sure that Adamov will understand and propagate what he has to say. What Artaud wants to say is that "what matters [...] is the ultimate purpose itself of the language of grammar *that I disorder*"[18] (O, 1631, emphasis in original). Artaud thus wants to thwart, disturb, or disorder—the French word "désaxé" ("disorder") mainly refers to a mentally unbalanced person—grammar in order to articulate the active void that animates him. What then follows are three lines of glossolalia: "yo kembi de lo poulaino / lo poulaino patentlu / lo poulaino patentlu" (O, 1631). Echoing a Portuguese or Spanish language (it could even allude to a Mexican tribe), Artaud continues his sentence by affirming that "I disorder it in such a way and in this respect that the necessity of a new/human *agony* appears from it,/ of a new way to sigh his body, *perpetually*"[19] (O, 1631, emphasis in original). He disturbs, disorders, and unbalances grammar thus in such a way that language, understood as the formalized system of signs, opens up to the necessity of a new human agony that is a new way to make the body perpetually breathe; the forces of a new agony revive the body.

Disturbing grammar thus brings us closer to a renewed struggle with death—we have already seen that death or "caca," which is essentially a state of arrest, was produced by the anus of being—territories and rust but, at the same time, offers us new ways to animate or revive our bodies with breath. This explanatory sentence is again followed by three lines of glossolalia that might well echo a Hindi language (or that could also evoke a Balinese theater): "ya garma yaur kautaurmo / naun no ko / ya garma yaurkautaurma" (O, 1631). Artaud then continues by noting that his disturbing of grammar comes from "a pure corporeal cry, on the edge of time and nothingness"[20] (O, 1631). In other words, his cries are at the borders of what language can express, at the borders of what language can communicate, and at the borders of what language can bear. His cries touch upon the outside of language; his cries echo a realm from which a new human agony is articulated. Denudating one's body through its cries and therewith "abolishing the mind, consciousness, *what is given*"[21] (O, 1631, emphasis in original) gives way to a new perpetual agony but also to "the establishment of a new corporeal anatomy, and of a new idea / of necessity, / of presence, / of void, / of essence, / of duration"[22] (O, 1631, emphasis in original). Artaud, again, is an intercessor for a new belief in *this* world, because his healing and curing enterprise of language in which he destabilizes and disorders grammar gives way to a new corporeal anatomy that presupposes necessity (an "amor fati"), presence (the actual presence of AND instead of IS, which is a commitment to absolute immanence), the void (the untranslatable forces or the unthinkable void that nevertheless incites us to think), essence (the perpetual difference that gives way to a new agony), and duration (hence focusing on the invitation to experimented, experienced and lived life).

The letter to Adamov is one of the few occasions where Artaud formulates *what* he *does* in his bodily practices of writing that are a "pharmakon" understood as a remedy. In his writings, he creates a material, corporeal and vital, that is a zoological language of the flesh that encapsulates forces, generated by and through the expression of matter, exceeding human life and evoking nonhuman, organic, and animal life. These genuinely creative writings are written in a vital and animated, that is, again, a zoological language echoing different languages without becoming intelligible as such. It is a language that is not principally guided by reason and is thus deprived from identity, unity, and thingness; it is an affirmative language that has disordered grammar; it is a genuinely creative language that is committed to the potentialities of matter, the hitherto unknown possibilities of *this* world, and the energetic fluxes within *this* life; it is an impersonal language that echoes the open-ended process of the generative vitality of life; it is the creation of a zoology of language that is an enterprise of auto-immunization and a healing practice of language.

"Only the Madman Is Really Calm"

In his long and enigmatic poem "Here Lies" (1947)—the poem that starts off in a megalomaniacal way by stating that *he* is his son, his father, and his mother—Artaud writes: "All true language/is incomprehensible,/like the chatter/of a beggar's teeth" (SW, 549) or "All true language/is incomprehensible/like the click/of clack teeth" (AN, 245) or, in yet another translation: "All true language/is incomprehensible/like the clap/of clapper dudgeons"[23] (WRS, 229). The original French lines schizophrenically vibrate because the almost onomatopoeic "la claque du claque-dents" can be translated as the slap of the whorehouse, the death of the pauper, or the noise of teeth—or a combination of these words. In a note to "Here Lies," Susan Sontag and Don Eric Levine therefore comment on these passages that they "contain many puns and plays on words, which are impossible to convey fully in translation" (SW, 657). All true language, following Artaud, vibrates is incomprehensible and untranslatable and is yet full of forces; all true language, that is, all vital and animated language is devoted to the potency of the expression of matter and the infinite potentialities of the realm of "zoe."

At the end of his "Manifesto in Clear Language," Artaud states that "[t]he truth of life lies in the impulsiveness of matter. The mind of man has been poisoned by concepts. Do not ask him to be content, ask him only to be calm, to believe that he has found his place. Only the Madman is really calm" (SW, 109). The order of things can only continue to exert its power, its suppression, and its confusion if we continue to cynically believe in its organization, believe in its rules, and believe in its grammar. Artaud reverses the order of things—he literally accuses us of being mad while he would be considered and diagnosed as such in the following years—and does not remain calm and believes that he has found his place. Artaud abandons his belief in grammar and starts writing with a hammer—in his room in Ivry, Artaud had a block of wood on which he literally used to smash with a hammer while writing his poems in order to rhyme them syllable for syllable—that, similar to the reflex hammer of a physician, cures the sick-making dominant language, structured by "Theos" and "bios," that is established and formalized by sets of rules. In this chapter, we have discussed, following Artaud (and Spinoza and Nietzsche), in what way we are confused by words and images, poisoned by concepts and lamentably tangled up in error by a firm belief in grammar. Language is, as he argues, at the base of this state, and it is only by disordering the functional rules of that suppressing language and by hollowing out a far more creative, vital, and animated language within that language of "Theos" and "bios" that we touch upon the impulsiveness of matter and the infinite potency of "zoe." Artaud's poetics thus consists of the creation of a zoology of language that opens up to a new human agony but that, at the same time, opens the cage that blocked our lungs and that, once opened, enables us to breathe and to affirm the joyous *and* terrible forces of life in the impulsiveness of matter. And although written in a zoological language, the style, form, and materiality of Artaud's later writings constantly change. In what way do these later works that have been considered for a long time as obscure and therefore irrelevant constantly change? And how can these later writings eventually be read or understood?

Notes

1   "La vérité de la vie est dans l'impulsivité de la matière. L'esprit de l'homme est malade au milieu des concepts" (OCI**, 54).
2   "Mon esprit fatigué de la raison discursive se veut emporté dans les rouages d'une nouvelle, d'une absolue gravitation. C'est pour moi comme une réorganisation souveraine où seules les lois de l'Illogique participent, et où triomphe la découverte d'un nouveau Sens" (OCI**, 53).
3   "le domaine de la chair pure" (OCI**, 53).
4   "ma chair irriguée par les nerfs" (OCI**, 53).
5   "Notre monde, Mr Albert Camus, est bien malade, et il *meurt* de quelque chose depuis longtemps, et très précisément de ce dont tant de génies sont morts, et parce que, quand ils ont voulu *parler*, on n'a pas voulu les croire" [my translation].
6   "je n ai jamais vu un homme plus bestialement feru/de ses principes aussi inverifies qu inverifiables que Spinoza" [my translation].
7   "de la tete du monsieur dont on/ne connaissait pas l existence et/qui s appelle parait il Mr Dieu" [my translation].

8   "les mots que l'on/utilise collent ils collent a la/pensée que l on vient d avoir comme/une colle miraculée" [my translation].
9   "c est très bien" [my translation].
10 "l'operation de reprendre/ce qu'on va enterre/au lieu de laisser circuler" [my translation].
11 "Mon esprit s'est ouvert par le ventre, et c'est pas le bas qu'il entasse une sombre et intraduisible science, pleine de marées souterraines, d'édifices concaves, d'une agitation congelée. Qu'on ne prenne pas ceci pour des images. Ce voudrait être la forme d'un abominable savoir. Mais je réclame seulement pourquoi me considère le silence, mais un silence intellectuel si j'ose dire, et pareil à mon attente crispée" (OCI**, 49).
12 "Je crois que la Mythomanie est à la base de tout langage entré dans l'histoire et grammaticalement organisé" [my translation].
13 "le voyeur du sommeil où la conscience se repose et où il fait naître des enfants déjà nés; qui ne purent suffire à vivre et que son vice a ressuscités du côté où ils étaient avortés" [my translation].
14 "la grammaire dans tous les pays où l'on parle des langages organisés n'est que la typification de nécessités prises non dans les affres directes d'une vie *expérimentée* mais dans je ne sais quelles nécessités stylistiques de mythes qui ne sont que l'issue larvaire d'un inconscient inorganique qu'on a voulu organiser" [my translation].
15 "homme non verbe mais animé" [my translation].
16 "Il y a dans ces poèmes un drame de l'esprit, de la conscience et du cœur mis en avant par les plus étranges consonances non de sons, non dans le registre auditif, mais *animé*" [my translation].
17 "c'est autour de ce point X que tourne tout le Pèse-nerfs qui est un livre écrit à vide et sur du vide, mais dont personne, spectaculairement parlant, pas même vous [...] n'a su déceler de quelle sorte crapuleuse et absolument (peut-on dire *inane*) du vide *il s'agissait*" [my translation].
18 "ce qui importe [...] c'est la raison d'être elle-même du langage de la grammaire *que je désaxe*" [my translation].
19 "je la désaxe de telle façon et sur un tel plan qu'il en apparaît la nécessité d'une nouvelle/*agonie* humaine,/d'une nouvelle façon de souffler son corps, *perpétuellement*" [my translation].
20 "un cri corporel pur, sur le bord du temps et du néant" [my translation].
21 "supprimant l'esprit, la conscience, *la donnée*" [my translation].
22 "l'instauration d'une nouvelle anatomie corporelle, et d'une idée nouvelle / de la nécessité, / de la présence, / du vide, / de l'essence, / de la durée" [my translation].
23 "Tout vrai langage/est incompréhensible,/comme la claque/du claque-dents" (OCXII, 95).

3

A Magical and Materialist Theosophy: On the Development of Artaud's Later Works

What I want to say Dr. Ferdière is this: that in the case of Antonin Artaud, there is no question of literature or theater, but of religion.[1]
—Antonin Artaud, *New Writings from Rodez*, ER, p. 28

The Man Crucified on Golgotha

In the previous chapter, we have discussed the problems to which our daily use of language, understood as a formalized system of signs, gives rise and how we can sustainably reengage with its still unexplored agential materiality. In especially his later writings, Artaud has disordered language in such a way that a far more creative, vital, and animated language, which we have called a zoological language, has been articulated that, in turn, reengages with the broken link between man and *this* world. Artaud's zoology of language manifests itself mainly in his later writings (in his earlier works, themes, concepts, and ideas are articulated that are put in motion in these later writings; there is thus not a radical difference between the earlier and the later writings, but rather a development in which language is set to work) and in constantly different styles, forms, and expressions. In this chapter we take a closer look at the development of these later writings and eventually discuss how we can read the impulsiveness of these works that, I claim, has still something to say to the reader of today.

In 1946 Artaud is finally transferred from the psychiatric hospital in Rodez to Paris where his friends excitedly welcome him. Nervously the poet Jacques Prevel looks forward to Artaud's return to Paris. Prevel had already corresponded with him because of the forthcoming publication of a selection of letters that Artaud wrote during his internment in Rodez and because of the already published and the forthcoming publication of Prevel's poetry. On April 29, 1946, he subsequently writes that "I am very curious to see Artaud" (34) and some days later he dramatizes his curiosity by claiming on May 1 that "I think I should see Artaud. I have been thinking a lot. It is not possible to do the opposite, I think" (35). The long-awaited Sunday approaches, and on May 26 at 9 o'clock in the sunny morning Artaud finally arrives at Austerlitz Station in Paris with the night train from Rodez. Artaud's psychiatrist Ferdière has accompanied him and two other patients from Rodez to Paris. With his beret pulled over his head, Artaud smokes cigarette after cigarette (see Danchin and Roumieux, 225) but is finally welcomed by his friends Henri and Colette Thomas, Marthe Robert and Jean Dubuffet who have discussed the general conditions for his return with doctor Ferdière and who have made, with the help of many others, his return to Paris possible, thanks to some fund-raising events. By some of his close friends Artaud's return to Paris is celebrated as a liberation and a victory over his psychiatrists. For Prevel it was a gloomy Sunday; he did not assist at Artaud's arrival, because he was too tired to get out of his bed.

The next day he finally has the opportunity to meet Artaud in the Café de Flore at the boulevard Saint-Germain. It will be a breathtaking day for Prevel and he even claims that this would be a day of great luck since his Buddhist friend Val Constantine had already mystically predicted the favorability of these events, because "this day passes in an explosion of events and shocks […] and I remember that Val had told me that my day of luck will slip from Tuesday to Monday and that all in all these events are favorable" (45). It is even as if Prevel finally meets his savior or his redeemer (maybe, we should call it: his intercessor) because on August 20, while humming a song that would have existed during the epoch of the Incas and while retelling the story of the magical stick of Saint Patrick that once belonged to Jesus Christ and that he has hidden in Dublin, Artaud tells him dramatically: "Do you know that it was I who was crucified on Golgotha. I especially remember the horrible moment at which I was nailed to the cross and when it was elevated" (91). Prevel's notices do not comment on these strange remarks, but we only know that Artaud's statements have not chased him away, because that day he does not leave Artaud until a quarter past noon. Some months later, on December 4, Artaud repeats what he earlier claimed and what he has already written and asserted in Rodez: "I am the man who was crucified on Golgotha. But the man who was crucified on Golgotha was not called Jesus Christ but Artaud" (Prevel, 122). It is thus not a Christ, the redeemer or savior who has been prophesied and who is both human and God, who has been nailed to a cross, but simply the man Jesus, a man of flesh and blood that has been persecuted for his ideas and who is, in that sense, the same man as Artaud. After some transpiercing chants and some enigmatic drawings that serve to illuminate his remarks, Artaud continues his reasoning on his way to another cafe by claiming that "formerly, I was crucified. In this life, I was imprisoned in an asylum. Don't you think that I must avenge myself terribly?" (Prevel, 123). Artaud then quickly slips into another cafe where Pierre Loeb and other friends would attend him. Again Prevel has not commented on these statements while many questions arise: What does Artaud mean by a terrible revenge? Does Artaud aim at a linguistic combat, struggle, or revenge? Or does he aim at a more militant and physical revenge?

"I Have to Laugh When You Talk about His Message"

The writings of Artaud give way to many responses. Some of his writings, especially those written during his various internments, are so delirious, unheard of, or mysterious that they provoke a responses ranging from admiration to disgust or disapproval.[i] For example, the pious psychiatrist Jacques Latrémolière, the doctor who administered many electroshocks on Artaud, states in an interview with Sylvère Lotringer that "I believe that Man will find nothing in Artaud's work. Nothing. It will not advance civilization" (68) and, focusing on Artaud's more religious texts, "God knows his ideas on religion were debatable. [...] I have to laugh when you talk about his message. There was nothing. [...] Moreover, it makes no sense. I was there. How many people read him? No one" (71). The more clinical reading of Latrémolière focuses on the surface of Artaud's debatable words and, from there, disapproves them while Prevel seems to ignore the play and the twists on the surface and rather dives into the depths of his words and statements. Indeed, Artaud's claims are megalomaniac or, as Latrémolière would characterize them as a psychiatrist, psychotic, but as many

---

[i] As already stated in the introductory paragraphs, the Anglo-Saxon literature on Artaud's writings have neglected for a long time these later works and rather focused on his period as a (Surrealist) playwright and his writings on the theater of cruelty. The reason for the negligence of these later works might have several explanations: the bad availability of many of Artaud's works in a good English translation, the unfamiliarity with close reading (or reading in depth) that, it seems to me, is required in reading Artaud's later works, or the fear of immorally defending the writings of an author or poet who is largely considered to be an alienated madman. Even in the French literature, the writings that Artaud produced in the early forties are largely disregarded.

textual analyses[ii] show, it is still interesting, important, and necessary to closely read and reread Artaud's writings in order to discover what forces are at work in his writings.

Artaud's writings develop a more mystical and religious tone after his journey to Mexico in February 1936. After his final return from Mexico in November, his works evolve from mainly theoretical works for the theater and the cinema; reviews of paintings and literary works and ingenious surrealist poetic writings to comments on his Mexican journey; letters full of complaints around the psychiatric hospitals; the treatments of his doctors and the stupidity of the Western civilization; writings that revolt against the therapies he underwent and reflections of his apocalyptic, religious, and earlier developed philosophically poetic visions; and corporeal, religious, and rebelling poetry. It is during this last period that Jacques Lacan visits Artaud in the psychiatric hospital of Sainte-Anne and where he declares in April 1938 that Artaud is "irrevocably fixed" and lost for literature (see Bousseyroux, 128). From this period until his return to Paris in 1946, Artaud has been interned in various French psychiatric hospitals. Positioning the beginning of the development of his later works in 1936 makes it possible to understand the influence Artaud's travel to Mexico has had on the performativity of the writings that would follow this journey. Understanding his experiences, his findings, and the impact that this Mexican voyage has had on his thinking, his writings and his behavior will also give us a better understanding of Artaud's later works in which he develops a more religious tone that gives way to so many divergent responses. How have his writings changed after his voyage to Mexico? What are these forces that work through Artaud's later writings? And why does the tone of his writings become more and more religious?

In this chapter, we take a closer look at the development of Artaud's later works. In doing so, we focus on Artaud's voyage to Mexico and his discovery of the rituals of the Tarahumaras Indians from which he formulates the principles of an organic culture. After discussing the aftermath of Artaud's experiences during which he develops a more revelatory reasoning and starts writing occult and prophetic texts that make him eventually derail, we finally focus on his writings from Rodez where Artaud formulates a theosophy that is based upon his Mexican experiences. I think that this theosophy, evoked in a zoological language, engages with forces that incite us to believe and thus heal the broken link between man and *this* world.

[ii] See Barber (1999 and 2008); Deleuze (1969/1990); Derrida (1967/1978); Garner (2006); Grossman (2003a and 2003b); Murray (2014); Tomiche (2002) or Weiss (1994) to mention only a few of the span of the many different readings.

Artaud in the Land of the Tarahumaras

On February 7, 1936, Artaud departs to Mexico where he is invited to lecture at the University of Mexico on surrealism, theater, anarchy, and revolution. At the end of August in that same year, he obtains a fund from a Mexican art association that gives him the possibility to travel to the Sierra Tarahumara. During his stay with the Tarahumaras Indians for one month, Artaud would have assisted at their rituals and would even have been initiated in their cult of the peyote. The peyote is a small cactus that, when chewing on it, produces hallucinogenic effects. In his article "Antonin Artaud, or the Mexican Dream," Jean-Marie Le Clézio asks: "Did Antonin Artaud really go to the Tarahumara Sierra?" (168). Le Clézio raises his question, because it must have been difficult to travel to Norogachic (the Tarahumara village), Artaud was sick and weakened by drugs, and he moreover did not speak the language of the Tarahumaras or Spanish at all. From these difficulties that would render his travel problematic if not impossible, Le Clézio contends that Artaud has only visited the Tarahumaras Indians in his dreams, visions, and imagination. In a sense, and we follow Le Clézio in this conclusion, it is not interesting, in the end, if Artaud has ever physically visited Norogachic to assist at the rituals of the Tarahumaras. More significant is that "[f]or him, describing the peyote ritual was to be aware of an enchantment, a magic which completely transformed him, which turned him into another man" (Le Clézio, 170). Physically present or not, Artaud's account of his travel to the Tarahumaras Indians testifies how deeply he was impressed by their culture. What matters is what *happens* within his writings and how they constitute eventually healing practices of language. Understanding "pharmakon," that is writing, as a remedy means that the actual assistance of Artaud at the rituals of the Tarahumaras is interesting, but not relevant for the potency of his writings.[iii]

In a letter directed to Jean Paulhan—Artaud writes his letter some months after his return from Mexico—Artaud describes the strange feelings he experienced while living with the Tarahumaras Indians, because "this lived organic experience reminded me of another, to which I felt linked perhaps indirectly, but by material threads in any case. They were reminiscent of a history that came to me, rock by rock, herb by herb, horizon by horizon"[2] (OCIX, 101). Artaud insists that his experience is not an experience of a strange, a new or a

---

[iii] In his account of Artaud's voyage to Mexico, Schafer speculates that Artaud's account "was in fact concocted out of readings, wish-fulfilment and his fertile imagination" (137). Since no record has been left of Artaud's voyage, Schafer's point is interesting, but, again, not significant for our reading of Artaud's texts on his Mexican journey.

better world; it is rather a reengagement with direct and personal memories, with life, earth and soil, and forces that he has already encountered and that have already passed through him and that are too great to conceive. On the other hand, Artaud similarly characterizes his experiences as "the dance of healing"[3] (OCIX, 42), "obscure tantalizations"[4] (OCIX, 45), or "Sickness"[5] (OCIX, 45). Searching for words and images to express his visions and his experiences, this organic experience is an experience of the body, the flesh, the earth, and the vital forces traversing them. It is an experience in which we are plunged into the "true nature of evil," which is the realm of "zoe," which is the vitality of nature or, for that matter, God, an ecstatic experience in which we are confronted with the vitality of animal, organic, *and* human life.

In his book *Perverse Desire and the Ambiguous Icon*, Allen Weiss describes Artaud's enchantment rather as an experience where it is "God himself who enters one's nerves" (54). As he interestingly reminds us, the rites of the Tarahumaras were derived from a syncretism of Catholicism and pagan rituals. In one of his last accounts on the Tarahumaras, Artaud equates peyote, the small cactus producing psychedelic effects and that was used during the rites of the Indians, with the vital fluxes of nature that the Indians call Ciguri. He moreover considers Ciguri as the God of the Tarahumaras (see OCIX, 19)—in another article devoted to the Tarahumaras, Artaud nevertheless nuances that "the Tarahumaras do not believe in God and the word 'God' does not exist in their language"[6] (OCIX, 68) and claims that they organize their cult around a transcendent principle of Nature—Jesus Christ (see OCIX, 86)—an assertion that is similarly criticized by himself, because in a letter to Henri Parisot, written shortly before the planned publication of his article on the Tarahumaras in September 1945, Artaud withdraws this comparison since "I had the stupidity to say that I was converted to Jesus christ [*sic*] while it is Christ that I have always mostly abominated"[7] (OCIX, 50)—or Matter (see OCIX, 46) that he equates with the concrete world (he even capitalizes the word "Concrete"). However various, plural, and grotesque Artaud's descriptions of Ciguri are, his struggle with this concept keeps echoing one constant: Ciguri is the expression of a void that is a realm of incessant vitality to which peyote opens up, that is, bare life or animal, organic and non-human life. In fact, the rituals of the Tarahumaras, especially the Dance of the Peyote, have impressed Artaud so deeply that he has never stopped searching words that would adequately express or evoke the organic and healing experience of Ciguri. More than two-third of his first article *On a Voyage to the Land of the Tarahumaras* (1937), published in *La Nouvelle Revue Française*, is devoted to the Dance of the Peyote. His posthumously published article—Artaud rejected the article, because he contended that he was too confused when he wrote his text—*Supplement to the Voyage to the Land of the Tarahumaras* (1943) is almost completely devoted to Ciguri and the Dance of the Peyote. One of his final articles *The Rite of Peyote at the Tarahumaras* (1947), published in *L'Arabalète*, is again entirely consecrated to the description of the organic experience that is provoked by peyote. This continuous rewriting makes the actual rites at which Artaud would have assisted diffuse, because he constantly changes, adds, and omits elements. The only element that is recurrent is the celebration of the peyote violating the organism and yet, or maybe, thus, heal the energetic mind of man that springs from the vitality of the flesh.

In an article that he wrote shortly after his return in Paris, Artaud describes the Dance of the Peyote as a dangerous but healing experimentation with the energetic vitality of the body. With fear and attraction, Artaud writes that the drugged dancer "moves deliberately into evil. He immerses himself in it with a kind of terrible courage, in a rhythm which above the Dance seems to depict the Illness [...] [T]his advance into the illness is a voyage, a *descent in order to* REEMERGE INTO THE DAYLIGHT.—He turns in a circle in the direction of the wings of the Swastika, always from right to left, and from the top"[8] (SW, 387, emphasis in original). The Dance of the Peyote effectuates a descent into the vitality of the body—Artaud plays with the *Dark Night of the Soul* by Saint John of the Cross who considered the dark nights of the body as a way for the soul to ascent and thus reunite with the light of God—and it is in this body that we can finally reunite with the lights of "organicity," the forces of earth and nature, and the vitality of *this* life. Artaud contends that the dance might appear as a manifestation of suffering or sickness, but this ecstatic and originary illness is essentially healing since it makes the dancer reengage with the vitality of this world, the forces of this life, and the hitherto unexplored capabilities of the flesh that is the infra-body. The dancer follows the Swastika not in a perverted way that closes off, restricts, and marks a stop to all movement. On the contrary, the dancer follows the Swastika in its original vitality that opens up to fluxes and offers new possibilities of life while exploring what a body is capable of. The drugged dancer does therewith not resemble the perverted Übermensch that stands on top of a hierarchized society, but rather an Übermensch that reveals inhuman forces that affirm the forces of life.[iv]

[iv] In his first study on Nietzsche, Deleuze similarly argues that this Übermensch marks "a sort of wrenching apart and transformation of human essence" (PI, 91). The Übermensch thus not only breaks with the human essence (this would only lead to a destructive nihilism), but at the same time creates new possibilities of life.

Our Advanced Civilization and the Search of an Organic Culture

In his article "The Theater and the Gods" (1936), Artaud states that "Europe is in a state of advanced civilization: I mean that she is very ill. It is in the spirit of the youth of France to react against this state of advanced civilization"[9] (OCVIII, 198). Artaud asserts that young French artists massively break with Surrealism in search of a culture that is not taught at public schools,[v] because "behind this idea of culture there is an idea of life that can only bother the Schools, because it ruins their teachings"[10] (OCVIII, 197). Opposed to the decadent culture of a festering civilization, Artaud introduces a healthier culture that reconnects to the primal forces of earth and nature, the infinite fluxes of the impulsiveness of the flesh, which is the creative and affirmative forces of *this* world and *this* life. He argues that "opposite to the culture of Europe that ties up with written texts and gives the appearance that the culture is lost when the texts are destroyed, I say that there is another culture on which other times have lived and this lost culture is based on a materialist idea of the mind"[11] (OCVIII, 200). Instead of a culture that propagates classical writing, which he considers to be a practice that "fixes the mind and crystallizes it in form, and, from the form, arises idolatry"[12] (OCVIII, 203), Artaud argues for a rather materialist approach to the mind—in other words, an approach that considers the mind as an expression of the vitality of matter, which is the depths of the body. Or, putting it differently, Artaud searches for an affirmative, generative, and open-ended culture that emerges directly from (and thus merges with) the vitality and agency of matter and that does not remain stuck in the abject practices of idolatry (which freeze the vitality of matter).

He consequently speaks of an organic culture that is connected with the forces of this life and which is "based on the mind in touch with the organs, and the mind bathing in all the organs while answering them at the same time"[13] (OCVIII, 201). This organic culture is thus the remerging of mind and matter, a plunging into the sole substance that is necessarily infinite and indivisible, which

---

[v] The resemblance with our current society that suffers under the structuring of advanced capitalism is striking, because we also face an enormous rise of escapism (we should think of games, virtual reality, or the continuing growth of social media that present their users often divergent realities), mindfulness, and detox retreats.

is traversed by vital and energetic fluxes, that is, nature or God. It is in this sense that the organization of the organs is disrupted and reversed, because whereas our (still) decadent culture constantly searches for therapies and remedies against dysfunctional organs—the most telling example in this case is of course the brain that should respond (if not via therapies, medicines, or surgeries) to a certain standard of normativity—Artaud rather praises the energetic mind that springs from the hitherto unexplored vitality of the organs. Concluding his discussion of Artaud's voyage to Mexico, Weiss rightly asserts that "[f]or Artaud, who will come to claim that 'I am infinity,' these events were a formative experience at the core of both his delirium at Rodez and the subsequent poetic reconstitution of his own body" (68). In constantly changing modes of expression, I think that Artaud's later writings are indeed devoted to this task that aims at formulating a healthier and more vital organic culture of life, understood as "zoe."

Intricately related to this formulation are Artaud's growing problems with the possibilities of expression within our daily language and his envisioning of a zoology of language in which words are cracked up to a new vitality. Artaud's later works show a development from a tone or an angle that strictly focuses on the healing and healthy organicity in all its joyous and terrible manifestations, the potency of the body, and on the vitality of matter to a tone that also involves occult and mystical and later more religious and Catholic concepts—it is a development toward a renewed, reanimated, or respiritualized theosophy or, better, a zoological theosophy expressed in a foreign, vital, and animated language that aims at connecting the organic culture with *this* life. We have already seen that Artaud equates Ciguri, the effects of peyote, with matter, but also with God or Jesus Christ. His poetics, which is Artaud's principles of his zoological language, remains more or less constant, which also goes for his search for an appropriate articulation of an organic culture, while his use of certain concepts slowly shifts. How do these concepts shift? And why do his writings adopt a more revelatory or religious tone within his materialist view on this world?

Expressing the Mexican Discoveries

Having experienced the healing practices of the rites of the Tarahumaras Indians, the revelation of a liberating organic culture, and the generative power of "zoe," Artaud searches for words and modes of expression to heal, reconvert, and reconnect the advanced civilization of Europe to *this* world. In July 1937,

Artaud therefore publishes the prophetic text *The New Revelations of Being* that is signed under the name "The Revealed." In the introductory words to his enigmatic and mystical or, for others, delirious text, the anonymous but enlightened author writes:

> That of what I have suffered from until now, it is of having denied the Void. The Void which was already within me. [...] I struggled trying to exist, trying to consent to forms (to all the forms) of which the delirious illusion of being in the world have redressed the world. [...] Now, being no longer, I see what is. I have really identified myself with this Being, this Being that has ceased to exist. And this Being has revealed everything to me.[14] (OCVII, 119)

The author asserts that he sees what *is* since he no longer *is*. He is now swallowed by this being that has ceased to exist, the void that he had denied for so long and that had made him suffer—it is the senseless, petty but vital void from which, as he would later assert,[vi] his writings stem. Artaud's suffering was thus primarily caused by a denial of the void and therewith by an active engagement with being. His refusal to dedicate his life to this void makes him verbal and unanimated instead of carnal and animated—in the sense of the Latin verb from which "animate" derives, that is "animare" meaning "to fill with breath or air," "to revive" or "to refresh," "to transforme into a living being," or "to give or bring life." Devoting himself to this healthy and healing void that, as he argues, is already in himself and refusing to consent to forms, that is, formations like judgments, imposed rules or conventions of thought, or preestablished structures and grammar, Artaud is swallowed by this being that encompasses everything that *is*; that is, he is immerged in a process of becoming-other within the realm of the healing practices of Ciguri, the vitality of matter, or the affirmative forces of an animal, organic, *and* human life, that is, "zoe."

Although the logic of *The New Revelations of Being* is similar to the logic of his writings on the Tarahumaras Indians—both writings are dedicated to the unthinkable forces traversing our bodies—what is interesting in the writings that follow his Mexican voyage is the tone that becomes more and more occult, mystical, and eventually religious. I even think that Artaud's *The New Revelations of Being*—which is also one of the first works in which Artaud plays with his name and his identity in signing the work under the pseudonym "the tortured," "the Recognized," and that dialectically develops into "the Revealed"—is one

---

[vi] See Chapter 2 for the discussion of Artaud's letter to Adamov in which he speaks of this void.

of his first attempts to articulate a pseudo-philosophical or mystical language that aims at contaminating its reader with the healing practices of Ciguri or the Dance of the Peyote, hence revealing a vital body. His enigmatic but prophetic text is however full of Kabbalistic notes and numerological references and therewith somewhat misses the point since it remains too cerebral—there do not seem to be any vibrating, disturbing, or healing forces at work in these writings. In the concluding notes for example, the reader gets an overwhelmingly well-reasoned overview of dates that are essential in the upcoming destruction of mankind and the construction of what "the Revealed" calls "the Abstract Man"[15] (OCVII, 144) or, as mentioned earlier, the animated and carnal man whose life is devoted to the void or even, following the drugged dancer of the Dance of the Peyote, the Übermensch. The author, as a genuine millennialist, precisely calculates when this destruction should take place; "if I add 3 from 3 June to the number of the sixth month of the year, I get 9, the Infernal Destruction which, that very day, begins. If I add 5, number of the Abstract Man, to 6 of the sixth month of the year, I get 11, which brings me back to November, and November is under the sign of the number 9 in the ancient calendar"[16] (OCVII, 133). The tarots—it is interesting to note the French phonetic resemblance between "artaud" (read phonetically as "arto") and "tarot" (and likewise the intricately related Italian word "teatro"); on a phonetic level, the tarots thus presuppose or generate Artaud's mystical practice—have revealed that it is "the Tortured" who has prepared the apocalyptic fate of mankind. "The Tortured" has been taken for a fool by everyone but has now the right to decide what *is* and what *is not*. And, in the end, "the Tortured has become the Recognized for everyone"[17] (OCVII, 144). However superficial Artaud's occult play with numbers, dates and Kabbalistic, occult and apocalyptic visions may appear, his *The New Revelations of Being* incite him to undertake a new journey.

Violating the Art of Caution

A month after the publication of his prophetic work, Artaud decides to undertake a voyage to Ireland and, on August 6, 1937, he writes a letter to the ambassador of Ireland in which he states "for some years I am searching for the sources of a very ancient tradition. I have sought them in Mexico. […] I designed the project to find in Ireland the living sources, and living among living man, of this very ancient tradition in its Western form" (qtd. in Penot-Lacassagne 2007,

145–6). Stimulated by his apocalyptic visions of the upcoming destruction of our advanced civilization and the emergence of the Übermensch, Artaud wants to find the organic culture that he envisioned in Mexico during his stay with the Tarahumaras Indians, in its Western and still living form in Ireland. On August 14, he embarks for Cobh, and on August 23, Artaud enthusiastically writes to Anne Manson that "my Life, Anne, realizes a Prophecy"[18] (OCVII, 200) after which he ends his letter with an enigmatic post-scriptum indicating "never lose your pen. It also contains something. It will protect you"[19] (OCVII, 200). Especially these words seem prophetic, because they are a reminder of the art of caution. In experimenting with the infinite depths of the body—the BwO— Deleuze and Guattari note that "[s]taying stratified—organized, signified, subjected—is not the worst that can happen; the worst that can happen is if you throw the strata into demented or suicidal collapse, which brings them back down on us heavier than ever" (TP, 178). Our combat against stratification, organization, and subjectification must thus always, following the true addict, that is, the true addict to life, as envisioned by Deleuze in the interview *Abécédaire*, stop "at the second-last glass, one removed from the fatal sip, or shot" (Braidotti 2006a, 218). Becoming drunk or destratified in the search, envisioning and formulation of a healthier organic culture are about making as many vital connections as possible, and it is certainly not about a fatal or suicidal disconnection. In critically combatting the overmedicalization of mental health care, writing can be a "pharmakon" understood as a remedy that is as vital, important, and relevant as the remedies and medicines proposed and prescribed by psychiatrists and physicians. Searching for a cure of detoxification of the modern fact that exposes us to a greater health implies an experimentation with the agential materiality of both body and language. In experimenting with this enterprise of auto-immunization, we must however respect the art of caution— for Artaud, this would have meant, following his letter to Anne Manson, that his pen should have protected him—since writing understood as a "pharmakon" can be turned out to be both a beneficial medicine or a suicidal drug. Artaud has respected the art of caution and created thresholds of sustainability during his voyage to Mexico by approaching the Dance of the Peyote as if it was a theater of cruelty. During his search in Dublin and the possible fulfillment of his prophecy that his pen should have protected him since his journey to Ireland has turned out to be a derailment.

On September 5, 1937, Artaud writes a long letter to André Breton in which he summarizes his plans. He apocalyptically starts his letter by asserting that "things will become serious and [...] I will go through to the end this time"[20] (OCVII, 206). Probably referring to the Druids—in a letter to his family on August 23, Artaud states that he is looking for "the last true authentic descendant of the Druids who possesses the secret of the Druid philosophy"[21] (OCVII, 202)— and echoing the rituals of the Tarahumaras Indians, Artaud then reasons that "it is Paganism that was right, but Men who are eternal bastards have betrayed the Pagan Truth. The christ then *returned* to bring to light the Pagan Truth, on which *all* christian Churches have then crapped with ignominy. The christ was a Magician who fought in the desert against the Demons with a stick"[22] (OCVII, 206, emphasis in original). Artaud has minusculed the word "Christ" and therewith implicitly denied the salvation, liberation, and holiness that goes with it but interestingly gives him an important role, because he brought to light the Pagan Truth that mankind has constantly betrayed. It is the whole range of different Christian churches—the word "Church" is capitalized to associate it, in its etymological sense of the gathering of people, with the similarly capitalized word "Men"—that has shamefully and abjectly betrayed Christ.

In her article "Knowing One's Enemy," Catherine Dale comments on Artaud's *To Have Done with the Judgment of God* and notes in passing that "it is not really God that Artaud rejects, but the judgment of god as instructed/constructed by man" (93). Artaud's later works are indeed not intended to reject, combat, or attack God or Christ, but rather to criticize, attack, and assault the transcendentalized (thus rendering it eternal and placing it beyond the infinity of nature) judgment of God that man imposes upon him.[vii] Artaud rather revitalized the concept of God or Christ by rendering it more generative, open-ended, and energetic.

Artaud's claims about a more truthful Christ are also interesting, because the Gospel according to Mark indeed speaks of impure spirits (Mark 5:2) and demons (Mark 5:12) that Jesus exorcises from a man and then sends into pigs. Artaud gives a twist to this story and places Christ, echoing the story of Saint-Anthony of Egypt, in the desert but, more interestingly, gives him a stick with which he combats the Demons. This stick that would also have belonged to Saint Patrick is in the hands of Artaud—the stick was bought on a flea market in Brussels by the Dutch artist Tonny Kristians and given to Artaud by René

[vii] After describing Artaud's often-changing moods, Schafer, from these observations, concludes that "Artaud's spiritual quest vacillated wildly between bouts of extreme religious devotion, pagan esotericism, non-sectarian spirituality and atheism" (24). I think that Artaud's immanent understanding of Christ and God is far more creative and interesting than Schafer advances in his conclusion. We will come back at this point later.

Thomas (see Danchin and Roumieux, 89); the stick plays an important role in *The New Revelations of Being*—who therewith associates himself with Christ or the magician who brings back and reintroduces the vital pagan truth. Artaud then continues his letter by explaining what this Pagan Truth entails:

> There is no God, but there are gods. And at the top of the Hierarchy of gods the greatest God of which Plato speaks, which like everything that is is victim of Nature. This is not a criminal, it is an Impotent, like Us. For, what is criminal, it is Nature, and Nature itself what is it. In itself Nothing. It is this Nothing of which Laozi speaks from which however stems Life.[23] (OCVII, 207)

Artaud thus asserts that we are confronted with a hierarchy of gods. At the top of this hierarchy is the greatest God—Artaud's reference to Plato is rather vague, but he probably refers to the work *Timaeus* where Plato identifies the greatest God with Cosmos that contains all the gods and non-gods—who is also subjected, like we all are, to nature. He is therewith as impotent and deprived from a free will—the French word "impuissant" also connotes "powerless"; by translating "impuissant" as "impotent" however I have wanted to focus rather on the deprivation of a free will instead of the alleged powerlessness—as we are, because we are all submitted to "the unconscious and criminal law of Nature"[24] (OCVII, 206). Artaud then goes on by reasoning that nature in itself is nothing and this is where life springs from—it is the void that Artaud has denied for so long. It is therefore absurd to revolt against the gods, because "when we revolt against this so-called God we revolt against ourselves, and it is our very loss that we create"[25] (OCVII, 207). We should combat what *is*, what has become rusted, what is *formed*: "The force of the law has expulsed beings, it has put them out of life. They are out of the infinity of Nothing since what is something has ceased to be infinite"[26] (OCVII, 207). We all stem from a nothing that is indivisible, infinite, necessarily existing, and uncaused, that is, a void that is full of potentialities, a nothing that is traversed by vital fluxes, but that becomes determined, fixed, and stratified when it is expulsed from the infinity of the void.

Artaud goes on by exposing the contradictions that are inherent to nature and the difference between the disputable eternity and the beneficial state of nonbeing and then suddenly boldly states:

> This is not a theory, but the Truth. It is a Truth that has been seen and translated as far as these things can be translated. Those who do not want to understand it; one will beat them up this time. For this Truth will be imposed by force. Being beneficial and salutary. And men do not understand the force of truth but the

truth of force, which will make them accept with all heart and consciously the force of truth. We will begin this work within two months.²⁷ (OCVII, 208)

Artaud wants to impose his salutary and healing truth by force and his project of conversion would start within two months; according to *The New Revelations of Being*, this apocalyptic enterprise must take place between November 3 and 7. Artaud takes his project seriously, because he reassures Breton that

> it may be that I go to prison at some future time. Do not worry, it will be voluntary and for a short time. I told you that I had read in the Tarots that I will have to fight with justice but that I didn't know if they would beat me up or if it would be me who would beat them up.²⁸ (OCVII, 208)

His words are sadly prophetic, and Artaud would get the worst of it.

A Sense of Persecution and Megalomania

It remains vague at what point Artaud imprudently derailed; we know that he has been imprisoned in the prison of Mountjoy in Dublin from September 23 to 29 and that he returns to France on September 30 where he is directly transferred to a special department in the hospital of Le Havre. We do not know what concretely happened during his journey in Ireland, but we should conclude that Artaud's mission failed. His mission has failed in such a way that, from this time on, Artaud would be constantly interned in various psychiatric hospitals. After the hospital of Le Havre, where he stayed for two weeks, Artaud is transferred to a psychiatric hospital in Sotteville-lès-Rouen where he will be interned for five and a half months. He is then transferred to the psychiatric center of Sainte-Anne in Paris where he is interned for more than ten months after which he is transferred to the psychiatric hospital of Ville-Évrard for three years and eleven months. It is during this turbulent period, a time in which Artaud hardly writes, that he starts to fight with his identity and play with his name.ᵛⁱⁱⁱ He signs his letters with a Greek version of his name "Antoneo Arlanapulos" (LET, 37, 38, 39, 44, 47) or "Antonin Artaud God the Nothingness"²⁹ (LET, 291), and from 1941 to 1943, he uses his mother's surname "Antonin Nalpas" varying on it on December 31, 1942, by adding megalomaniacally "Antonin Nalpas—J-C"

ᵛⁱⁱⁱ Artaud's play with his identity is also reflected in his passport from 1935 that he had started to use as a notebook (see De Mèredieu 1992, 141–76, for a reproduction of this passport).

(LET, 460). This play with his name and identity was not a momentary crisis but rather a prediction that Artaud already made in a letter written in Ireland to Breton: "I sign one of the last times with my Name, afterwards it will be another Name"[30] (OCVII, 209). Neglecting this conscious enterprise of becoming-other, a medical report has been made up in the hospital of Sainte-Anne stating that Artaud would suffer from a "double personality, he knows little and from hearsay the personality that bears his name, Artaud; he knows much better, and from familiar memories, another personality that bears another name" (LET, 59). Artaud—for the sake of readability we use his official name—comments on his struggle and play with his name and his identity in a letter that he writes on December 31, 1942, to his mother. After he claims that his mother is dead, he asserts that "the mother of Nanaqui [Artaud's nickname during his childhood], Euphrasie Nalpas is my daughter, because I cannot have a mother, and calling oneself my mother in this very world is to insult me. I have no other mother than the Virgin Mary"[31] (LET, 460). Artaud reverses the order of things and makes himself the producer instead of the product or the creator instead of the created. By signing his letter with "Antonin Nalpas—J-C.," Artaud fulfills a project that began in 1936. Claiming that he is initiated in the rituals of the Tarahumaras Indians and asserting to be the revealed author who has apocalyptic visions of a new truth to come and going to Ireland with a stick that once belonged to Saint Patrick and Christ, it is but a small step to claim to be the son of Mary. And yet this step is programmatic and even necessary in the development of Artaud's later writings.

During his internment in Rodez, Artaud writes some poetic lines that concisely summarize his enterprise: "And so it is like being suspected of being god / and of having therefore a unique body and the body from which all has come / that I have thus been pursued, / that I have thus been intruded and bitten, / by hordes of parasites (of souls), / of microbes, / of vile erotic intruders of the ass, / of thick-lipped and barbed vampires, / and by them filed, planed, / shredded, sheared, / pumped, sucked, / picked, drilled, perforated, / broken, etc., etc."[32] (OCXIV**, 136). The reason for Artaud's persecution, internment, or, as he would later claim, crucifixion was that he has been suspected of being god and thus of having a unique body. His body, an expression of matter that has infinite and hitherto unexplored possibilities and potentialities, has been persecuted, invaded, and bitten by hordes of parasites (even from souls) but also of thick-lipped yokels or bearded savants, doctors, or psychiatrists who have eventually sucked him out, brought him down, and who have broken him

(Artaud uses many riming and alliterating—this play gets mainly lost in my translation—qualifications). Artaud's claims around his suffering and sickness are essentially an ironic appropriation of the passion and the suffering that he endured. In his writings, it is actually Artaud himself who is the vampire that sucks out the narrow-minded life of words, which is the denoting function of language, in order to play with the empty carcasses and eventually refill them with a more vital, energetic, and animated breath. This linguistic vampirism is the most important feature of Artaud's crusade since he wants to plunge the various arrests and judgments of God that man formalized back into the realm of infinity and vitality that is the realm of "zoe," where they can re-enable man to breath and reaffirm *this* world; where they can re-plunge man back into the Dionysian barrels of this life from which man becomes drunk of nature or God; where they enable man to reengage with the hitherto unexplored capabilities of the impulsiveness of the flesh. From this linguistic vampirism, the writings of Artaud begin to develop a more religious and theological tone. It is a period that doctor Latrémolière describes as a time in which Artaud "was only interested in himself. Throughout the period when I knew him, he was Christ, the center of the world. So don't tell me he advanced society. It was quite the opposite. And it never changed" (in Lotringer, 70–1).

The short time that Latrémolière takes care of Artaud is a period of an astonishing literary, poetic, and, one might say, religious production; it is the period of his internment for more than three years in a psychiatric hospital in Rodez. From 1942 onward, Euphrasie Nalpas tries to transfer her son to another psychiatric hospital because of the worse living conditions in Ville-Évrard. It is the Surrealist poet Robert Desnos who manages to transfer Artaud to Rodez where doctor Gaston Ferdière—who was also part of the Surrealist group and the initiator of art therapy—was the head of psychiatric hospital. The living conditions improve for Artaud because Rodez is situated in the unoccupied zone of France during the Second World War, and the progressive psychiatric and medical ideas of doctor Ferdière give much more freedom to him. Artaud arrives in Rodez on February 11, 1943, and directly writes an extensive word of thanks to doctor Ferdière the day after his arrival. It is this letter from February 12 that concisely summarizes his project or, better, his theosophy—we should keep in mind that Artaud is still exploring the healing practices of Ciguri, nature or God—and clearly reveals how one could read and reread the later writings of Artaud.

A New Religion

Artaud's letter is preceded by an enigmatic epigraph: "Inemi tenter monientan / Inemon ton tarinan" (ER, 27), echoing in a strange twist some parts of the Trinitarian formula or evoking the murmuring of an old priest after which he praises the importance of Ferdière's decision to transfer him to Rodez. He begins by claiming that Ferdière would "do justice to a writer interned against any rights"[33] (ER, 27), but, more importantly, the psychiatrist in Rodez would also have been led by "an occult inspiration that comes from above, I mean Dr. Ferdière that it comes from *God*, and that it is he who inspired you to rescue the unrecognized man"[34] (ER, 27, emphasis in original). Artaud then starts to objectify himself and states that he *was* a writer, a dramaturg, and a reputed actor who has been interned for more than five years after which he complains that he was interned "without any easing and without any movement of *effective* disgust that did not raise in his favor the consciousness of honest people"[35] (ER, 27, emphasis in original). According to Artaud, there were, for sure, various revolts in France—"there have been countless bloody encounters on the streets of Paris about Antonin Artaud"[36] (ER, 28)—but it is only thanks to the godly inspired Ferdière that he is now in safer hands. In what follows, Artaud sets forth the reasons for his internment, because "in the case of Antonin Artaud, there is no question of literature or theater, but of *religion* and that it is for his religious ideas, for his religious and mystical attitude that Antonin Artaud UNTIL HIS DEATH [Artaud declares himself dead in 1939] has been pursued by the French crowd"[37] (ER, 28, emphasis in original). Artaud accentuates the word "religion," and its constitutive etymology is important, because on the one hand, "religion" is etymologically derived from the Latin verb "religare" ("to connect") or the noun "religio" ("veneration") while on the other hand, the word is also rooted in the Latin word "relegere" ("to recollect" or "to reread," but also with its stem "legere," "to read").[ix]

Already in his earlier works from the Surrealist period, but intensified after his journey to Mexico, Artaud wants to cure our Western civilization that he finds too advanced. Following Frédéric Neyrat, this advanced civilization is the

---

[ix] In *The Natural Contract*, Michel Serres interestingly notes that the etymological opposite of the word religion is "negligence" and thus asserts that "[w]hoever has no religion should not be called an atheist or unbeliever, but negligent. The notion of negligence makes it possible to understand our time and our weather" (48). Etymologically, Artaud's accentuation of the word "religion" thus already suggests the cynicism, passivity, or negligence that he perceives in our Western civilization.

expression of a society that is conducted by a bewitchment "from the alloy, more than from the alloy, between capitalism, monotheism and techno science" (13). It is precisely this "lethal alloy" (13), attacked by Artaud in *To Have Done with the Judgment of God*, that sustains the bewitchment "which causes famine and pain" (15). Neyrat considers Artaud's later writings as an attempt to replace a culture of famine by a culture of hunger. It is interesting to elaborate on Artaud's writings on hunger, famine, and his eventual affinity with Naess's "deep ecology," as Neyrat contends, but for our discussion we consider famine mainly as a phenomenon of scarcity, which is a lack of vitality, causing pain, suffering, and death—in this understanding, the nuanced argument of Neyrat's reading of Artaud still stands up. In our Western civilization, following Artaud, no one escapes from this bewitchment that functions through magic. Neyrat argues that "[t]o the 'civic magic' that starves, abhors and suicides [...], Artaud opposes an 'alchemical' magic, a 'ritual and magical' theater, a poetry that forms new shadows that are able to restore the desire to eat to the one who feels no more than *hunger without appetite*" (16, emphasis in original). Following Neyrat, Artaud thus wants to cure our Western civilization by alchemically manipulating an already civically manipulated society. Neyrat's allusion to the formation of new shadows hints at Artaud's article "The Theater and Culture" in which he explains that "[f]or the theater as for culture, it remains a question of naming and directing shadows: and the theater, not confined to a fixed language and form, not only destroys false shadows but prepares the way for a new generation of shadows, around which assembles the true spectacle of life" (TD, 12).

Magically combatting the Platonic order of things—we should keep in mind that magic never changes the *nature* of things—and hence creating new shadows that restore the appetite for life, Artaud urges that

> [w]e must believe in a sense of life renewed by the theater, a sense of life in which man fearlessly makes himself master of what does not yet exist, and brings it into being. [...] Furthermore, when we speak the word "life," it must be understood we are not referring to life as we know it from its surface of fact, but to that fragile, fluctuating center which forms never reach. (TD, 13)

Artaud's magical theater is thus a religious enterprise and therewith a healing practice because it aims at curing and reconnecting the spectator or the reader to a forgotten sense of life that relentlessly resists any form or formation. Artaud's project is to reconnect society to the vital forces traversing the void, Ciguri or matter. He wants to heal the broken link between man and *this* world, *this* life, and *this* body. This healing, reconnecting, or revitalizing is still an important task of our time, because, as we have discussed earlier, Deleuze observes that we are becoming more and more passive with regard to our cultural, social, and mental environment. We should madden and defamiliarize our accustomed and thoughtless sensory-motor circuits of our habits, customs, and values in order to reengage with the vital, incessant, and creative fluxes of thinking, being, and life. Deleuze therefore asserts that we should "[b]elieve, not in a different world, but in a link between man and the world, in love or life, to believe in this as in the impossible, the unthinkable which none the less cannot be thought" (C2, 164). To believe essentially means believing in the potentialities of *this* world or, following Bogue, "[b]elief in this world is a view through the present and toward the future, one that envisions nothing specific in that future, but that trusts in the possibilities immanent within the real to produce something genuinely new" (2007, 11). Deleuze's immanent conversion is essentially about believing—we should bear in mind that a belief is something different than a consolidated knowledge—in the hitherto unexplored and infinite potentialities of *this* body, *this* life, and *this* world and an engagement with the agential materiality of language, the body, and our therewith intricately related thinking. Elaborating on this belief, Deleuze explains that "it is simply believing in the body. It is giving discourse to the body, and, for this purpose, reaching the body before discourses, before words, before things are named [...]. Artaud said the same thing, believe in the *flesh* [...]. Give words back to the body, to the flesh" (C2, 167, emphasis in original). Believing in *this* world and in *this* body and therewith engaging with being and life means that we should create words that are the direct expressions of matter, revalorize the singular expression of the body and—Deleuze is also aware of the healing forces at work in Artaud's writings—critically read and reread the works of Artaud.

Artaud indeed disorders the functional rules in the dominant biological and theological language by hollowing out a far more creative, vital, and animated language. In articulating a zoology of language, Artaud essentially wants to heal our sick and worn-out society ruled by civic magic and bewitchment, but violated, mainly during his voyage to Ireland, the art of caution and did not create safer or effective thresholds of sustainability. His vital theosophy of matter, which is the programmatic search for the incessant fluxes and the hitherto unexplored capabilities in the realm of the commonly denied void or the zoological enterprise that aims at creating vibrating words that are expressions of the vitality of Ciguri, nature, or God, did therewith not completely fail but, for a long period of various internments, made the sick-making, cynicism-stimulating and worn-out strata fall back on him. It is thus indeed for his religious ideas, in its common but more importantly and constitutively in its etymological sense, that Artaud "has been pursued by the French crowd" (ER, 28).

The Healing Powers of Magic

His letter to doctor Ferdière goes on by asserting that one might find it incredible but he is "deeply religious and *Christian*. He has been in this world the most qualified and the purest representative of the true Religion of Jesus Christ of which the exoteric Catholicism has for a long time only be the shameful caricature" (ER, 28, emphasis in original). It is evident that Artaud calls himself deeply religious, but also deeply Christian[x]—the most qualified and purest representative of the true religion of Jesus Christ. He is thus not so much a disciple of Christ, but more a Christ-like figure who stands in opposition to the caricature of the general doctrine that is exoteric and that therewith only focuses on obedience to the imposed rules and laws. Artaud then shifts to his resurrection, because "Antonin Artaud died in sorrow and in pain in Ville-Évrard in the month of August 1939 […]. I succeeded him and added myself to him soul to soul and body to body that has formed in his bed even concretely and really but by magic in his place" (ER, 28). Like Christ, Artaud dies as a martyr from the punishments that are imposed on him after which his dead body is magically respiritualized by a man who claims to be the son of the Virgin Mary.

In the foreword to Artaud's artistic and poetic work "50 Drawings to Murder Magic," Grossman notes that it unfolds

> on the one hand, the contemplative stopped gaze, the visual stasis: the image. On the other, the energy that acts at a distance, the rise of the act: the magic. *Image/Magic*. Is it an anagram [the French words for "image" and "magic" are "image" and "magie"]? It is an anagram, and more. Reverse the order of letters, twist them, petrify in it the visual and sound matter, it is also treating words as things: psychosis, diagnoses psychiatry; *poetry in space, theater of cruelty, affective athleticism*, retorts Artaud. (DM, 6, emphasis in original)

---

[x] See also Derrida 2002, who considered Artaud as a "hyper-Christian" (27).

Grossman thus contends that Artaud's material, phonetic, and semantic twist of words and his later play with sound and images are a form of magic[xi] that treats words as things and thus equalizes signs with ideas. They are a form of magic that changes the sense of words by changing the matter that composes them. Focusing on his magic, Grossman quotes a relevant passage from *Mexico and Civilization* in which Artaud remarks that "if magic is a constant communication from the inside to the outside, from the that act to thinking, from the thing to the word, from matter to spirit, one could say that we have lost for a long time this form of lightning inspiration, of nervous illumination, and that we need to re-soak ourselves in still living and unaltered sources"[38] (DM, 6). Grossman comments on this passage by asserting that "the magic is thus for him a *link*, a power of 'communication' to the formidable efficiency. Magic alone can cure this 'painful separation,' this rupture between things and words, ideas and signs, this separation between culture and life—this deadly petrification that Artaud sees at work everywhere in the Western world" (DM, 6, emphasis in original). Magic, understood as an enterprise that creatively plays with the vitality of matter, can thus heal the broken link between man and this world, because it engages with genuine thinking that is creation, being, and life. Magic is a feature of this vital and healthy religion that is devoted to matter, to Ciguri, to nature, or to God—this healing liquor that makes us drunk of the relentless stream of forces traversing this world, this life, and this body, which is this immanent and inexhaustible God that encompasses everything. A magic that sublimates brings us in a state where we become drunk of God, where we are plunged into the creative and incessant fluxes of life, and where we are thrown into a healthy delirium that gives us reasons to believe in a vital link between man and *this* world, *this* life, and *this* body.

Artaud's magical and materialist theosophy engages with the infinite expressions of matter and is eventually a healing practice of language that aims at restoring the broken link and the painful and sick-making separation between the organic culture and our Western civilization. The word "magic" might have the negative connotation of being exerted by a sneaky wizard or of weird paranormal activities, but its actual meaning is that of producing, through material procedures and incisions, hitherto unexplored phenomena; magic thus changes the phenomena that determine our comprehension of the world; magic

---

[xi] We must note that this magic is not alchemical, as Neyrat would have it, but rather sublimated (see Grossman 2003a, 82), because this magic engages with the same matter of which it does not change its nature.

combats the false shadows that keep us from "the true spectacle of life" (TD, 13). Artaud's use of the word "magic" must be read in this literal meaning. Magic does not change the world as such; it changes our narrow-minded and cynic perception of the world.

A Magical and Materialist Theosophy

Artaud continues his letter to doctor Ferdière by asserting that Antonin Nalpas has entered the dead body of Antonin Artaud who possessed already another spirit in its body, because "the real name of Antonin Artaud is Hippolytus and Saint Hippolytus was, as you know, the bishop of Piraeus in the early centuries of the Christian era after the death of Jesus Christ of who Antonin Artaud Hippolytus has transported the body *in time*"[39] (ER, 29, emphasis in original). Being a true magician, Antonin Artaud's body is thus actually the body of Hippolytus of Rome. Having transported and reincarnated Hippolytus of Rome is significant, because Hippolytus, who foresaw a soon apocalypse that he estimated to take place around 500, also combatted the rusted doctrines of the Catholicism of his time, criticized the politics of pope Callixtus I, and was later on elected bishop of Rome and therewith became the first antipope. Artaud ends his letter by claiming that it is Antonin Nalpas who is talking to doctor Ferdière and that "it is Heaven *from which you come yourself actually* that have sent you to me. And I have only written this letter to you in order to ask you to remember yourself of this literarily and objectively because what is actually your soul is an Angel and you are an Angel of Jesus Christ"[40] (ER, 29, emphasis in original). It is the salutary and infinite heaven, this void that is above, around, beneath, and within us, that would have brought Artaud's psychiatrist in contact with him. Artaud's letter is an expression of his thanks and a literal and objective reminder for Ferdière to remember his origins. Artaud's use of the words "literally" and "objectively" is important, because Artaud asks Ferdière to take his words literally and thus not metaphorically, symbolically, and abstractly and thus not arbitrary or subjectively—as if his words were only a hallucinatory psychosis of a madman. Artaud finally notes that Ferdière's soul is an angel, an intermediary between heaven and earth and a messenger of God. For having enabled his transference from Ville-Évrard to Rodez, Artaud considers doctor Ferdière a benevolent and Christian angel who has seen and acknowledged the profoundly religious attitude of his patient.

However impressive this letter is, Ferdière writes on April 17 to Artaud's mother that "his psychosis seems indeed very serious to me but I think that an exit in good conditions can be attempted later" (Danchin and Roumieux, 321) and the first electroshock would be administered on June 20, 1943. Four days later, when the third electroshock is administered on Artaud's body, the therapy causes a vertebral compression fracture after which the electroshock therapy is stopped for some time. Following the history of his internment, it seems that Artaud has again failed in his articulation of a magical and materialist theosophy where the drunkard of God—that is, the productive and creative delirium of him who submits himself to the healing powers of matter, nature, or God—magically combats the deadly petrification that is the modern fact in order to heal the painful separation or the broken link between man and this world. It seems that he has again failed in his search for words that express what he has experienced during his stay with the Tarahumaras Indians.[xii] We do not discuss the disputable administering of the electroshocks, which has also turned out to be physically healing for Artaud in a way, since that would lead to a specialist neurological, psychological, and psychiatric discussion.[xiii] More fruitful, interesting, and necessary is a critical and close reading of Artaud's later writings in order to understand his development toward a magical and materialist theosophy of immanence that he practices by using a zoological language that aims at restoring our belief in God, which is *this* indivisible, infinite, necessarily existing and uncaused world, *this* life, and *this* body.

"Man Will Find Nothing in Artaud's Work"

Latrémolière couldn't be more right when he asserted that "I believe that Man will find nothing in Artaud's work. Nothing" (Lotringer, 68). There are forces at work in Artaud's later writings evoking the infinite possibilities of nature,

---

[xii] Camille Dumoulié signals the same failing in asserting that "[e]verything has failed: the theater of cruelty, the cinema, poetry, the journey to the land of the Tarahumaras, and so on. In short, existence was a failure. But at the same time, everything testifies it [...]. It is too much life that can not enter the frame, which does not want to let itself flow in the mold as in an excremental offering" (18). Artaud's engagement with life and matter is indeed a perpetual experimentation that leaves traces, writings, and works that only give a glimpse of the forces of life that are too great to conceive. In this sense, his writings are indeed excrements—in his last notebooks, therefore, there is a constant recurrence of the word "shit." However impossible his writings are, they nevertheless bear witness, as Dumoulié notes, to the vital forces with which Artaud engaged.

[xiii] See De Mèredieu 1996 for a thorough analysis of the electroshock therapy that Artaud underwent.

this nothing that is traversed by vital forces and that is full of potency, and, in that sense, man will indeed and hopefully find nothing in Artaud's work. This nothing, or this void, is evoked in a foreign language that is hollowed out in the dominant language and that vibrates in such a way that it is the expression of this nothingness. Focusing on Artaud's zoological language, Dale asserts that

> [i]nvented language, says Artaud, must issue from torment, words (Artaud's "howl-words", which act at the level of pure phonetics and his unwritable "breath-words" must have value in themselves, which in effect means that at some level they must be meaningless. [...] The language of the depths of the body is before and after the judgment of man (it is not really God that Artaud rejects, but the judgment of god as instructed/constructed by man). (2002, 93)

As argued in this chapter, it is indeed the judgments, stoppages, and arrests of a transcendental, and hence humanly constructed, God that Artaud combats. Despite the appearances, Artaud does not reject this immanent God (cf. Penot-Lacassagne 2002, 112) in which vital and animated forces of nature and matter energetically flow. Being an expression of matter, his zoological language aims on the contrary at evoking and suggesting this God that encompasses everything, this God or nature that is infinite, indivisible, and uncaused; this is what his magical and materialist theosophy essentially aims at. Some weeks before Artaud's arrival in Paris, Prevel formulates an adage to which this magical and materialist theosophy might give rise: "Live it. One should live it. And I want to try this card that fate hands me. A magic card, I feel it" (19). Artaud's magical and materialist theosophy of immanence aims at a "sacred yes-saying" (Nietzsche 2006, 17) to the forces of *this* world, or following Derrida, a "yes" that "should be anything except the rest of a stabilization and [that] is beyond 'yes' and 'no'" (2002, 30). This religious, curing, and joyful "yes" is an inevitable submission to the joyous and terrible forces of life and the "true nature of evil."

Prevel does not dramatize Artaud's premature death on March 4, 1948, but rather dramatizes his own fate, and on March 9, he sadly writes to his aunt Germaine Chéron that "Antonin Artaud was my only friend. It was the only man I loved. Now I have nobody" (210) and in the few years that were left until Prevel's own death, he has not stopped writing about Artaud. On August 22, 1950, Prevel even claims that

> the intensity of his life has led me to an absolute; to his life. I was caught in its vortex. I followed him like a sleepwalker. And when I left him at Jussieu or somewhere in the night, I returned drunk, strangely obsessed by his words, by

the songs he chanted, with his unique face, with its poignant look. [...] My life was transformed, illuminated. There was Antonin Artaud. I lived. (242–3)

Artaud's words, gestures, and appearances, being those of a genuine intercessor, have thrown Prevel into a delirium, a vortex, or a state where he becomes drunk without alcohol and that have thrown him off the rails into life; he has been drunk of God. In what way Prevel's life has been transformed remains vague and is only hinted at in two words: "I lived."

In this chapter, we have traced the development of the early period of Artaud's later writings that are deeply influenced and inspired by Artaud's experiences from his journey to Mexico. Searching for the articulation of an organic culture, Artaud constantly searches for new forms of expression to envision this healthier culture. Considering writing as a "pharmakon" that can be both a beneficial remedy and a destructive drug, the majority of Artaud's later writings are devoted to a magical and materialist theosophy that he expresses in a zoological language and that aims at restoring our belief in *this* world. This magical and materialist theosophy of immanence is therewith an enterprise of auto-immunization and likewise a cure of detoxification of the modern fact.

Notes

1   "Mais ce que je veux dire Dr Ferdière est ceci: c'est que dans le cas d'Antonin Artaud il n'est pas question de littérature ni de théâtre mais de *religion*" [my translation].
2   "cette expérience vécue m'en rappelait un autre, à laquelle je me sentais lié indirectement peut-être, mais tout de même par des fils matériels. C'étaient des réminiscences d'histoire qui venaient à moi, rocher par rocher, herbe par herbe, horizon par horizon" [my translation].
3   "la danse de guérison" [my translation].
4   "obscure tantalisations" [my translation].
5   "Maladie" [my translation].
6   "Les Tarahumaras ne croient pas en Dieu et le mot « Dieu » n'existe pas dans leur langue" [my translation].
7   "j'ai eu l'imbécilité de dire que je m'étais converti à Jésus-christ alors que le christ est ce que j'ai toujours le plus abominé" [my translation].
8   "avance délibérément dans le mal. Il y plonge avec une sorte d'affreux courage, sur un rythme qui, au-dessus de la Danse, semble dessiner la Maladie. [...] cette avance

dans la maladie est un voyage, une *descente pour* RESSORTIR AU JOUR.—Il tourne en rond dans le sens des ailes de la Swastika, de droite à gauche toujours, et par le haut" (OCIX, 45).

9. "L'Europe est dans un état de civilisation avancée: je veux dire qu'elle est très malade. L'esprit de la jeunesse en France est de réagir contre cet état de civilisation avancée" [my translation].

10. "derrière cette idée de culture il y a une idée de la vie qui ne peut que gêner les Écoles parce qu'elle détruit leurs enseignements" [my translation].

11. "En face de la culture de l'Europe qui tient dans des textes écrits et fait croire que la culture est perdue si les textes sont détruits, je dis qu'il y a une autre culture sur laquelle d'autres temps ont vécu et cette culture perdue se base sur une idée matérialiste de l'esprit" [my translation].

12. "l'écriture fixe l'esprit et le cristallise dans une forme, et, de la forme, naît l'idolâtrie" [my translation].

13. "une culture basée sur l'esprit en relation avec les organes, et l'esprit baignant dans tous les organes, et se répondant en même temps" [my translation].

14. "Ce dont j'ai souffert jusqu'ici, c'est d'avoir refusé le Vide. Le Vide qui était déjà en moi. […] J'ai lutté pour essayer d'exister, pour essayer de consentir aux formes (à toutes les formes) dont la délirante illusion d'être au monde a revêtu la réalité. […] Or, n'étant plus je vois ce qui est. Je me suis vraiment identifié avec cet Être, cet Être qui a cessé d'exister. Et cet Être m'a tout révélé" [my translation].

15. "l'Homme Abstrait" [my translation].

16. "si j'ajoute 3 de 3 juin au chiffre du 6ᵉ mois de l'année, j'obtiens 9, la Destruction Infernale qui, ce jour-là, a commencé. Si j'ajoute 5, chiffre de l'Homme Abstrait, à 6 du 6ᵉ mois de l'année, j'obtiens 11 qui me ramène à Novembre, et Novembre est sous le signe du chiffre 9 selon l'ancien calendrier" [my translation].

17. "Le Torturé est devenu pour tout le monde le Reconnu" [my translation].

18. "Ma Vie, Anne, réalise une Prophétie" [my translation].

19. "Ne perdez jamais votre stylo. Il contient lui aussi quelque chose. Il vous protégera" [my translation].

20. "les choses vont devenir grave et […] j'irai cette fois jusqu'au bout" [my translation].

21. "la dernière descendante authentique des Druides, celle qui possède les secrets de la philosophie druidique" [my translation].

22. "le Paganisme a eu raison, mais les Hommes qui sont d'éternels saligauds ont trahi la Vérité Païenne. Le christ ensuite est *revenu* pour remettre au jour la Vérité Païenne, sur laquelle *toutes* les Églises chrétiennes ont chié ensuite avec ignominie. Le christ était un Magicien qui a lutté dans le désert contre les Démons avec une canne" [my translation].

23. "Il n'y a pas de Dieu, mais il y a des dieux. Et au sommet de la Hiérarchie des dieux le plus grand Dieu dont parle Platon, lequel comme tout ce qui est est victime de la Nature. Ce n'est pas un criminel, c'est un Impuissant, comme Nous. Car ce qui est criminel c'est la Nature, et la Nature elle-même qu'est-ce que c'est. En elle-même Rien. Elle est ce Rien dont parle Lao-Tseu, d'où pourtant est issue la Vie" [my translation].
24. "la loi inconsciente et criminelle de la Nature" [my translation].
25. "quand nous nous révoltons contre ce soi-disant Dieu nous nous révoltons contre nous-même, et c'est notre perte même que nous créons" [my translation].
26. "La force de la loi a expulsé des êtres, elle les a mis dehors dans la vie. Ils sont sortis de l'infini du Rien car ce qui est quelque chose n'est plus l'infini" [my translation].
27. "Ceci n'est pas une théorie, mais la Vérité. C'est la Vérité vue et traduite autant que ces choses peuvent se traduire. Ceux qui ne voudront pas la comprendre, on leur cassera la gueule cette fois. Car cette Vérité sera imposée par la force. Étant salutaire. Et les hommes ne comprennent pas la force de la vérité mais la vérité de la force, qui leur fait accepter ensuite de tout cœur et en conscience la force de la vérité. On commencera ce travail dans deux mois" [my translation].
28. "Il se peut que j'aille en Prison d'ici quelque temps. Ne vous inquiétez pas, ce sera volontaire et pour peu de temps. Je vous ai dit que j'avais lu dans les Tarots que j'aurai à me battre avec la justice mais que je ne savais pas si elle me casserait la gueule ou si ce serait moi qui la lui casserais" [my translation].
29. "Antonin Artaud Dieu Le Néant" [my translation].
30. "Je signe une des dernière fois de mon Nom, après ce sera un autre Nom" [my translation].
31. "la mère de Nanaqui, Euphrasie Nalpas est ma fille, car je ne peux avoir de mère, et se dire ma mère en ce monde-ci c'est m'insulter. Je n'ai d'autre mère que la Vierge Marie" [my translation].
32. "Et c'est donc comme prévenu d'être dieu / et d'avoir par conséquent un corps unique et le corps d'où tout est sorti / que j'ai été ainsi poursuivi, / que j'ai été ainsi envahi et mordu, / par des hordes de parasites (D'esprits), / de microbes, / d'ignobles intrus érotiques du cu, / de vampires lippus ou barbus, / et par eux limé, raboté, / râpé, tondu, / pompé, sucé, / pioché, percé, troué, / rompu, etc., etc." [my translation].
33. "rendre justice à un écrivain interné contre tout droit" [my translation].
34. "une inspiration occulte qui vient d'en haut, je veux Dr Ferdière qu'elle vous vient de *Dieu*, et que c'est lui qui vous a poussée à porter secours à l'homme méconnu" [my translation].
35. "sans aucun adoucissement et sans qu'un mouvement de dégoût *efficace* n'ait soulevé en sa faveur la consciences des honnêtes gens" [my translation].

36 "il y a eu d'innombrables rencontres sanglantes dans les rues de Paris au sujet d'Antonin Artaud" [my translation].
37 "dans le cas d'Antonin Artaud il n'est pas question de littérature ni de théâtre mais de *religion* et que c'est pour ses idées religieuses, pour attitude religieuse et mystique qu'Antonin Artaud JUSQU'A SA MORT a été poursuivi par la foule des Français" [my translation].
38 "Si la magie est une communication constante de l'intérieur à l'extérieur, de l'acte à la pensée, de la chose au mot, de la matière à l'esprit, on peut dire que nous avons depuis longtemps perdu cette forme d'inspiration foudroyante, de nerveuse illumination, et que nous avons besoin de nous retremper à des sources encore vives et non alternées" [my translation].
39 "Le véritable nom d'Antonin Artaud est Hippolyte et Saint Hippolyte fut vous le savez évêque du Pirée dans les premiers siècles de l'ère chrétienne après la mort de Jésus-Christ dont Antonin Artaud Hippolyte *dans le temps* a transporté le corps" [my translation].
40 "c'est le Ciel *dont vous venez vous-même en réalité* qui vous a envoyé à moi. Et je ne vous ai écrit cette lettre que pour vous demander de vous en souvenir littéralement et objectivement car en réalité ce qui est votre âme est un Ange et vous êtes un Ange de Jésus-Christ" [my translation].

4

The Writing of Cruelty: On the Art of Crescive Writing

The first manifestation / of the theater of cruelty / can only be / the departure of / the vengeance of / my eternal / history of / sempiternal / persecuted.[1]
—Antonin Artaud, *Notebook 375*, CI, p. 1999

Artaud's Return to Paris

In the previous chapter, we have discussed the form, that of a magical and materialist theosophy, with which we can understand the development of Artaud's later writings. This magical and materialist theosophy is a theosophy of immanence that creatively engages with language in its agential materiality (it has, again, nothing to do with alchemy but rather with sublimation). We have also concluded that Artaud's journey to Mexico has been constitutive in the constant search, especially in his later writings, for an articulation of a healthier and happier organic culture to come. In this chapter, we will focus on the content of Artaud's later writings that are, I argue, essentially concerned with the writing of "cruelty."

At the end of February 1946, Marthe Robert and Arthur Adamov visit the psychiatric hospital in Rodez not only to see their friend but also to discuss the conditions for Artaud's return to Paris with his doctor and psychiatrist Ferdière. In the following months, the Committee of Friends of Antonin Artaud is formed in Paris under the presidency of Jean Paulhan. The committee is responsible for the arrangement of Artaud's new life after nine years of treatments in psychiatric hospitals. Knowing Ferdière's conditions for Artaud's return to Paris, Marthe Robert and Arthur Adamov ask André Berne-Joffroy and Paule Thévenin to find a new home for Artaud. Spending his Easter holidays of 1946 with his cousins in Aveyron, Berne-Joffroy travels, on the insistence of Colette Thomas, to Rodez where he visits Artaud. In an interview with Jean-Claude Fosse from 1996, Berne-Joffroy admits that he didn't know much about Artaud or his works and that he was surprised and struck by his "very weird and strange behavior. His ridiculous appearance, his agitation and his vociferations aroused the astonishment of passersby" (Danchin and Roumieux, 767). Berne-Joffroy's surprise turns into astonishment as he hears Ferdière's proposal to accommodate Artaud in a small hotel on the Rue de Grenelle in Paris. Fearing another internment for Artaud, he rather looks for a pension that is specialized in psychiatric patients. Berne-Joffroy finds this pension in Ivry-sur-Seine, a suburb in the south of Paris, in a nursing home that is under the direction of doctor Achille Delmas. In an interview with Laurent Danchin that was broadcasted on January 14, 1986, at *France Inter*, Ferdière nuances and criticizes Berne-Joffroy's way of acting and claims that he wanted to release Artaud from Rodez if two conditions were met: his friends should, first of all, find a pension or a clinic that could properly accept Artaud in order to give him the right food so that he would not suffer again from being underweight and, secondly, that the pension or clinic should be well monitored because of Artaud's bad hygiene. With a sense of delusion, Ferdière remarks that Berne-Joffroy and Thévenin came up with "the only clinic in the Parisian region where the doctor—it is not worth mentioning his name[i]—gave toxins to the patients as long as they wanted" (Danchin and Roumieux, 695). This intentional or accidental miscommunication between doctor Ferdière and the Committee of Friends of Antonin Artaud would create a final altercation upon Artaud's arrival in Paris. Jacques Prevel, although he couldn't assist at Artaud's arrival because of his sudden sickness, notes in his diary that "Marthe Robert and Henri Thomas were waiting for him. They were nearly having a row with Ferdière, who advised Artaud against entering the clinic" (46). However right Ferdière's objections might have been, Artaud praises the progressive and liberal policy of doctor Delmas and even claims in a letter from May 1947 that he wrote to his doctor, after a long praise of opium, that "[y]ou are the only doctor to know something about that [the working and the apparently positive effects of opium] because you have felt it with the rest of a lacerated heart that another doctor does not have"[2] (O, 1620).

Not only Artaud's way of living—he is transferred from a strict regime in the countryside of Rodez to a far more liberal treatment in the cosmopolitan

---

[i] In a later interview with Lotringer, Ferdière would boldly assert that "Dr. Delmas was an idiot [...]. I consider him to be a mediocre psychiatrist—Achille Delmas" in order to finally conclude that "[i]t's the most horrifying clinic in the Parisian region—the most horrifying" (191).

capital of France—and his social network—he had moved from an environment of doctors and patients to the presence of equally minded friends—change after his return to Paris, his writings also develop into a more theatrical, energetic, and violent form of writing. In his notebooks, he continues to use the paper as an object or a tactile in which he sometimes almost carves his words and in which he stabs holes with his pen and on which he draws sketches, small images, signs, lines, or glossolalia that are as important as the more readable and intelligible words. For Ferdière, this more frequent use of glossolalia[ii] is a clear sign of Artaud's deteriorating state that was caused by the treatment of doctor Delmas. In an interview with Lotringer, Ferdière asserts that "it is a sign of aggravation, a sign of a breakdown. At that point it is doubtful if the patient will improve" (189).

Besides his reproach to the policy of Delmas's clinic, Ferdière also doubts if it was Artaud himself who has written the hundreds of notebooks in Ivry: "I think they were doctored. It is not possible that he concealed so many things. They must have arranged and tweaked them. Paule Thévenin is a woman who can easily imitate the writings of others" (164). In a letter to Bettina Knapp in 1965, Thévenin pins down her critics by claiming that

> [w]hat I can tell you, is that he worked all the time. At any moment, wherever he was, whether at a table, in the subway, surrounded by friends, how inconvenient his position might be, he would take from his pocket one of those little school notebooks that he was carrying everywhere with him, and write or draw in it. In doing so, he would accompany his work with rhythmic chanting in a language invented by himself. (Thévenin, 64)

In our discussion of Artaud's eventual participation in the rituals of the Tarahumaras Indians, we have concluded that it is, in the end, not interesting to know if Artaud really physically participated in the Dance of the Peyote; the same argument is valid for Ferdière's suggestion of Thévenin's participation in Artaud's writing. What is interesting is the development of a use of language that becomes more theatrical, energetic, and violent, a writing that uses the paper as a tactile and the pen or the pencil as a burden, a sign, or a mark. The question whether Thévenin would have assisted during Artaud's writing is interesting and

---

[ii] See Tomiche (2003) for an analysis of the glossolalia that develops from a religious phenomenon to a pathological phenomenon and eventually a poetic experimentation. See also (2012, 234–61) in which she relates Artaud's usage of the glossolalia to his mystical and religious crisis (2012, 238) during the first months of his treatments in Rodez.

important but not relevant to a textual analysis of the development of Artaud's later writings. What genuinely matters is, again, what *happens* in these later works and the more theatrical, tactile, and material approach to writing that comes into being in his later writings.

"I Ended Up Hanging/a Door in Language"

Language has always played an important role in the works of Artaud. From the correspondence with Rivière to his writings on the theater, cinema, and the visual arts and from his letters, poems, and notebooks written in the psychiatric hospitals to the works written after his return to Paris, something is at work in Artaud's use of language. In a notebook from February 1947, Artaud reflectively writes that

> the rational
> grammatical modern
> actual language
> is far too approximative
> with its way of tightening
> ~~a false subject~~
> clearly a false
> subject
> it obliges to edify only
> in the directory of
> lucid things, that is
> to say already illuminated [things]
> instead of going to seek
> in the obscure at each
> time an unknown to
> which will be given
> his lucid life by
> effort and by willingness
> What I do is to
> flee the light
> to illuminate the obscure.[3] (CI, 34–5)

Our daily and rational language with its modern grammar would, following Artaud, tie and narrow the subject and turn it into a false subject—Artaud intensifies his reasoning by adding that it is obviously a false subject. This rational language excludes and undermines the unknowns of the obscure, the hitherto unexplored and therefore marginalized, dangerous, and delirious forces of the "true nature of evil," and therefore hinders to give them a clear life.

It is Artaud's task and project—we have called it a cure of auto-detoxification and an enterprise of auto-immunization articulated within a religious and a healing practice of language (Chapters 1 and 2) or a magical and materialist theosophy of immanence (Chapter 3)—to broaden language, to hollow out in this language a far more vital and animated language in order to give words and hence life to these unknowns in the still obscure fields that are excluded by our rational language. These obscure fields are the realm of untranslatable, unimaginable, and unthinkable cries of a void that thinks, suffers, and yet lives life to its fullest potential. We have already discussed how our rational language is an ideological, political, biological, and a theological enterprise that participates in the eventual stimulation of confusion, cynicism, and illness; its structuring grammar posits unity and identity and consequently postulates an obviously false subject. In order to liberate his tongue from the burden of this theological and biological language, Artaud engages with a zoological language, which is a minor and foreign but healing, affirmative, and generative language encompassing "Theos" (the discourse of reason, unity, and opposition), "bios" (the political discourse of human and discursive life), *and* "zoe" (the animal, organic, pre- and nonhuman, and vital life). This zoological language engages with forces that are the expressions of matter and thus broadens what language can *say* and what language can *do*, but to enlighten, develop, and emancipate language, or to create a far more materialist and vital language, we should, finally, also focus on what Artaud's language *does* on a more vertical axis.

As discussed earlier, Artaud's zoology of language is expressed in a magical and materialist theosophy that investigates and explores mainly Ciguri, nature, or God and magically plays with ideas by materialistically treating words as things. This theosophy of immanence, however, is only the form within which a reciprocal but not yet discussed content or, better, a not yet investigated theology is expressed. The discussion of the theology (the word "logos" in "theology" means "word" as well as "reason," "thought," or, interestingly, "language") within Artaud's magical and materialist theosophy is stirred from a passage in a notebook that also dates from February 1947 in which he writes:

> By dint of pushing outside the written
> with the written

> I ended up hanging
> a door in language, by
> taking down a wall, by
> moving a partition
> and that this partition, this new
> plan where I ended up by
> unblocking,
> as a lost body,
> has been
> the death that I really
> knew helping me,
> this swarming,
> catapultuous, hateful,
> dreadful
> acrimonious world of the uncreated,
> where, through speech,
> the words, the aborted syllables,
> I felt moving
> the epidermic body
> of beings and forms,
> which having never
> existed, wanted
> to live
> although never
> having the right to.[4] (CI, 177–8)

The French word "pousser" (translated as "pushing") can be read literally because it might well refer to Artaud's use of a hammer that he would smash on a block of wood during his writing. Apart from this anecdotal and literal reading, the word "pousser" is furthermore interesting, because it is etymologically derived from the Latin verb "pulsare" meaning "to hit" or "to put into movement." In other words, Artaud puts his writings into movement (he pushes it to the outside, which is beyond the limits[iii]) through and with writing. It is this impossible movement that matters for Artaud, because, following Tomiche, "[i]t is no longer a question of finding a fundamental and immediate language, but [...] of turning language, to make it turn, to shape it differently" (2002, 152).

[iii] This reminds us of the third aspect of literature that Deleuze distinguished in the practice of literature (see CC, 5 and Chapter 2 for a short discussion).

As already discussed, Artaud's zoology of language encompasses "Theos," "bios," *and* "zoe" and is thus articulated *in* and *through* the formalized system of signs that is our daily and common language. Artaud *does* and *creates* something in his language, because, as he contends, he has hung a door in it and he has achieved to move the wall that has been his death. He then comments on the acrimonious world of the uncreated, which paradoxically exists without having being created, which has come into being through words and aborted syllables, hence without life. Artaud continues that he has felt the epidermal and thus superficial body of beings and forms, which wanted to live without ever having existed and who had never the right to, moving on this world of the uncreated. In other words, the wall that Artaud has torn down was the wall that kept him inside the world of the uncreated—that was maintained by speech, words, and aborted syllables—and on which epidermal bodies wanted to exist. What realm is then disclosed by Artaud's fall of the wall and to what sphere does his door open up to? In this final chapter, we first discuss Artaud's references to the theater of cruelty with which he reengages in his later writings (notably in the notebooks in which he continues to write after his return to Paris) after which we investigate what the concept of "cruelty" entails. We finally argue, from a schizoanalytic perspective that especially focuses on the invention and creation of new possibilities of life, that Artaud's later works are religious practices of bodily writings that go beyond the practices of creative, performative, and asemic writing but are more adequately covered by the practice of what we call "crescive writing," which is a rather critical creative writing or, better, an affective and cruel writing. This writing of cruelty is essentially about Artaud's engagement with the joyous *and* terrible forces of the wound that constantly invites us to embody it.

The Theater of Cruelty and Language

In the beginning of November 1947, the art director of *Radiodiffusion française* Fernand Pouey asks Artaud to write and perform a poem for the cycle "The Voice of the Poets." Writing new lines and poems, Artaud finally reads his texts on November 28. Artaud's performance was meant to be broadcasted on February 2, 1948, at 10:45 p.m., but after listening to the words, screaming, and strange sounds that Artaud, in collaboration with Maria Casarès (she replaced Colette Thomas who found the performance too exhausting), Paule Thévenin, and Roger

Blin, had created, the general director of the radio station Wladimir Porché decided to put a ban on the poem. More than twenty-five years later, Artaud's last major work was broadcasted by *France Culture* for the first time on March 6, 1973. In an article devoted to Artaud's envisioning of a new theater, Thévenin refers to the interdiction to broadcast *To Have Done with the Judgment of God* by quoting a letter of Artaud in which he writes to Paulhan that "you will not hear the sounds, / the sonic xylophony, / the cries, the guttural sounds and the voice, / all that constituted a 1st rehash of the Theater of Cruelty. / It is a DISASTER for me"[5] (qtd. in Thévenin, 129). The cycle of poems that constitute *To Have Done with the Judgment of God* is not only interesting for its words, but also for its actual manifestation: the readers or executers of the poems rhyme and alternate their words, jabber, and screams with the xylophone, gongs, and other sounds.

Commenting on the language used in Artaud's cycle of poems, Jean-Christophe Bailly rightly asserts that we are faced with a

> language which is written only to be said, uttered, triturated by the voice [...] according to the idea of a sonic efficiency based on a nervous basis—the idea that was the one before, that was that of *The Theater and its Double*, but that has now no time to lose [...]. The necessity, the urgency, the will to act immediately, all that could have appeared as a watchword in the works of the avant-gardes becomes here pure effectiveness, full employment. (21)

In addition to Bailly, I argue that this flexional language is the expression of an organic culture where the mind is intricately related to the body and where thinking is hence related to "a nervous basis."

Bailly also notes the similarities between the language in *To Have Done with the Judgment of God* that is based on the nerves and the ideas that Artaud exposed in his concept of the "theater of cruelty." Artaud's final major work is indeed a complex play of language and sounds from which an estranging energy springs that confronts its auditors with an immense joy of life, creativity, and yet also a then and still today marginalized, disvalued, and disputed sense of violence, gloominess, and suffering. Stephen Barber suggests a similar fulfillment of the "theater of cruelty" by claiming that "Artaud's last work, finally, is theology of a virulent and pure kind—an anti-religious language of the scream made new, vivid flesh" (1999, 94). This conclusion foregrounds the religious aspects of *To Have Done with the Judgment of God* by claiming that this work is pure theology, which is the language and words of and from God (understood as nature or matter); it is in this sense that the work is, for that very reason, religious. Although

Artaud harshly criticizes Catholicism and their God,[iv] his language, stemming from the scream and that becomes vivid flesh, is a genuine religious language—it is only anti-religious, as Barber suggests, in the sense that it critically fights against the institutionalized religions—because it creatively and dramatically reengages with the potency of the materiality of words and sounds. In doing so, this work participates in healing the broken link between man and this world.

An Impossible Theater

Returning to Thévenin's remark on Artaud's last works, we follow her characterization of the "theater of cruelty" that stages the incessant combat of man—she calls it more pathetically "a bloody war" (127)—with his badly constructed body—she also specifies it as "moron" (127); it is a combat that strives for liberating man from his anatomy. Thévenin thus concludes that "[y]ou have the feeling that this impossible theater of which Antonin Artaud had once dreamed, he finally realized it […]. It is a theater that refrains itself from the stage boards, […] it is a theater whose place is the body of man uttering his very life" (127–8). Artaud's theater is impossible in the sense that it cannot and should not ever achieve what it strives for: the actual victory over this badly constructed body would paradoxically cause his death and hence destroy life. In this sense, Artaud's theater is the stage of becoming the BwO, a stage where one experiments in playing with the actual construction of the body. As Artaud claims in the final lines of *To Have Done with the Judgment of God*:

> Man is sick because he is badly constructed.
> We must make up our minds to strip him bare in order to scrape off that animalcule that itches him mortally,
> god,
> and with god
> his organs.
>
> For you can tie me up if you wish,
> but there is nothing more useless than an organ.

[iv] Neyrat contends that *To Have Done with Judgment of God* criticizes "the immediate facts of the West" (17). For his interesting reading of the five parts of the cycle of poems, see Neyrat, 17–26, or see Dolphijn, 24, for a more philosophical discussion of the implications of this work. However interesting and useful the criticism in Artaud's cycle of poems is, what interests us for this part are the forces that are at work in his writing and his use of language.

When you will have made him a body without organs,
then you will have delivered him from all his reactions and restored him to his true freedom.[6] (SW, 570-1)

These programmatic lines conclude the impossibility of Artaud's project: one cannot *be* a BwO and hence free of all constraints, which does not imply that one should never stop *becoming* a body without organs and thus free of all constraints. Striving for liberation involves the art of caution and the creation of thresholds of sustainability that we can find on the stage—whatever the form of this stage may be—of the theater of cruelty.

Artaud himself considered *To Have Done with the Judgment of God* to be a first rehash of the theater of cruelty. Thévenin contends however that all of Artaud's later works, in one way or another, engage with the theater of cruelty. Focusing on the act of writing along with a textual analysis of its production, Alain Jugnon also rightly argues that "[t]he writing of Antonin Artaud between 1946 and 1948, until the very moment of his death, is a continuous fire, the political and poetic staging of the living theater of our creative life: it does so because everything is written" (42). In addition to Jugnon, we claim that the theater of cruelty manifests itself in the ongoing fire, which is the ungraspable but energetic forces, of Artaud's later writings (at the end of this chapter, we argue that these later writings are thus practices of what I call "crescive writing"). Commenting on Artaud's rehash of the theater of cruelty, Thévenin describes it as an impossible theater.[v] Derrida similarly asserts the impossibility of Artaud's theater of cruelty, since his theater aims at the resistance of repetition (see 1978, 248); his theater searches for the flexional singularity that cannot be caught in reflection. Putting it differently, his theater aims at the articulation of a perpetual AND instead of a repeatable IS. Looking at Artaud's notebooks—he writes almost continuously in the hundreds of notebooks after his return to Paris—the reader indeed discovers what I call a writing of cruelty. Before turning to a discussion of these notebooks in order to see how this "cruelty" works through language, we first discuss the concept of cruelty that Artaud first coined in a letter to Jean Paulhan from 1932.

---

[v] Alain Virmaux perceives the same impossibility in Artaud's theater of cruelty and contends that this theater is full of antinomies, "dissonances and correspondences, multiplicity and unity, double and cruelty. If all the attempts of Artaud bring us back to the theater, it is that the theater expresses the fundamental distress of its nature" (99).

Cruelty as Necessity and Life

In his letter to Jean Paulhan, Artaud comments on the title that he wants to give to his manifest of a renewed theater—"The Theater of Cruelty"—and explains that cruelty does not exclusively concern sadism or blood. He wants to broaden the word "cruelty," to dive into the depths of the words, because "I claim, in doing this, the right to break with the usual sense of language, to crack the armature once and for all, to get the iron collar off its neck, in short to return to the etymological origins of speech which, in the midst of abstract concepts, always evoke a concrete element"[7] (TD, 101). He specifies that he wants us to imagine a pure and authentic cruelty that "[f]rom the point of view of the mind, cruelty signifies rigor, implacable intention and decision, irreversible and absolute determination"[8] (TD, 101). Specifying that one of the images of cruelty is philosophical determinism, Artaud continues that "[c]ruelty is above all lucid, a kind of rigid control and submission to necessity"[9] (TD, 102). Over the years, the basis of Artaud's understanding of the concept "cruelty" remains unchanged, because in a poem that he wrote for *To Have Done with the Judgment of God*—the poem was finally excluded from the recording because of the total length of the actual broadcast—he writes that "[t]he Theater of Cruelty / is not the symbol of an absent void, / of a dreadful inability to realize oneself in his life as man. / It is the affirmation / of a terrible / and otherwise inescapable necessity"[10] (OCXIII, 110). This terrible and inescapable necessity, of which "cruelty" is the affirmation, also challenges the bad construction of man in its engagement with the becoming of a BwO that is a non-organized and vital body that is liberated from its automatisms. Dale similarly concludes that "[c]ruelty makes us move, it wakes up the heart and nerves and tests our vitality in order to confront us with our potential, in order to force us into combat with our chaos. Deleuze follows Artaud's schizophrenic thought as it plunges into universal depths where the word loses its meaning but not its affect" (2002, 92). In this combat that is stimulated by an affective cruelty, Artaud fathoms the depths of words on which Dale elaborates by contending that "[t]he language of depths of the body is before and after the judgment of man (it is not really God that Artaud rejects, but the judgment of god as instructed/constructed by man)" (2002, 93).

As we have already seen, Deleuze indeed contends in *The Logic of Sense*: "Artaud is alone in having been an absolute depth in literature, and in having discovered a vital body and the prodigious language of this body" (LS, 105). Taking a closer look at Artaud's schizophrenic words, Deleuze contends that they are the manifestation of the theater of cruelty and he continues:

> The duality of the schizophrenic word has not been adequately noted: it comprises the passion word, which explode into wounding *phonetic* values, and the action-word, which welds inarticulate *tonic* values. These two words are developed in relation to the duality of the body, fragmented body and body without organs. They refer to two theaters, the theater of terror or passion and the theater of cruelty, which is by essence active. They refer to two types of nonsense, passive and active: the nonsense of the word devoid of sense, which is decomposed into phonetic elements; and the nonsense of tonic elements, which for a word incapable of being decomposed and no less devoid of sense. Here everything happens, acts and is acted upon, beneath sense and far from the surface. (LS, 90, emphasis in original)

Deleuze's conclusion is interesting because it stresses again the duality, or the apparent impossibility, of Artaud's theater: the theater of cruelty is a stage where energetic forces of suffering and joy play together; it is a theater of passion and action and a theater where some words are blessed and other words yet armed. It is in this sense that the theater of cruelty does not represent something but, following Derrida's reading of Artaud, presents "life itself, in the extent to which life is unrepresentable. Life is the nonrepresentable origin of representation" (1978, 294). In other words, the forces of life that are too great to conceive are staged in the theater of cruelty. This does not mean that the theater of cruelty stages a mute void, but it rather engages with words whose affects are far more important than their actual meaning or, in the words of Derrida, "[t]he word is the cadaver of psychic speech, and along with the language of life itself the 'speech before words' must be found again" (1978, 303). In other words, this language of life is thus the flexion that resists repetition. Bouthors-Paillart similarly reads Artaud's theater of cruelty as a practice that "is not artificial imitation of reality, it *is* the reality because the enunciation on stage is, properly speaking, novel creation of reality" (96–7, emphasis in original). It is from this enunciation that the actual reality of *this* world, *this* body, and *this* life magically springs. The theater of cruelty is thus both about the articulation of the unrepresentability of life and the creation of reality in which language plays a key role.

Cruelty as a Healing Practice

Artaud found his inspiration for the theater of cruelty in the Balinese theater and actually experimented with this theater of cruelty by staging *The Cenci* in 1935. Some weeks before the staging of his theater piece, Artaud writes to André Gide that the spectator should not so much focus on the behavior of the Cenci family, because "[a]ll that is attacked is much less on the Social plain than on the Metaphysical plain"[11] (OCV, 241). Despite the murder in the play, Artaud thus contends that this is not what the play essentially is about. On May 6, 1935, the day of the first staging, Artaud repeats in *Comœdia* that "[m]y heroes [...] are set in the realm of cruelty and must be judged beyond good and evil. [...] Cruelty which also acts against the spectator and that must not allow him to leave the theater intact, but, rather, exhausted, engaged, transformed perhaps"[12] (OCV, 309). His theater thus stages a terrible and inescapable necessity that engages the spectator affectively in order to make him struggle with the metaphysical presuppositions of good and bad. After this explosion of and exposition to cruelty the spectator will leave the theater exhausted and transformed. Artaud therewith conceives the theater of cruelty as a healing practice that works through affection. In a conference at the Sorbonne in 1933, Artaud compares his theater with the plague. Elaborating on his conception of a renewed and affective theater, he states that "[i]f the essential theater is like the plague, it is not because it is contagious, but because like the plague it is the revelation, the bringing forth, the exteriorization of a depth of latent cruelty by means of which all the perverse possibilities of the mind, whether of an individual or a people, are localized"[13] (TD, 30). His theater of cruelty is thus the revelation of what the mind is capable of—as we have discussed earlier, Artaud considered the mind as the energy, the force, and the consciousness (understood as "con-sciousness") that emanates from the actions, expressions, and movements of the participants. This turns the theater essentially into an enterprise of health or a healing practice, because it is a catharsis against the grain, since it ultimately reveals the vitality and infinite possibilities and hitherto unexplored potentialities of the expulsed cruelty. The theater is like a plague that directly affects the nervous system of its spectators. It is in this sense that Artaud's theater of cruelty is a religious enterprise because it reconnects man with the forces of *this* world and the vitality of the "true nature of evil."

Submitted to the cruelty of Artaud's exorcism, the spectators will be contaminated with the demonic but vital forces of the body. For this reason, the theater of cruelty is a theater of the affect that Deleuze and Guattari define as "man's nonhuman becomings" (WP, 183), thus exploring the still neglected and underestimated perversities of a corporeal mind. Garnet suggests that Artaud's theater of cruelty, like the plague, is "efficacious, exteriorizing psychic states, changing the nature of the real, and re-embodying metaphysics in transformative theatricality" (11). I think that Artaud's theater of cruelty is far more radical, affective, and active than Garnet suggests in his assertion that the exteriorization of psychic states is staged. Garnet's argument somewhat underestimates the healing powers that are at work in the theater of cruelty, because in his conference at the Sorbonne, Artaud contends in fact that

> [a] social disaster so far-reaching [the outcome of the plague or the theater of cruelty], an organic disorder so mysterious—this overflow of vices, this total exorcism which presses and impels the soul to its utmost—all indicate the presence of a state which is nevertheless characterized by extreme strength and in which all the powers of nature are freshly discovered at the moment when something essential is going to be accomplished.[14] (TD, 27)

Artaud's theater thus not stages an exteriorization of psychic states but rather articulates and suggests an extreme force that reveals the powers of nature, which is life, and therewith experimenting with the perverse possibilities of a mind that emanates from the movements and actions of the materiality of the body, hence creating reality.

The Cenci was only staged for seventeen times and is considered to be a failure. Some months after his revolutionary but failed project, Artaud embarks for Mexico because, as he argues in a letter to Jean Paulhan, "I believe that in Mexico there are still forces which are moving, and which hamper the blood of the Indians"[15] (OCVIII, 336). On April 23, 1936, Artaud enthusiastically writes again to Jean Paulhan and insists that Gallimard should publish *The Theater And Its Double* quickly, because "[w]hat I see in Mexico proves to me that I have always been on the right track"[16] (O, 664). Some weeks later, the University of Mexico suggested that he visited the Tarahumaras Indians during which Artaud explored a corporeally and dramatically staged Dance of the Peyote that was however dangerous for his fragile health. After the discovery of this energetic and healing practice, Artaud finally sets on realizing the theater of cruelty in different ways (we have discussed these developments in Chapter 3). However different these experimentations may be, they vary from drawings, sketches, and poems, but also inadmissible behavior in Ireland, a different use of language—a use in which the body plays a primordial role—keeps playing a key role in his works. Situating his later works in mid-1936 (the year of his explorations in Mexico), Artaud's writings develop into a constant rehash of the theater of cruelty, a practice in which a twisted language, sounds, images, and gestures are staged. Before discussing Artaud's last notebooks in which the reader discovers the articulation of the body within these practices of the writing of cruelty, we first have to investigate more thoroughly the constitutive role of language in Artaud's conceptualization of the theater of cruelty.

A Concrete and Physical Language

Already in his earlier texts on the theater of cruelty, Artaud insists that he wants to fathom the depths of language and to reengage with the etymology of language that would always reveal a concrete notion. This is an interesting enterprise that echoes the Stoic conception of language. In an overview of the Stoic views on poetry, Phillip DeLacy asserts that

> [t]he name of an object imitates the object in that the name is derived from some word which denotes a quality of the object. So the etymology of the name reveals the nature of the object. [...] The etymologizing process, however, is regressive, and ultimately elements must be reached that cannot be further analyzed. Such elements would be the various sounds of the language, and at this stage the imitation is either onomatopoetic or in some other way directly expressive of the meaning. (257–8)

The onomatopoetic basis or the otherwise directly expressive meaning of the origins of words is interesting because it necessitates a cutting or digging in language. In order to reconnect to these origins, language must be estranged to itself in order to critically consider its rusted meaning or usage. Following Deleuze's reading, Artaud would have explored this infra-sense—Deleuze's use of the prefix "infra-" is constitutive because it means "below" or "under"— and these depths of language through suffering (LS, 105). This revaluation of suffering is an important and productive virtue for the Stoics, and in a footnote to Nietzsche's identification with the Stoics, Karl Simms notes that "[t]his admiration of suffering is replicated by Deleuze in his canonization of

Artaud [...]. Deleuze [1990c: 23–7] explicitly characterizes this suffering as 'Stoic'" (109). As we have already seen, Artaud has tried in vain to combat his suffering and his sickness but at a certain point—his voyage to Mexico could again have been a turning point in the acceptance of his suffering—more and more accepts the forces of life traversing his body in an inevitable submission to its necessity. It is in this "sacred yes-saying" (Nietzsche 2006, 17) or in this affirmative resignation that Artaud's suffering can be seen as Stoic. We will come back at the Stoic's vision of language later. For now, we elaborate a bit more on the role of language in Artaud's theater of cruelty.

In an early conference at the Sorbonne in 1931, Artaud reads a text entitled "Metaphysics and the Mise en Scène" in which he contends that

> this concrete language, intended for the senses and independent of speech, has first to satisfy the sense, that there is a poetry of the senses as there is a poetry of language, and that this concrete physical language to which I refer is truly theatrical only to the degree that the thoughts it expresses are beyond the reach of the spoken language.[17] (TD, 37)

The concrete and physical language—this suggests a naked, skinned, and pure language or, following Klossowski, an impure language (see Chapter 1)—of the theater of cruelty is thus addressed to our senses and is only theatrical, which is affective, when the thoughts and forces that spring from it cannot be voiced in our ordinary, abstract, and, what Artaud calls, articulated language. At the end of his conference, Artaud notes that this concrete and physical language is however voiced through the articulated language. In other words, this concrete and physical language of the theater of cruelty is the animation and spiritualization of the tortured and sucked-out words; it is the turning and reshaping of language in order to articulate the onomatopoetic basis or the otherwise directly expressive meaning of the origins of words. Attacking the metaphysics of this articulated language, Artaud specifies that it

> is to make the language express what it does not ordinarily express: to make use of it in a new, exceptional, and unaccustomed fashion; to reveal its possibilities for producing physical shock; to divide and distribute it actively in space; to deal with intonations in an absolutely concrete manner, restoring their power to shatter as well as really to manifest something; to turn against language and its basely utilitarian, one could say alimentary, sources, against its trapped-beast origins.[18] (TD, 46)

Artaud's exploration, struggle, and play with language mean that he revalorizes the materiality of words and thus gives language back its possibilities of physical affection. In doing so, he therewith also attacks the utilitarian use of language—our common and habitual use of language in which language is treated as a piece of food, which is a word having an intrinsic meaning, or as a caged and trapped beast. The language of the theater of cruelty, the concrete and physical language, liberates the forces of the beast that dwell within language and transforms it into something that eats rather than something that is eaten; it renders language active, affective, and vital again in its articulation of a zoology of language. Artaud then goes on by claiming that this new poetic language of the theater of cruelty can bring about "the religious and mystic [acceptance][vi] of which our theater has completely lost the sense"[19] (TD, 46). The theater is thus a religious enterprise and therewith a genuine healing practice of language because it heals the broken link between man and his body and reengages with the forces of life, the unexplored possibilities of the expression of matter, and the infinite potentialities of *this* world.

Returning to the word "cruelty," the constitutive role of language in the unfolding of the concept becomes clear. In a letter to Jean Paulhan from November 1932, Artaud writes that "I have therefore said 'cruelty' as I might have said 'life' or 'necessity,' because I want to indicate especially that for me the theater is act and perpetual emanation, that there is nothing congealed about it, that I turn it into a true act, hence living, hence magical"[20] (TD, 114). Artaud's concept of "cruelty" has thus two important synonyms: "life" and "necessity," because, following Artaud, the theater is a perpetual emanation (the French word "émanation" also connotes the more physical meaning of "exhalation") of incessant fluxes and vital forces. Following Braidotti, we consider life, and hence cruelty, as "cosmic energy, simultaneously empty chaos and absolute speed or movement. It is impersonal and inhuman in the monstrous, animal sense of radical alterity: *zoe* in all its powers" (2006a, 216). Cruelty is thus life understood in terms of "zoe," a vitality that brings about suffering and pain but also joy and creativity, hence the infinite potencies of life. The other term that Artaud uses in his description of "cruelty" is "necessity," which we read as "amor fati." Again following Braidotti, we consider "amor fati" as "the recurrence of difference in successive waves of repeated, successive and excessive becomings, in which 'I' participates and gets formatted, whereas *zoe* acts as the motor" (2006a, 258) or, as she later puts it in terms of dealing with "amor fati:" "It is a way of living up

---

[vi] Artaud uses the French word "acceptation" instead of using the word "preference" that is used in the translation of Mary Caroline Richards and which implies a subjective choice. I use the word "acceptance," which more effectively describes the compelling religious character of the theater of cruelty.

to the intensities of life, to be worthy of all that happens to us—to live fully the capacity to affect and to be affected" (2006a, 271). "Amor fati" is thus the ethical position that one can take in relation to "life"; "cruelty" then stages and plays with these forces. From this definition, it is as a matter of course that Artaud firstly explored the possibilities of the theater, but considering the "theater of cruelty" as an act, a magical and materialist practice and a religious enterprise, it is logical that Artaud continued, after the failure of *The Cenci*, his exploration in poetry, drawings, and sonic experiments. As we have already seen, Artaud considered his cycle of poems *To Have Done with the Judgment of God* as his first rehash of the theater of cruelty. In a notebook from April 1947, Artaud interestingly notes that "[t]he theater of cruelty has / died before / living / but nothing ever appeared / to be more alive to me / than it does now"[21] (CI, 594). In other words, while Artaud has seen his theatrical project failing in Paris, he feels it however acting and living all the time. I think that his later works are indeed a constant rehash and an incessant search for a realization of the theater of cruelty with other means.

The Writing of Cruelty I: From a Mechanized Anatomy to a Machinic Anatomy

On January 13, 1947, Artaud can finally hold his conference at the Vieux-Colombier Theater where he tries to read some of his poems after which he speaks of his voyage to Dublin and the subsequent internments. The audience is so crowded that some people must even stand. Prevel assists at the conference but suffers from the swelling heath in the theater. He nevertheless remarks on an agitated Artaud who "speaks in jerky way taking again the words to support them but his reading is chopped, bumped and incomprehensible" (133). However fragile and incomprehensible Artaud's lecture must have been, Prevel remains impressed by him and looks out for Artaud some days later with Georges Bataille at the Rue Jacob. Prevel notes that "I told Artaud how impressed and distressed I was. He writes and above all draws these extraordinary magic drawings that seem to come out from his notebook" (135). Artaud does not react and seems to be preoccupied by the theater, because four months later, Prevel writes on May 9 that "Artaud has just read me a text on the theater: the Theater of Impiety. The theater of what does not exist, what will never exist, which has no place to be" (159). The theater of impiety is, like the theater of cruelty, a theater of merciless forces that will never know a fixed form, a theater that will never *be* but that perpetually *becomes*.

As we have discussed earlier, Artaud's later writings articulate a magical and materialist theosophy that are devoted to God, understood as nature or matter, that encompasses everything, that is infinite, indivisible, and uncaused. This theosophy—that is inspired by Artaud's discoveries and experiences in Mexico—is unfolded in a zoological language of which the theosophy is only but the form, but of which we have not yet discussed the content or the activism that is at work *under* this theosophy. As discussed above, Artaud writes that he has moved a wall through language and hung a door within language. But again, what realm is disclosed by this fallen wall? And to what sphere or theology does his door open up? For our approach, a Stoic view on poetry is again interesting, because the Stoics distinguish speech ("phone") into articulated sounds or noises, those sounds or noises that can be written ("lexis"), and those sounds or noises that have a meaning ("logos").[vii] DeLacy consequently states that "[a] poem can be considered as both *lexis* and *logos*. As *lexis*, it is a pattern of sounds and words; as *logos* it signifies a certain meaning" (243–4). From this formal distinction, DeLacy concludes that "Stoic poetics was divided into these two parts: the study of the poem as a form of language or speech, and the study of the poem as the expression of meaning" (244). We have already discussed the form that is the "lexis" of Artaud's speech: his later works are written, in conclusion from a textual analysis, as a magical and materialist theosophy. As for the "logos," we more closely read some passages from Artaud's notebooks in order to investigate the theology to which the door that he hung in his language opens up. I think that it is this theology or this healing—and therefore maybe scary—activism that is at work under the written or spoken words of Artaud and has been disvalued for a long time in many readings within the Anglo-Saxon literature on Artaud.

In a notebook from June 1947—a notebook that he would finish at the end of July and mid-August—Artaud starts with the text "The Human Face" that was published in the catalogue to his exposition "Portraits and Drawings by Antonin Artaud" at Gallery Pierre from July 4 to 20, 1947. He comments his

---

[vii] The distinction made by the Stoics is interesting and already foregrounds the Saussurian distinction between "signifier" and "signified" that was later fleshed out by Louis Hjelmslev who further differentiated the "signifier" and the "signified" or, what he calls, "expression" and "content." For my analysis of Artaud's language, I however turn to the Stoic's views on language because of their insight that nature, and hence matter, is the guiding principle in everything. Language, in their view, is thus first and foremost an expression of matter whose meaning evolves over time and thus often loses the contact with the source from which it originated.

own portraits and drawings and contends that "[t]he human face indeed carries a kind of perpetual death on his face of which it is precisely up to the painter to save him by giving him back his own features"[22] (O, 1534). Artaud criticizes other portraitists and claims that he wants to capture the lived secrets that traverse any face. For this reason, he argues, some portraits are interjected by poems and other visual objects. After his text "The Human Face," Artaud continues his notebook on the seventh page by sketching a figure that severely stares to its right. Different lines flow inside or outside its body and he or she is surrounded by three or four small sketches (sketches of which it remains unclear what they represent—if they do *re*present anything at all—but that return in other sketches and drawings). On the back of the seventh page, Artaud continues by writing on the soul, his father Lucifer, and his son. This son would be the father of everyone who believes in being and who tortures the idea that there is a life, a thought, a consciousness, and death (he even capitalizes the words "LA MORT"). His incoherent story is suddenly interrupted in the middle of the eight page by a direct address to the reader that is not finished either. As thoughts that move at an enormous speed, the back of the eight page then reflects on the notebooks because

> [t]hese notebooks
> have not been
> put under glass
> in the intention
> to be fitted
> as museum
> pieces.
> They will still serve me,
> but
> I show them
> so that a
> man who
> searches like
> me a truth
> and a lost
> <u>mechanism</u>
> will finds them again,
> as I have been
> searching them in
> these notebooks.[23] (CI, 1267–8)

Artaud's notebooks are thus no objects or pages to simply look at from behind a glass in a museum but are rather tools that the reader may use if he or she is looking for a truth or a lost mechanism (it is, for this very reason, that Artaud can be considered an intercessor for those who want to heal the broken link between man and this world). The word "mechanism" is underlined and is interesting because it is closely connected to our mechanized anatomy that Artaud wants to liberate in order to touch upon a lost and more machinic anatomy.

In his poem "The Theater of Cruelty," which was written some months after this notebook, Artaud writes programmatically:

Make the human anatomy dance at last,

from high to low and from low to high,
from the back to the front
from the front to the back,
but even more from the back to back,
elsewhere, than from the back to the front
[…].
We made the human body eat,
we made it drink,
to prevent us
from making it dance.[24] (OCXIII, 109)

In other words, Artaud searches for a machinic anatomy that dances, connects, disconnects, creates, sings, and dances instead of a mechanized anatomy that is submitted to various sets of preestablished rules. It is the search for the depths of the body, the infra-body, or the BwO that contests the badly constructed body and that should function willingly in a human and intelligent life governed by reason, unity, and identity. Considering the notebooks rather as tools is also what Barber suggests when he rightly asserts that "[t]he unique physical form of Artaud's notebooks […] refuses reduction, and cannot be adapted, amended or assimilated. The notebooks bear, as an essential component, their multiple gestural scarifications, abrasures and incision, which amass at the instants in Artaud's work when his fury against representation bursts" (2008, 139). In other words, the notebooks should not be read passively or be considered reflectively, but Artaud's search—Barber calls it even "his anatomical work" (2008, 138)—must rather be experienced as a theatrical stage where different forces are at work that affect, exhaust, and transform the reader or spectator. It is in this sense that they stage reality and articulate life.

Artaud's underlined name appears at the end of the front of the ninth page. He then speaks of his daughter (that he never had[viii]) that has come out of him. He pluralizes or, better, renders schizophrenic, his "daughter" by stating:

[t]he things that came out
of me
are
my daughter
my child
they
are
not
my
gaghasse.[25] (CI, 1268)

The word "gaghasse" does neither exist in French nor in English but might well be derived from the French (and likewise the English) word "gaga" that indicates a person that becomes senile. If Artaud hints at the state of senility, he thus claims that his output, his creations, and his writings should *not* be considered as senile. The mysterious word "gaghasse" however maintains the tension how the reader must approach his writings. The speed of thoughts continues and Artaud changes the course of reasoning by reducing man to his digestive system who is also an antidigestive system because, as Artaud reasons, he also pisses and shits. What follows on the eleventh page is an enlisting of what man inhales and exhales, and at the bottom of the page, Artaud writes some enigmatic lines that seem to comment the physiological élan. He writes that "it is not the equilibrium / of the breath of 2 lungs / they are it is the buttress / of gothic churches / prove of an immense theft"[26] (CI, 1268). In other words, our physiology is not the outcome of the harmonious and autonomous functioning of the body,—"the equilibrium/of the breath of 2 lungs"— but is rather constructed by the buttress—that is a reinforcement of a wall—without which everything will collapse. This buttress is the proof of an immense, quoting the French original, "vol." The French word "vol" can be translated as "theft"— which is most consistent with Artaud's reasoning—but also with "flight." Reading the word "vol" as "flight" radically changes the sense of these lines, because it would render the reinforcement of the wall, the buttress, laudable. Artaud again confronts the reader with different, conflicting, and yet vital forces whose tension make these lines escape from any fixity. In doing so, these lines escape from a fixed meaning

---

[viii] See Poulet for an analysis of these "daughters of the heart" that Artaud invented in his later writings.

and continue to circle around a plurality of meanings. The other sixty pages of the notebook continue with this ambiguous reasoning where the meaning of words remains unstable, paradoxical, or conflicting and where different forces are at work since Artaud underlines, capitalizes, and encircles words, uses glossolalia and neologisms, makes sketches in the margins or in the middle of the pages, and writes alternately with a pen and a pencil.

On the eleventh page of a notebook from February 1947, Artaud writes that what he knows and thus writes down is the "chanted / secular / humming / non-liturgical / non-ritual / non-greek // between negro / chinese / indian / and français [sic] villon"[27] (CI, 150). He continues that if he wants to attain this chanted and secular humming, he must start from what he is and knows, which is the French language, because "it will always be me speaking a foreign / language with an always recognizable accent"[28] (CI, 150). In her critical analysis of these enigmatic lines, Tomiche notes that Artaud emphasizes the vocality, and thus the materiality, and the mixture of languages in his "other" language—what we have called his zoological language. Focusing on the particularities of this "other" language, Tomiche interestingly analyses that "negro" recalls the French expression "speaking little negro," meaning "speaking grammatically incorrect French" (2002, 142); "chinese" evokes the expression "that is Chinese," meaning that is incomprehensible; "indian" refers without any doubt to his Mexican experiences, and for "français villon," Tomiche argues that

> the formula suggests both a medieval and archaic French, a transgressive language in the image of the "outlaw" that the poet was [the fifteenth century poet François Villon], or even, more precisely, a jargon as little comprehensible as "the jargon of Villon," which Pierre Guiraud analyses as a "secret language" whose "words do not exist in French but which are directly related to French by determined methods of morphological or semantic derivation (and often both combined)." (2002, 142)

Artaud's zoological language, a healing practice where the body participates in the ongoing process of writing, in which different forces are at work, is thus a grammatically incorrect, incomprehensible, and organic language, a foreign, magical, and material language that is hollowed out in his mother's tongue that creates, within the formalized system of signs, unstable, paradoxical, and conflicting words that, as vacuoles, continue to vibrate. It is this foreign language that engages with the vital forces of life, the impulsiveness of matter, and the "true nature of evil" in staging them and hence creating reality. In this sense, Artaud's zoological language is the writing of cruelty that is finally articulated within language.

The Writing of Cruelty II: The True Story of Jesus Christ

In another notebook from July 1947, Artaud again fathoms the depths of words, explores their ambiguity, writes glossolalia, and makes sketches in the margins or over the written text. More interestingly, he reworks his "The True Story of Jesus Christ," a project that he already started in Rodez. Artaud begins his notebook with a text from which the start is unknown to the reader. After six lines and a horizontal line, Artaud writes a reflexive statement: "I'm not an/initiated one/but an inventor,/creator/author/whatever you like"[29] (CI, 1750). What then follows is an incoherent reasoning that is suddenly interrupted because the back of the page is left blank. The second page starts again with the story of Christ in which Artaud focuses on the ridiculousness of the myth around his supposed divine birth and death. After some bombastic reproaches, Artaud lists eight names of people from whom—according to the annotation by Grossman—Artaud needs laudanum. What then follows is a discussion about the differences between the myth and the true story of Christ, the fact that someone else had been crucified on Golgotha (in contrast to other versions of this story, Artaud does not immediately identify this crucified person with himself) and the toughness of the myth. Artaud then finally concludes that Jesus was, according to the myth, the son of God, but in reality he was not even the son of a man but rather the son of a donkey. To consolidate his conclusion, Artaud argues that in Hebrew the word "Christ" would actually mean "donkey" or, better, as he specifies, "donkey keeper" or "donkey fart." Following Artaud, the true story of Christ is that he was actually a released donkey-spirit that was incarnated in a donkey-man. Again Artaud consolidates his story by arguing that, in those days, animals copulated frequently with man and that this bestialization of man was normal. It was even sacred if a man would be the husband of a female donkey—as would have been the case for Christ's parents. Artaud then focuses again on Golgotha and contends that Christ has fled away from his crucifixion. The thirteenth page then starts off with the words "The bodies are"[30] (CI, 1756) after which twelve lines of glossolalia follow.

The story continues with Christ's flight from Golgotha, because when Christ saw that things turned bad, he fled away—according to Artaud, this reaction is explicable because Christ was a black magician whose major characteristic was cowardice. Instead of Christ, someone else was crucified on Golgotha. This person remained loyal to his ideas that concerned the denial of the existence of an infinite and eternal God. The one crucified on Golgotha instead believed in the immortality of man and his superiority over the spirit of angels (which are also donkeys that surround God). God—who was, as Artaud continues, an innate cow—was eternally jealous of this crucified person because he knew that the immortality of man would imply the mortality of the animal. As mentioned above, the person that was actually crucified denied the existence of God and therewith also denied that man would copulate with animals. The supposed copulation with animals, the cow-God, and the donkey-Christ are interesting themes in Artaud's story that contains, apart from the apparent Surrealist and blasphemic effect, some conflicting elements: how must the reader value the cow or the donkey? Looking at the course of history or the development of different religions and societies, it is not clear whether the equalizing of God with a cow or Jesus Christ with a donkey is positive or negative. This tension, along with the identity of the man crucified on Golgotha (who was, in earlier versions, Artaud himself), remains dominant in the text, because Artaud continues to blame Jesus Christ—he significantly writes "Jesus christ" who is thus the person crucified on Golgotha and *hence* not the true Christ—to have left many descendants who have constituted a race of untouchables, repugnant and truly abominable pariahs. These descendants are left by this so-called Jesus christ, the person crucified on Golgotha and who denied the infinity and eternity of God and who maintained that man does not copulate with animals. Related to these descendants, Artaud claims that "I believe that all / initiation is the / fruit of a crime / on the astral of / the universal matter / to which we have given / a world / that it [= universal matter] did not / want to give and that / the initiates have / forced it to give"[31] (CI, 1757-8). Being a Christian—if we follow Artaud's reasoning, every Christian is a fake Christian since he or she is the follower of a surrogate person that was crucified on Golgotha—would thus mean that one is initiated in a circle of criminals who impose a form on the world—the reader must remember that they believed in the immortality of man—of which Artaud claims that "it is on this world / that they have constructed / their kabbalistic / numbering supposedly / secret and / it is so but infernal / because from a / wanted world and which / does not exist"[32] (CI, 1758). These criminals have thus falsely constructed a world that does not actually exist and in which man *must* nevertheless live enslaved. Artaud continues by claiming that he is looking for a reality in which things do not lose their residue and in which man can walk freely and in the way he wants to—this might well be the world of the true Jesus Christ.

Some pages later, Artaud contends that we are still confronted with some important questions concerning man's anatomy and in particular

> that of regressive
> organic involution

> of the human being;
> man wants to become
> bad again and to
> release himself in the
> holding of his internal
> organs, but his major
> vital purpose is
> nothing else
> than to get to
> bestialize himself.[33] (CI, 1760–1)

The regressive rusting of anything that suffers from organization reduces man to a simple radar, a piece of meat in the mincer or a mechanized organism—it stimulates the bad feelings of man, which means that he wants to explore the limits that are imposed on him. Man is created in the image of God and he thus wants to explore his bestiality again, and Artaud therefore argues that man's "major / vital purpose is / nothing else / than to get to / bestialize himself"[34] (CI, 1760–1). Combatting one's mechanized organism in order to experiment with a machinic organism indeed implies an engagement and a reconnection with the nonhuman and animal forces of *this* life; man's major and vital purpose would then be that he reengages with an animal dance through which his flesh dances again vitally around the bones. Exploring the animal spirit of man then bears witness to a greater health. Commenting on this process of bestialization or becoming-animal, Braidotti asserts that it "is connected to an expansion or creation of new sensorial and perceptive capacities or powers, which alter or stretch what a body can actually do" (2006a, 103). Becoming-animal is thus an exploration of the hitherto unexplored capabilities of the body and a devotion to the vital forces of life. According to Deleuze and Guattari, this becoming-animal must not be reduced to a bestialization in the common sense of the word and has nothing to do with making love to animals—as Artaud's story suggests—but is rather about reaching the point of indiscernibility where the distinction between animal and man is pushed to its limits (see TP, 342). Following Artaud's reasoning, he contends in the final pages of his notebook that the medical world is but one monstrous, cynical, and scientific dupery because it is based on a human crime. This dupery turns the medical world into the main instigator of a world from which man is detached. Artaud claims that upon the day of the crucifixion of the person that replaced Jesus Christ, the circulatory system did not exist because

> the blood from
> the heart did not

yet return
always
and invariably
to the heart
that is to
that is to say that a
certain organic
automatism was not
yet irreme
diably
established and
that liberties
were left
to the exercise of this
spontaneous and
deaf
temperament.[35] (CI, 1761–2)

In other words, any deviation (of an automatism that was not yet fully conceived) was respected and the freedoms of the body were fully respected as being the product of a deaf and spontaneous energy.

The Writing of Cruelty III: The Laboratory of Life

Artaud's notebook is not only interesting for his alternative and creative reading of the story of Jesus Christ, but also for the way in which he lucidly treats and creatively plays with his words. Artaud writes in his notebook with a pencil and a green pen, underlines words, capitalizes letters, and plays with sounds, different lines, and sketches. He moreover treats the paper itself as an autonomous object that also participates in the expression of this theater of cruelty. In his materialist reading of Artaud's last notebooks, Barber claims that "[b]y damaging that page, with pencil-incisions and cigarette-burn holes, as he had with his spells, Artaud not only renders the page still more visually dense, but also accentuates its status as an entity through which the body can pass" (2008, 50). Barber contends that the pages of Artaud's notebooks launch the body toward other bodies because of a "transformational aperture" (2008, 50) that functions like a spell. The spell that Artaud magically writes in the paper is interesting but the argument can be enforced by returning to his concept of "flesh." Artaud actually uses the paper as a tactile in which he stabs holes and carves some of his words. The paper is therewith not only the medium and the support of his words and sketches but genuinely participates in the expression and articulation of Artaud's religious enterprise. As a theater of cruelty where different forces are at work, the materiality of the damaged paper also experiments, investigates, and plays its agential role in the exploration of the still unknown possibilities of what a body, in this case a body of writing, is capable of. As discussed earlier, Artaud's concept of "flesh," which was articulated in his earlier writings, designates the integral body where matter and thinking meet. "Flesh" is thus the not yet broken continuum of body and thinking or, following Grossman, an "organic crucible of thinking" (2017, 10). In this sense, Artaud's tactile use of the paper puts indeed a spell on it, a spell that transforms the paper into an integral body, that is "flesh," that is traversed by "undefined forces"[36] (AN, 58) and from which emanates a mind as "quick as lightening"[37] (AN, 59). Artaud's use of the paper as a tactile that he damages and transforms and on which he writes schizophrenic words along with abstract and yet concrete sketches and lines that follow the quickness, the paradoxes, and the ambiguity of thinking, transforms the paper and the notebook into a vital and vibrating materiality from which a mind, energy, and forces arise; it transforms the paper and the notebook into an integral body, which is body-thinking continuum; it transforms, to conclude, the paper and the notebook into Artaudian "flesh" (which we have discussed, focusing on his earlier works, in Chapter 1 and which is finally performatively articulated in these later writings). This affective flesh of language differs only relatively from the flesh of the body because, following Grossman, "[f]rom body to language, for Artaud, the material is the same, only the density, which is more or less large, changes [...]. From the 'substantial' body to the 'subtle' body, the difference is of degree, not of nature" (2003a, 82).

In another notebook from July 1947 that we now briefly discuss, Artaud comments again on the theater that it

> is in fact
> a sort of laboratory
> or factory
> where man comes periodi
> cally,
> in the
> most real
> sense

> of the term
> to change himself
> bodily
> and dynamically.³⁸ (CI, 1422)

The comparison of the theater with a laboratory is interesting—the word "laboratory" is derived from the Latin noun "labor," which means "work"; in this etymological sense, Artaud's comparison with a laboratory would thus mean that the theater is a working place where one does research and experiments and explores life. Comparing the theater with a factory is also constitutive—the French word "usine" is etymologically developed from the Latin noun "officina," which also means "workshop." Both the laboratory and the factory are thus, following Artaud, different names for the theater in which man comes to change corporeally—from a mechanized anatomy to a machinic anatomy—and dynamically—from a fixed "I" to an "amor fati" where the "I" is constantly generated and transformed.

Some pages later Artaud again plays with the importance of the theater by saying that

> the true purpose of the
> authentic theater lies
> thus in this transfer of a
> body, this passage of a
> body acknowledged as bad
> and gangrened to a superior
> body where
> the actor
> can find again
> at least
> the man he was
> before this obscene
> passage on him of the
> body of the whole
> society.³⁹ (CI, 1429)

The authentic theater, the affective theater of cruelty, should thus render the bad and gangrene—the infection that kills the tissue because of an insufficient supply of blood from the circulatory system, a system that, as Artaud suggested in his constantly rewritten "The True Story of Jesus Christ," came into being after the crucifixion of the person that replaced Christ on Golgotha—body into a superior body in which the actor, or in this case the reader, touches again upon his freedom and upon whom he was before the corruption of his body. The theater is thus a healing and creative working place where the lost body of man is given back to him. It is a religious practice from which forces emerge that affect the spectator or the reader who is subsequently confronted with the imposed automatism of his mechanized anatomy. In Artaud's later writings, this theater of cruelty is an enterprise that has found its last stage within the affective flesh of language. This "flesh," understood as the integral body, is the theology to which the door opens up that Artaud, as a genuine intercessor, has hung in his foreign language. This language of matter, nature, or God is the affective flesh of language. It is a vital theology of life that is open for experimentation with the fall of the wall that Artaud has caused in his later writings. From a Stoic point of view, we conclude that Artaud's later writings thus engage—however various and contradictory these works may appear—with a magical and materialist theosophy analyzed and considered as "lexis" and yet a bodily practice of the writing of cruelty, which is a genuine and vital theology of "life" and "necessity" or "zoe" and "amor fati," analyzed and conceived as "logos." What the two viewpoints share is the language in which these later works are written: a religious and affective flesh of language that is a zoology of language; a healing practice of a creative, vital, and animated language that remains unstable that keeps on vibrating and that is the expression of the impulsiveness of matter.

Practices of Creative Writing

Having discussed Artaud's bodily practices of language and his writing of cruelty, it is interesting to consider if and how his writings fit with the ongoing rise of various creative, performative, and asemic writing practices.[ix] In his reading of Artaud's correspondence (1923–4) with Jacques Rivière—a correspondence that started because of Rivière's refusal to publish Artaud's early poems in *La Nouvelle Revue Française*—Samuel Delany compares Artaud's letters with "the belligerent creative writing student's protests [that] throw into question all the underlying percepts of artistic craft, content, reference, and communication that, unspoken, nevertheless and always underlie, support, and allow any location of artistic

---

[ix] Creative, performative, and asemic writing are, I think, the three most institutionalized practices of writing that can be associated with Artaud's later works.

value in its connotations, suggestions, and resonances" (30). However right his comparison could be, Delany's remark in relation to the practices of creative writing is interesting, because Artaud's writings, and not specifically his later works, are indeed engaged with creation and the art of writing. The conclusion presses itself forward that Artaud's writings could thus be considered as a form of creative writing. This conclusion however underestimates other aspects that are active in his later works.

Since especially Artaud's later writings are engaged with the articulation of vital forces, the poetic creation—etymologically, "poetic creation" is a pleonasm—of compounds of percepts and affects, and the renewed staging of the theater of cruelty, it seems logical to describe Artaud's later writings as an ultimate or genuine form of creative writing. Such a characterization fits well with the ongoing rise of creative writing courses and education in high schools and universities. Creative writing is not solely a literary form of writing but can also manifest itself in academic writing. Tim Mayers defines the practice of creative writing as

> the academic enterprise of hiring successful authors (with success defined as publication in 'approved' journals and magazines and by "approved" university and trade presses, along with the winning of prestigious literary prizes for such publication) to teach college-level creative writing courses. Creative writing has a dual purpose: first, it aims to train aspiring writers to produce publishable work, to find success in the literary marketplace; second, it operates as a *de facto* employment program for writers who are unable to earn a living simply by writing. (218)

Mayers opposes the emerging "creative writing studies" in universities against this conception of "creative writing" since it addresses the contradictions that may arise from the practices of "creative writing." Dealing differently with texts compared to interpretative criticism, Mayers considers "creative writing" to be the instigator of a "more active, engaged citizenship among students" (224). This engaged citizenship is an integral part of "creative writing," because, following Graham Mort's understanding of its practices, "[it] is also a source of human understanding, offering insights into the wider human experience of signification and culture, creating new perspectives and new configurations, experimenting with form while engaging with literary tradition or canonical texts" (204). It is in this sense that "creative writing" is not only about the application of (literary) techniques to written texts in order to effectively capture the attention of the reader; it is also about rereading, reengaging, and eventually rewriting the canonized texts. "Creative writing" thus also challenges our accustomed and thoughtless sensory-motor circuits of our habits, customs, and values in offering alternative perspectives.

Characterizing Artaud's writings as a practice of creative writing would enrich and develop the current practices of creative writing: it would expand the tools and the fields upon which the notion of "creation" can be exerted because Artaud's writings are not solely concerned with language, but also with sounds, screams, sketches, and the materiality of the media with which one works. It would furthermore mean that the carefully learned techniques should be loosened in order to give way to a more free and spontaneous way of writing that does not aim at persuading, manipulating, or diverting the reader but that rather aims at confronting, affecting, and transforming the reader. Considering Artaud's writings as practices of creative writing would then especially develop the engagement that is part of its practices. It would stimulate the student's task of rewriting the present in creating new possibilities of life and especially emphasize the constitutive role of language.

However challenging such a characterization would be, the main problem lies in the word "creation." The word "creation" comes from the Latin noun "creatio" which means "producing" or "bringing forth." Artaud's later works indeed bring forth something genuinely new, but the word "creation" misses somewhat the forces and the activism that is also at work within and through his writings. Following Derrida's reading of Artaud's writings, the reader of Artaud's later works is rather confronted with a work that "refuses to signify, or by an art without works, a language without a trace" (1978, 174, emphasis in original). Artaud's later writings are thus rather traces that contest representation or the actual production of a work. Artaud essentially wants to give form to life and yet tries to resist repetition and reflection. It is precisely this process that the writing of cruelty entails, which the word "creation" does not cover.

Practices of Performative Writing

Another popular term that presses itself forward in characterizing Artaud's writings is the term "performative writing." Focusing on the performativity of language recalls Austin's speech acts. Austin approves that speech acts can be considered from three points of view: a speech act is a locutionary act when it is "the performance of an act *of* saying something" (99, emphasis in original), when it is an illocutionary act, or a performative utterance, when it is "the performance of an act *in* saying something" (99, emphasis in original), or the speech act can be considered a perlocutionary act when it effects "what we bring about or achieve *by* saying something, such as convincing, persuading, deterring, and even, say, surprising or misleading" (108, emphasis in original). Whereas perlocutionary acts are found in what can be termed "affective writing," illocutionary acts are used in "performative writing"; by writing, we *do* something; an act is performed in writing. Following Benveniste, Deleuze and Guattari flesh out this idea of performative utterances, because "the performative relates not to acts but instead to a property of *self-referentiality* of terms (the true personal pronouns, I, YOU ..., defined as shifters). By this account, a preexistent structure of subjectivity, or intersubjectivity, in language rather than presupposing speech acts, is adequate to account for them" (TP, 86, emphasis in original). This preexistent structure of linguistic subjectification nuances Austin's idea that illocutionary acts cause performative utterances, because the performatives are rather self-referential properties of words. In other words, language understood as a formalized system of signs contains a preexisting theological (the discourse of reason, unity, and identity) and biological (the discourse of human and intelligent life) structure. Language thus governs the processes of subjectification and subjugation by constituting order-words[x] that, in the words of Deleuze and Guattari, are "the relation of every word or every statement to implicit presuppositions, in other words, to speech acts that are, and can only be, accomplished in the statement" (TP, 87). Order-words are thus the performatives that realize the preestablished structure in language. Whereas Benveniste thus concludes that "[i]t is in and through language that man constitutes himself as a *subject*, because language alone establishes the concept of 'ego' in reality, in *its* reality which is that of the being" (224, emphasis in original), Deleuze and Guattari straightforwardly contend that "*I* is an order-word" (TP, 93, emphasis in original). The performativity of order-words thus shows the preestablished privileging of theological and biological discourses in language over the forces of "zoe"; it ultimately shows that language speaks through us rather than that we speak through language.

---

[x] Van der Tuin reads the same logic in Bergson's *The Creative Mind* in which he asserts that "[l]anguage transmits orders or warnings. It prescribes and describes .... But in either case the function is industrial, commercial, military, always social" (Bergson qtd. in Van der Tuin 2011, 24). Because of its social functioning, we must, as we have already discussed, be cautious not to throw these order-words into a destructive collapse.

Eluding the preestablished order-word assemblages does not mean that the artist, writer, or poet can only produce trivial, incomprehensible, and incoherent noises. Deleuze and Guattari assert that "[o]ne should bring forth the order-word of the order-word. In the order-word, life must answer the answer of death, not by fleeing, but by making flight act and create" (TP, 122). In other words, one should carry language away from its stability and its preestablished structures through that very language. This becoming-foreign of language recalls Artaud's chanted and secular humming that is a language "between negro / chinese / indian / and français villon"[40] (CI, 150). Artaud reinforces this becoming-foreign of language also typographically, because as Tomiche rightly notes: "[B]y another strategy, linked to the orthographic deformations that he regularly practices, especially at the time of proofreading, Artaud makes French *look* like a foreign language[xi] [...]. Artaud visually deforms (and correlatively phonetically) French to the point where it appears as a foreign language" (2012, 145, emphasis in original). This becoming-foreign or becoming-other of language thus carries away language through that very language. This process of creating tensions within language is possible since the order-word is but a function of language. Deleuze and Guattari argue that words are always double-layered, because "[t]here are pass-words beneath order-words. Words that pass, words that are components of passage, whereas order-words mark stoppages or organized, stratified compositions. A single thing or word undoubtedly has this twofold nature: it is necessary to extract one from the other—to transform the compositions of order into components of passage" (TP, 122). By creating openings that undermine the stable units—the order-words—within language, one can effectuate change within a collective assemblage of enunciation. As we have discussed earlier, this is exactly what Artaud's zoological language does: disordering the functional rules of a suppressing language by hollowing out a far more creative, vital, and animated language, a foreign language, in order to articulate the vitality of "zoe" and therewith exploring the hitherto unknown possibilities of the expression of matter.

Characterizing Artaud's later writings as practices of "performative writing" would indeed emphasize the energy and forces that *do* something in and through what we have earlier called his affective flesh of language. Considering however Benveniste's along with Deleuze and Guattari's understanding of performatives, using the term "performative writing" to describe Artaud's later writings creates

---

[xi] As an example, Tomiche recalls Artaud's "la volonté psygique" (instead of "la volonté psychique"), "lam" (instead of "l'âme") or "saimble," "simbleu," and "simpleu" (instead of "simple"). It is mainly in his later writings that Artaud experiments with these linguistic deformations.

confusion because Artaud rather combats the performativity of order-words; his writings rather aim at the healing of the detachment from the singularity of body, expression, and desire to which they give rise. His zoological language that consists of a magical and materialist theosophy along with a theology of "zoe" and "amor fati," which is the writing of cruelty, is rather affective and aims at disordering the performativity of language. In this sense, Artaud's writings twist the performativity of language by suggesting and articulating a "performative writing" that creatively dismantles the performativity of order-words from which a different reality, that is another possibility of life, is expressed. Considering Artaud's works as a practice of rather creative and critical "performative writing" would then emphasize the constitutive process of becoming-foreign or becoming-other of language that is at work in Artaud's writings.

Practices of Asemic Writing

A last still less theorized term that could characterize Artaud's writings is "asemic writing." "Asemic writing" is a more or less spontaneous practice of writing that, following Tim Gaze, "does something to us. Some examples have pictograms or ideograms, which suggest a meaning through their shape. Others take us for a ride along their curves. [...] They tend to have no fixed meaning. Their meaning is open" (Gaze 2013). The practices of "asemic writing" thus play with the established semantics in language in order to create an open language that only suggests meaning. In the first and for the time only anthology of asemic handwriting, the editors write that "[t]hese writings are not completely 'meaningless' or 'illegible,' but challenge our common notions of reading, writing, and the meaningfulness of language. Therefore we prefer the adjective 'asemic'" (2013, 5). They characterize "asemic writing" a bit further as "closely linked to a poetic practice that first liberated itself from the linearity of the verse, and subsequently from the conformity of the sign" (2013, 6). In other words, the practices of "asemic writing" empty words and signs from their preestablished meaning—what the Stoics considered as "logos"—in order to turn them into autonomous words and signs that challenge the fixity of meaning—from a Stoic viewpoint they would thus only become "lexis."

The anthology of asemic handwriting is an overview of almost 200 pages filled with sketches, images, and expressions made by different authors or artists like, among others, Max Ernst, Isidore Isou, and Roland Barthes. Some writings are only made up of lines, others are constituted of smears, and there are also works that consist of self-created symbols. These writings indeed challenge our way of reading and looking at words, signs, and sketches because there is often no beginning or central point upon which the reader may focus. Any intelligible or communicative language has been undone and dismantled in order to create an autonomous work that speaks for itself. In his reading of Artaud's struggle with language, Alain Milon concludes that his writings are a likewise attempt to unfix language. Milon specifies that "[t]o unfix, a term invented by Gaston Bachelard to speak of Henri Michaux's *The Distant Interior*, amounts to entering under language as one would enter a dance, not to find the presence of a word but to strip the meaning until the discovery of the absence that it carries" (2016, 19). From this definition, characterizing Artaud's later writings as a practice of "asemic writing" would be a logical conclusion. Considering Artaud's use of language, sketches, sounds, and the materiality of the paper would add an interesting element to the practices of "asemic writing"; it would not only challenge our ways of reading and looking at works but also challenge our notion of what actually constitutes the work: Artaud's later writings suggest that the materiality of the paper that he uses as a tactile also participates in the expression of the forces of life.

The problem is however the word "asemic" in the practices of "asemic writing," because it suggests, as Milon argues, the absence of a fixed meaning. Artaud's schizophrenic words indeed unfix the rusted meaning of words by diving into the etymological or vocal depths of the words in order to attain a more concrete meaning. Instead of the absence of a fixed meaning, Artaud materialistically plays on the surface, phonetically, and with the depths, semantically, of words that he characterizes as speaking "français villon." In doing so, he unfolds the plurality of meaning within words along with the absence of a fixed meaning. In Artaud's later writings, words are thus forces, stemming from matter, with unstable and vibrating meanings that, finally, is the practice of a theology of "zoe" and "amor fati." The term "asemic writing" does not cover this vital aspect in Artaud's later writings.

The Art of Crescive Writing

Instead of a practice of creative, performative, or asemic writing, I characterize Artaud's later writings as practices of "crescive writing," bodily practices in which an affective flesh of language is articulated. The term "crescive writing" encompasses creative, performative, *and* asemic writing but emphasizes an important element: the spontaneous, generative, and open-ended development within and through Artaud's writings. The word "crescent" is etymologically related to the word "creation" but is derived from the Latin word "crescere" meaning "to come forth," "to grow," "to thrive," "to swell," or "to increase in numbers or strength." "Crescive writing" is thus a practice of an enhanced or genuine creative writing that creates an artwork that is traversed by vital forces and from which affective fluxes of life keep on emanating. Putting it simply: in the art of "crescive writing," life matters![xii] Characterizing Artaud's later writings as practices of "crescive writing" is a conclusion that can only be drawn after a textual analysis from a schizoanalytic perspective. This method that focuses on the invention and the creation of new possibilities of life along with a close reading of both the form and the content of Artaud's creative language enables us to conclude that Artaud's later writings are traversed by unstable and vital forces from which life is generated.

After the failure of *The Cenci*, Artaud keeps on searching for an articulation of his theater of cruelty in poetry, drawings, and sonic experiments and he eventually develops his theater of cruelty within a language of life, understood as "zoe." The thus developed practice of "crescive writing" is also present in his earlier works— where words materially and phonetically generate each other in order to suggest a new assemblage of meaning—but germinates in his later works where Artaud more and more experiments with his chanted and secular humming that is a material language "between negro / chinese / indian / and français villon"[41] (CI, 150). This material language participates in the becoming-foreign or becoming-other of the dominant and formalized system of signs and in challenging our sensory-motor circuits that are related to the performatives of language. Thus encompassing the practices of creative, a rather critical performative writing *and* asemic writing, the practices of "crescive writing" bring forth a perpetually swelling, growing, and vibrating foreign language that is a zoological language, which is traversed by the forces of the "true nature of evil" that they affirm in its plural manifestations. The practices of "crescive writing" consist of the creation of integral bodies that is body-thinking continuums or affective words of flesh. In this sense, "crescive writing," thus understood as the minor expression of

---

[xii] The word "matter" is etymologically derived from the Latin noun "mater," which means "mother," but also "origin" or "source." In an etymological reading, the art of "crescive writing" thus articulates life from a play with matter.

the body, stages cruelty, understood as "zoe" and "amor fati," in an affirmative, generative, and open-ended process. Enhanced or genuine creative writing is thus the *art* of crescive writing that is essentially a magical, materialist, and religious enterprise of auto-detoxification and auto-immunization that heals the broken link between man and *this* body, *this* life, and *this* world. It is a healing practice that is articulated in a zoology of language and that engages with a magical and materialist theosophy as well as with a theology of "zoe" and "amor fati," which is cruelty.

"[Life] Is Only Worthy/to the Extent/ That It Changes"[xiii, 42]

On Thursday, March 4, 1948, the gardener of the pension in Ivry who gets Artaud's breakfast every day finds him dead at the foot of his bed. In February 1948, Artaud is diagnosed with anal cancer, a late but logical diagnosis because he already suffers from cramps and intestinal bleeding in 1944 (see Danchin and Roumieux, 696). Because of the malignancy in his cancer, Artaud is not treated in a hospital. Thévenin thus comments on his death that

> [w]hen Mondor [Artaud's doctor] gave him a letter that allowed him all the opium he wanted at the clinic, he must have known what it meant. He didn't die from cancer, but it was inoperable. It was something he had endured for a long time. (Lotringer, 206)

Ferdière goes even a step further and suggests that Artaud's cause of death lies mainly in his friends, because "[w]hat Artaud has in his belly, and what one sees on the X-rays of Artaud that I have seen and examined, is what we call 'scybala:' it means goat's droppings![xiv] That is to say, when drinking laudanum or opium in high doses, one is extremely constipated. Then one ends up having in the folds of the intestine small material balls that are as hard as this table. But that is what Mondor saw. This allowed him to leave the doctor with a spectacular prescription of laudanum. [...] Well, he died of an excess of laudanum [...]. If they had looked for a serious clinic, Artaud would still be alive! I finally have one regret, that is to have let Artaud leave the psychiatric hospitals!" (Danchin

---

[xiii] *Notebook 326* (CI, 1433).
[xiv] Ferdière refers to the Greek word "σκύβαλα" from which "scybala" is etymologically derived.

and Roumieux, 695–6). Berne-Joffroy, who proposed the pension in Ivry to house Artaud, however criticizes Ferdière's denial and concludes that "there is no doubt that Artaud died of cancer, although Ferdière never wanted to believe it" (Danchin and Roumieux, 780).

Whatever the cause of Artaud's premature death—a malignant disease, an accident, or suicide—might have been, Thévenin contends that Artaud would have died exactly in the way he wanted and when he wanted to. She even argues that "[t]he last few weeks he repeated frequently: 'I have nothing more to say, I have said all that I have to say.' He declared that he would no longer write" (Thévenin, 69). Artaud's last notebook from March 4, 1948, indeed uncannily seems to support Thévenin's conclusion. On the cover of his notebook, Artaud writes with his pencil the title "The execration of an <u>innate</u> magician"[43] (CI, 2325) after which the first pages assert that magic exists. After two pages of glossolalia follow again some pages that resume the theme of magic, God, and the gang of criminals that force Artaud in an unwanted life. The notebook ends on the eleventh page where Artaud states that

> the same character
> thus comes back every
> morning (it is an other)
> to accomplish his
> revolting, criminal
> and murderous, sinister
> function which is
> maintaining
> <u>the spell</u> on
> me
>
> continuing to
> make me
> this eternal
> bewitched one.[44] (CI, 2328)

As we know, the gardener of Ivry would get Artaud's breakfast every day and he, an ordinary man that simply obeys the rules that are imposed on him, continues to give him his daily food—in order to maintain his mechanized anatomy—and that therewith upholds his eternal bewitching. Artaud uses the word "envoûtement" and "envoûté" (translated as "spell" and "bewitched one") which are interestingly derived from the old French words "volt" and "vout," meaning "face." In other words, the gang of criminals, and the person that comes back every morning, thus wants to give Artaud a face.[xv] Following his lamentation, it becomes clear that Artaud complains about the man—by adding "it is an other," this complaint may concern anyone maintaining the spell upon him—who every morning confirms the preestablished structures of subjectification and subjugation that therewith appropriates the singularity of his body, expression, and desire. Artaud ends his notebook with his last words: "etc etc" (CI, 2328). Using the word "etcetera" two times implies that this ongoing action of bewitchment can be doubled and therewith eternally repeated. The doubling of "etcetera"—which Artaud slightly justifies to the right therewith suggests that it not really belongs to the main text—could also indicate that he has already told this story and that the end is thus predictable. Finally, this doubling of etcetera could also suggest that it is up to the reader to combat the before-mentioned processes—one should remember that Artaud considered his notebooks rather as tools—and hence to be engaged in exploring new ways to develop this execration. A third of the pages of this last notebook is left empty and can consequently be seen as an invitation to the reader who, as Artaud earlier suggested, is looking for a truth or a lost mechanism. It is up to the reader to interpret "etc etc," and it is hence up to us how to engage with these later writings. Are they the words of a madman or genius? And are they the writings of a patient or a physician? These last words are an open invitation.

Artaud's notebooks are written in an untranslatable language. His usage of the glossolalia and phonemes along with a play with the etymology of French words makes his zoological language difficult to understand and difficult to adequately translate. Artaud's later works even question our will to understand or to reflect on a text, because his writings are, as we have discussed, engaged with the vital, flexional, and singular forces of life, the becoming-foreign or becoming-other of language, and the expression of the impulsiveness of matter, which is "zoe" and "amor fati," or cruelty. The exploration, struggle, and play with language in these later writings necessitate a close reading and, if the reader wants to reengage with the thus created vital forces that are hollowed out in language, ask

---

[xv] This bewitching, or this process of giving a face to someone, echoes what Deleuze and Guattari have termed "faciality," which they characterize as "a horror story" (TP, 187). The burden of "faciality" is that "[f]acialization operates not by resemblance but by an order of reasons. It is a much more unconscious and machinic operation that draws the entire body across the holey surface, and in which the role of the face is not as a model or image, but as an overcoding of all of the decoded parts" (TP, 189). Similar to the functioning of order-words, this facialization organizes, overcodes, and restricts the vitality and singularity of the head. In his study of the paintings of Francis Bacon, Deleuze asserts that this head "is a spirit which is body, corporeal and vital breath, an animal spirit; it is the animal spirit of man" (FB, 15).

for a schizoanalytic approach that focuses on the emergence of something new rather than on the reiteration of something that is already postulated. Artaud's healing language of the flesh is an integral body, a crucible, that cruelly cries in a practice of an enhanced and genuine creative writing that is the art of crescive writing which gives us back our belief in this world. If we translate this last sentence in Artaud's mother tongue—"Le langage guérisseur d'Artaud, venant de la *chair*, est un *corps* intégral, un *creuset*, *criant* d'une façon *cruelle* dans une pratique d'*écriture créative* améliorée et authentique, qui est l'acte de l'*écriture croissante*, ce qui nous redonnera notre *croyance* au monde"—it becomes all the more clear that the French words, put in italics, phonetically generate each other—flesh, body, crucible, cry, cruelty, creative and crescive writing, and belief—and therewith suggest an intricate relationship that Artaud's later writings stage, explore, and heal. Pure coincidence or a delicate composition? Again, it is up to the reader how to engage with these writings that are, and that is for sure, scary to study.

Notes

1   "la première manifestation / du theatre de la cruauté / ne peut être que / le depart de / la vengeance de / mon eternelle / histoire de / sempiternel / persecuté" [my translation].
2   "Vous êtes le seul médecin à savoir quelque chose de cela parce que vous avez senti cela avec un reste de cœur lacéré qu'un autre médecin n'a pas" [my translation].
3   "le langage rationnel
    grammatical moderne
    actuel
    est beaucoup trop approximatif
    avec sa manière de serrer
    ~~un faux sujet~~
    clairement un faux
    sujet
    il oblige à n'édifier que
    dans le répertoire des
    choses claires, c est
    a dire déjà eclairée
    au lieu d'aller chercher
    dans l'obscur à chaque

fois une inconnue à
laquelle sera donnée
sa vie claire par
fort et par volonté
Ce que je fais est de
fuir le clair
pour eclairer l'obscur [my translation].

4 "A force de pousser hors l ecrit
avec l ecrit
j'ai fini par accrocher dans
le langage une porte, par
decrocher un mur, par
remuer une paroi
et que cette paroi, ce plan
neuf où j ai fini par
déboucher,
à corps perdu,
a été
la mort que j'ai vraiment
connue m'y aidant,
ce monde grouillant,
catapultueux, haineux,
epouvantablement
acrimonieux de l'increé,
où, a travers la parole,
les mots, les syllabes avortées,
j'ai senti remuer
le corps epidermique
des etres et formes,
qui n'ayant jamais
existé, veulent
vivre
bien que n y ayant
jamais eu droit" [my translation].

5 "on n'entendra pas les sons,
la xylophonie sonore,
les cris, les bruits gutturaux et la voix,
tout ce qui constituait une 1re mouture du Théâtre de la Cruauté.
C'est un DÉSASTRE pour moi [my translation].

6. L'homme est malade parce qu'il est mal construit.
   Il faut se décider à le mettre à nu pour lui gratter cet animalcule qui le démange mortellement,
   dieu,
   et avec dieu
   ses organes.

   Car liez-moi si vous le voulez,
   mais il n'y a rien de plus inutile qu'un organe.

   Lorsque vous lui aurez fait un corps sans organes,
   alors vous l'aurez délivré de tous ses automatismes et rendu à sa véritable liberté (OCXIII, 104).
7. "je revendique, ce faisant, le droit de briser avec le sens usuel du langage, de rompre une bonne fois l'armature, de faire sauter le carcan, d'en revenir enfin aux origines étymologiques de la langue qui à travers des concepts abstraits évoquent toujours une notion concrète" (OCIV, 121).
8. "Du point de vue de l'esprit cruauté signifie rigueur, application et décision implacable, détermination irréversible, absolue" (OCIV, 121).
9. "La cruauté est avant tout lucide, c'est une sorte de direction rigide, la soumission à la nécessité" (OCIV, 122).
10. "Le Théâtre de la Cruauté
    n'est pas le symbole d'un vide absent,
    d'une épouvantable incapacité de se réaliser dans sa vie d'homme.
    Il est l'affirmation
    d'une terrible
    et d'ailleurs inéluctable nécessité" [my translation].
11. "Tout ce qui est attaqué l'est beaucoup moins sur le plan Social que sur le plan Métaphysique" [my translation].
12. "Mes héros […] se situent dans le domaine de la cruauté et doivent être jugés en dehors du bien et du mal. […] Cruauté qui agit aussi contre le spectateur et ne doit pas lui permettre quitter le théâtre intact, mais, lui-même, épuisé, engagé, transformé peut-être !" [my translation].
13. "Si le théâtre essentiel est comme la peste, ce n'est pas parce qu'il est contagieux, mais parce que comme la peste il est la révélation, la mise en avant, la poussée vers l'extérieur d'un fond de cruauté latente par lequel se localisent sur un individu ou sur un peuple toutes les possibilités perverses de l'esprit" (OCIV, 30).
14. "Un désastre social si complet, un tel désordre organique, ce débordement de vices, cette sorte d'exorcisme total qui presse l'âme et la pousse à bout, indiquent la présence d'un état qui est d'autre par une force extrême et où se retrouvent à

vif toutes les puissances de la nature au moment où celle-ci va accomplir quelque chose d'essentiel" (OCIV, 29).

15 "je crois qu'au Mexique il y a encore des forces qui bouent, et gênent les Indiens" [my translation].

16 "Ce que je vois au Mexique me prouve que j'ai toujours été dans la bonne voie" [my translation].

17 "ce langage concret, destiné aux sens et indépendant de la parole, doit satisfaire d'abord les sens, qu'il y a une poésie pour les sens comme il y en a une pour le langage, et que ce langage physique et concret auquel je fais allusion n'est vraiment théâtral que dans la mesure où les pensées qu'il exprime échappent au langage articulé" (OCIV, 36).

18 "c'est faire servir le langage à exprimer ce qu'il n'exprime pas d'habitude: c'est s'en servir d'une façon nouvelle, exceptionnelle et inaccoutumée, c'est lui rendre ses possibilités d'ébranlement physique, c'est le diviser et le répartir activement dans l'espace, c'est prendre les intonations d'une manière concrète absolue et leur restituer le pouvoir qu'elles auraient de déchirer et de manifester réellement quelque chose, c'est se retourner contre le langage et ses sources bassement utilitaires, on pourrait dire alimentaires, contre ses origines de bête traquée" (OCIV, 44).

19 "l'acceptation religieuse et mystique dont notre théâtre a complètement perdu le sens" (OCIV, 44).

20 "J'ai donc dit « cruauté », comme j'aurais dit « vie » ou comme j'aurais dit « nécessité », parce que je veux indiquer surtout que pour moi le théâtre est acte et émanation perpétuelle, qu'il n'y a en lui rien de figé, que je l'assimile à un acte vrai, donc vivant, donc magique" (OCIV, 83).

21 "le Theatre de la cruauté / est mort avant de / vivre / mais jamais je ne l ai / senti plus vivant / que depuis qu il n a / jamais pu exister" [my translation].

22 "Le visage humain porte en effet une espèce de mort perpétuelle sur son visage dont c'est au peintre justement à le sauver en lui rendant ses propres traits" [my translation].

23 "Ces cahiers
n'ont pas été
mis sous verre
dans l'intention
d'être enchâssés
comme des pièces
de musée.
Ils me serviront
encore, mais
je les montre
pour qu'un

homme qui
recherche comme
moi une vérité
et une mécanique
perdue
les retrouvent,
comme je les ai
cherchées dans
ces cahiers [my translation].
24 "Faites danser enfin l'anatomie humaine,
de haut en bas et de bas en haut,
d'arrière en avant et
d'avant en arrière,
mais beaucoup plus d'arrière en arrière, d'ailleurs, que d'arrière en avant
[…].
On a fait manger le corps humain,
on l'a fait boire,
pour s'éviter
de le faire danser" [my translation].
25 "les choses sorties
de moi
sont
ma fille
mon enfant
elles
ne
sont
pas
ma
gaghasse" [my translation].
26 "ce n est pas l equilibre
du souffle des 2 poumons
ce sont est le contrefort
des eglises gothiques
preuve d'un immense vol" [my translation].
27 "le chantonnement
scandé
laïque
non liturgique
non rituel
non grec

　　　　entre nègre
　　　　chinois
　　　　indien
　　　　et français villon" [my translation].
　28　"ce sera toujours moi parlant une langue
　　　　etrangère avec un accent toujours
　　　　reconnaissable" [my translation].
　29　"je ne suis pas un
　　　　initié
　　　　mais un inventeur,
　　　　createur
　　　　auteur
　　　　tout ce qu'on voudra" [my translation].
　30　"Les corps sont" [my translation].
　31　"Je crois que toute
　　　　initiation est le
　　　　fruit d'un crime
　　　　sur l astral de
　　　　la matière universelle
　　　　a qui on a fait donner
　　　　un monde
　　　　qu elle ne voulait
　　　　pas donner et que
　　　　les initiés l'ont
　　　　forcée à donner" [my translation].
　32　"c est sur ce monde
　　　　qu ils ont construit
　　　　leur numerotation
　　　　kabbalistique soi
　　　　disant secrete et
　　　　elle l'est mais infernale
　　　　car venue d un
　　　　monde voulu et <u>qui</u>
　　　　<u>n'existe pas</u>" [my translation].
　33　"celui de l'involution
　　　　organique regressive
　　　　de l être humain;
　　　　l'homme veut redevenir
　　　　mauvais et se
　　　　relâcher dans la

tenue de ses organes
internes, son but
vital majeur n'est
plus autre chose
que de parvenir
à se bestialiser" [my translation].

34 "son but / vital majeur n'est / plus autre chose / que de parvenir / à se bestialiser" [my translation].

35 "le sang sorti du
cœur ne retournait
pas encore
toujours
et invariablement
au cœur
c est a
c'est-à-dire qu'un
certain automatisme
organique n était
pas encore irreme
diablement
etabli et
que des libertés
etaient laissées
à l exercice de cette
humeur
spontanée et
sourde" [my translation].

36 "forces informulées" (OCI*, 50).

37 "prompt comme la foudre" (OCI*, 51).

38 "est en réalité
une sorte de laboratoire
ou d usine,
ou l homme periodi
quement,
vient dans le sens le
plus réel
du terme
se faire
corporellement

et dynamiquement
changer" [my translation].

39 "le but vrai du
theatre authentique est
donc dans ce transfert de
corps, ce passage d un
corps reconnu mauvais
et grangené à un corps
superieur ou
l acteur
puisse retrouver
au moins
l homme qu il était
avant cet osbcène [*sic*]
passage sur lui du
corps de toute la
société" [my translation].

40 "entre nègre / chinois / indien / et français villon" [my translation].

41 "entre nègre / chinois / indien / et français villon" [my translation].

42 "elle [= life] ne vaut que / dans la mesure / où elle change" [my translation].

43 "L execration / du / magicien / inné" [my translation].

44 "le même personnage
revient donc chaque
matin (c'est un autre)
accomplir sa
revoltante, criminelle
et assassine, sinistre
fonction qui est de
maintenir
l'envoutement sur
moi" [my translation].

Conclusion:
Toward a Postsecular Religion of Language.
Or, etc., etc.

The earth paints and describes itself under the action of a terrible dance which has not yet given epidemically of its fruits.[1]
—Antonin Artaud, "The Theater of Cruelty," OCXIII, p. 115

A Treatment of Auto-Detoxification

After an early stopped detoxification treatment, Artaud again starts to take drugs in April 1947 and subsequently writes in his notebook from the same month that

I am more and more
tired with suffering
and I know
that I can
1° detoxify myself without
suffering
2° having the courage and "boldness" (oh!)
to <u>detoxify</u> myself
more profoundly.[2] (CI, 715)

In other words, Artaud criticizes the administered detoxification treatments since he can detoxify himself and, more interestingly, he has the courage and audacity to detoxify himself more constitutively. The word "boldness" (Artaud uses the word "audace") refers to a courage that knows neither obstacle nor limit but mainly indicates the act of violating the imposed rules; his auto-detoxification is thus both courageous and presumptuous. This auto-detoxification is essentially an engagement with the forces of life, because four pages later he writes that

the ineluctable life is
the
force
that can not
~~can~~ not burst out
leap
go out
now this force
<u>it's me</u>
it must go out at all costs
it can not
not
<u>be there</u>
<u>be</u> everywhere
occupy everything
if we suffer
it's because people
prevent it from
going out
and keeping it
for themselves.[3] (CI, 716–17)

A treatment of auto-detoxification thus consists of boldly assuming these powers of life that traverse our body.

Artaud contends that *he* is this force of the ineluctable life that, whatever one tries, strives to burst out of conventions, formalizations, and codes. Artaud consequently continues: "Evil is but an/imbecile and crapulous/invention/of beings/who have wanted//to signify/to give sense/to an invented/supposed thing/calculated in all/corners and which/absolutely did not/exist"[4] (CI, 717). The forces of life are thus caught in a web of signification that is but an invention and that gives way to genuine evil and suffering. Artaud's treatment of auto-detoxification is, as we have discussed in this book, a cure of auto-immunization through a treatment of language. It is a treatment that detoxifies man from his mechanized anatomy in order to experiment more healthily with a machinic anatomy that engages with the forces of life. In this sense, these treatments of auto-detoxification strive for a greater health that combats the imposed suffering by society—who does so by a tendency of overmedicalization within the field of medical health care and through the structuring of advanced capitalism that catches the forces of life and cages them in conventions, formalizations, and codes—and reassume and reaffirm both the joyous *and* terrible forces of life. These treatments imply, as we have discussed in Chapter 1, an intricate relationship between flesh, mind, and expression. In considering the flesh in his earlier works, Artaud discovered that it was traversed by "undefined forces"[5] (AN, 58) from which a mind emanates that is as "quick as lightening"[6] (AN, 59). By phonetically playing with words, Artaud investigated how a creative play with the sound, form, and restricted meaning of linguistic units can bring about a new meaning that is the expression of their materiality. This rewriting of the dualism of words suggests an intricate relationship between flesh, mind, and expression because meaning is essentially generated by matter in an openended way. Thus fathoming the depths of the body, Artaud discovered yet another treatment to engage with the forces besieging him and that are too great to conceive. In his "theater of cruelty," he subsequently envisioned to stage these vital forces of life in an affective play "that must not allow him [the spectator] to leave the theater intact, but, rather, exhausted, engaged, transformed perhaps"[7] (OCV, 309). Confronted with a new corporeal anatomy that should affect the spectators under the skin, man would again feel and discern the link with the vitality of his body and with the "true nature of evil," which is the forces of *this* life.

The first staging of this theater of "life" and "necessity," or "zoe" and "amor fati," hence "cruelty," turned out to be a failure with only seventeen performances of *The Cenci*. Persisting in the idea of the generative vitality of matter, that is the intricate relationship of flesh, mind, and expression, Artaud decides to travel to Mexico in order to investigate, among others, another expression of "cruelty" in the Dance of the Peyote in which the drugged dancer "moves deliberately into evil. He immerses himself in it with a kind of terrible courage, in a rhythm which above the Dance seems to depict the Illness"[8] (SW, 387). Back again in Paris, Artaud undergoes two detoxification treatments from February to March and another in April but, as was ultimately the purpose of the "theater of cruelty," he seems to be engaged and transformed by his Mexican experiences and leaves for Ireland in August 1937 in order to investigate "the living sources, and living among living man, of this very ancient tradition in its Western form" (Artaud qtd. in Penot-Lacassagne 2007, 145–6). Conscious of his changed behavior, Artaud writes to Anne Manson in September that "[i]f they think me crazy, megalomaniac or maniac, so much the worse for them. […] Tell them that I have hated them for years, they and their political social, moral, amoral and immoral ideas"[9] (OCVII, 226). After his derailment in Dublin, Artaud will be interned for nine years in various psychiatric hospitals in France. Diagnosed with a delirious syndrome with paranoid structures, schizophrenia, and graphorrhea, Artaud, against all expectations, reengages with writing during his internment in Rodez from February 1943 to May 1946. Still indebted to the articulation of his Mexican experiences—the healing and healthy culture of organicity that is devoted to cruelty—Artaud again engages with the untranslatable, unimaginable, and unthinkable forces of thinking and life, but explores them, this time—and this is what characterizes his later writings—more sustainably within and through language.

Understanding language as a deprivation of life, because of its structuring through the discourse of reason, unity, and opposition ("Theos") and the political discourse of human and discursive life ("bios"), which creates confusion, cynicism, and illness, Artaud creates a language in suspense, which is a foreign language that also engages with animal, organic, and nonhuman forces ("zoe"). This zoology of language is articulated within and through the dominant system of signs, and thus demands a close reading if we want to discern it, and is a healing practice since it reaffirms and reassumes the link between man and *this* world, *this* body, and *this* life. Putting it differently, this zoological language that is articulated in Artaud's later works is a healing practice of the body, and in this sense a religious enterprise, because it reengages with the generative vitality of the expression of matter. It is for this reason that we have considered Artaud an intercessor for those longing for the healing of the vital link with *this* world that is still broken. Artaud's vibrating language is a creative and animated language where words are used as material forces that remain unstable, paradoxical, conflicting, and hence vital. We have called this spontaneous, generative, and open-ended development within and through Artaud's later writings the practices of "crescive writing." In this book, we have mainly discussed Artaud's play with language in his later writings through a critical textual analysis, based on a close reading from a schizoanalytic approach. In doing so, this book is only exploratory and an invitation to further research because for a more complete understanding of what these practices of "crescive writing" entail, it would be necessary to consider, from a similar schizoanalytic approach, his images, sketches, and his tactile use of the paper more thoroughly as well. Investigating, analyzing, and rereading his "50 Drawings to Murder Magic," for example, will then give us a more thorough understanding of Artaud's still relevant way of writing. Another omission in this book is the only briefly mentioned role of sound in Artaud's recitation of his poems. Besides the famous registering of

To Have Done with the Judgment of God, Artaud has also recorded his poems "Alienation and Black Magic" and "The Patients and the Doctors" in 1946. Focusing on the particular use of the voice, screams, and his interpretation of the glossolalia, which often differs from the written phonemes, along with different other sounds, may also enhance our understanding of the practice of "crescive writing." A close reading, a critical analysis, and a schizoanalysis of the sounds, images, and the tactilely approached paper used in his later writings will then, I think, unfold that Artaud's zoology of language or his practice of "crescive writing" question the dominant role and status of language in our current understanding of his works.

In this book, we have contended, in conclusion from a close reading, that Artaud's later works are written as a magical and materialist theosophy. This magical approach to language sublimates matter by treating words as things and thus changing the formalized sense of words. This vital theosophy thus searches for the hitherto unexplored potentialities of the agential materiality of language and its capacity to create vibrating words that express the impulsiveness of matter, nature, or God. This magical and materialist theosophy is therewith an important part of Artaud's treatment of auto-detoxification and his enterprise of auto-immunization because it reconsiders the forces of life that are in a state of deprivation in our advanced civilization. Considering his notebooks as tools, Artaud also claims that

> it
> is not for me that I
> speak, it is not for
> the happiness of speaking
> in my name and to
> rise in the name of my
> name but for a few dozen
> others who are like me,
> and who are in the same position
> as me
> and when I speak it is they
> these somber and hidden
> unknowns, but very alive,
> and breathing and especially
> suffering, alas
> it is they who speak
> in me.[10] (CI, 751)

Artaud's works are thus collectively produced writings that voice the suppressed but living and breathing bodies of those who engage with the forces of life. In other words, Artaud zoological language is not *his* language; it is a collective language of a suffering and subjugated people.

Considering literature as an enterprise of health, Deleuze asserts that writing

> consists in inventing a people who are missing. [...] This is not exactly a people called upon to dominate the world. It is a minor people, externally minor, taken up in a becoming-revolutionary. Perhaps it exists only in the atoms of the writer, a bastard people, inferior, dominated, always in becoming, always incomplete. (CC, 4)

Writing for a people to come is also about inventing a language for these minor people that are subjugated and suffering from the developments within medical health care and the structuring and functioning of advanced capitalism. Always in becoming, as Deleuze contends, these people find their expression in the enterprise of health that is literature or, following Artaud, a treatment of auto-detoxification within an enterprise of auto-immunization. It is this creation of a language for a people to come that Deleuze and Guattari call a "minor literature," which "doesn't come from a minor language; it is rather that which a minority constructs within a major language" (K, 16). Minor literature is thus created from a minor use of language and has consequently three characteristics: "the deterritorialization of language, the connection of the individual to a political immediacy, and the collective assemblage of enunciation" (K, 18). In other words, a minor literature is created from a becoming-foreign or becoming-other of the dominant system of signs, from a combat against the political discourse of human and discursive life and is written for a people to come (see also Bogue 2003b, 91–114 for a good and thorough discussion of what minor literature entails). It is in this sense that Artaud's later writings can well be considered a minor literature conceived as a minor expression of the body. Focusing a bit more on the political dimension of this minor literature or, better, this minor expression of the body, we more clearly understand the importance and relevance of Artaud's later works for the reader of today.

The Contract with Nature

In *The Natural Contract* Michel Serres comments on our cynic attitude toward environmental engagement and then confronts the reader with a modern version of Pascal's Wager: "If we judge our actions innocent and we win, we win nothing, history goes on as before, but if we lose, we lose everything, being unprepared for some possible catastrophe. Suppose that, inversely, we choose to consider ourselves responsible: if we lose, we lose nothing, but if we win, we win everything, by remaining the actors of history" (1995, 5). Pascal's Wager concerned the bet that God exists or does not exist but was criticized since it was essentially not an ontological argument that proved God's existence. Serres's Wager differs, of course, since it does not aim to prove the existence of environmental problems—for this reason, Serres argues that it concerns a wager "since our models can serve to defend the two opposing theses" (1995, 5)—but rather incites us to act and engage with environmental and ecological problems. Serres rewrites Rousseau's *The Social Contract* and also plays with his famous conclusion—"Back to nature"—which means for Serres that "we must add to the exclusively social contract a natural contract of symbiosis and reciprocity in which our relationship to things would set aside mastery and possession in favor of admiring attention, reciprocity, contemplation, and respect; where knowledge would no longer imply property, nor action mastery, nor would property and mastery imply their excremental results and origins" (1995, 38). It is thus a shift from the lifeless and forceless excrements of property and mastery to the vital flesh that is full of forces and that makes connections in a nonhierarchical, hence rhizomatic way.

Elaborating on this contract of symbiosis, Serres contends that "a symbiont recognizes the host's rights, whereas a parasite—which is what we are now—condemns to death the one he pillages and inhabits not realizing that in the long run he's condemning himself to death too" (1995, 38). The rewritten social contract, the natural contract of symbiosis, thus makes us all accountable for what we do. This contract holds us back from outsourcing our ability to act by blaming a system that indeed suppresses, overcodifies, and restricts our behavior, actions, and expressions but that, at the same time, also offers us small degrees of freedom and inventiveness—without which the system cannot be sustained—which therewith compels us to be accountable for our actions. In other words, the natural contract of symbiosis is a contract with which we critically reconsider advanced capitalism as an ally in the becoming-posthuman where man becomes a symbiotic host instead of a parasitic intruder. This contract allows us to dive into the depths of nature or, as we have earlier discussed and following Spinoza, God and from there to express "the simultaneously materialist and vitalist force of life itself, *zoe* as the generative power that flows across all species" (Braidotti

2011a, 91). The natural contract of symbiosis is thus a contract with the forces of *this* life, a contract with the vitality of the expression of matter and a contact with the hitherto unexplored possibilities of *this* world; it is an engagement with absolute immanence in a posthumanist ethics of becoming; it is a commitment to the vital forces of Ciguri, nature, or God.

The difficulty of this contract is that "[n]ature lies outside the collectivity, which is why the state of nature remains incomprehensible to the language invented in and by society—or that invents social man" (Serres 1995, 85). The task to which this natural contract of symbiosis gives way is thus also to create a language that is the genuine expression of nature. In *Biogea*—"Biogea" is a contraction of "bios" (life) and "Gaia" (Mother Earth)—Serres contends that "[t]he world resonates with a common language, no doubt formal, I don't know if it's poetic but what does it matter, the essential thing remains sharing these codings, this universal language, music and science" (172). In other words, nature has one common language that needs to be shared and that is the language of life, of necessity, of matter, hence of "zoe." The art of expressing and sharing this language that reveals, following Artaud, the "perverse possibilities of the mind"[11] (TD, 30) is an ethico-aesthetic practice that results from the natural contract of symbiosis. Apart from the ethical and aesthetical components of these practices, we have seen that this enterprise of language is also religious, because it reengages, in its devotion to absolute immanence, with nature and therewith wants to heal the broken link between man and *this* world. Using the word "religion" in its etymological sense—that of "reconnecting" and "rereading"—Serres's natural contract of symbiosis thus gives way to a religo-ethico-aesthetic practice where a zoology of language needs to be expressed and shared. It is in this sense that a critical revaluation of Artaud's practices of "crescive writing" is still relevant for the reader of today since it shows the affective, potential, and powerful forces that are still at work in his minor use of language, which is the minor expression of the body.

To Believe in the Flesh

Serres's Wager is a rational argument that engages with environmental and ecological concerns. From its logic results a reconnection with this world that eventually leads to a natural contract of symbiosis. Apart from this rational argument, there is however also a more ontological argument that constitutes the reconnection of man with this world. This argument is related to the impossibility of thinking. In his correspondence with Rivière in the 1920s, Artaud claims that his readers should believe in "a sickness which touches the essence of being and its central possibilities of expression, and which applies to a whole life. A sickness which affects the soul in its most profound reality, and which infects its manifestations. The poison of being. A veritable *paralysis.* A sickness which deprives you of speech, memory, which uproots your thought"[12] (SW, 44, emphasis in original). In other words, Artaud incites us to believe in a "true" sickness that disrupts thinking, paralyzes our soul, and modifies its manifestations. In this sickness we are confronted with the "essence of being" or the "true nature of evil" that maddens and immobilizes any fixity, stability, and rootedness. Some months before his praise of this "true" sickness, Artaud contradicts, in another letter to Rivière, the stupidity that he would be just a madman—Artaud's treatments started already in 1915—because "I am not stupid. I know that it possible to think further than I think, and perhaps differently. All I can do is wait for my brain to change, wait for its upper drawers to open"[13] (SW, 36). These superior drawers of our brain think the incessant fluxes that precede thinking and think the screaming void from which genuine thinking emerges. In a short article devoted to his writings, Blanchot argues that Artaud does not cease to struggle against this distressing experience of genuine thinking. This combat oscillates "between thought as lack and the impossibility of bearing this lack, between thought as nothingness and the plenitude of upsurgence that hides in thought, between thought as separation and life as inseparable from thought" (1993, 294). In other words, the impossibility to think forces us to think. We must constantly scratch open the itching wound from which life emerges and that bears witness to a greater health. Genuine thinking is a shock that disrupts and maddens the supposed fixity and stability of any being. Similar to the productive delirium of a true sickness, thinking engages with what Artaud called "essence of being" or the "true nature of evil."

In *The Time-Image*, Deleuze logically concludes that

> if it is true that thought depends on a shock which gives birth to it (the nerve, the brain matter), it can only think one thing, *the fact that we are not yet thinking*, the powerlessness to think the whole and to think oneself, thought which is always fossilized, dislocated, collapsed. A being of thought which is always to come. (C2, 162, emphasis in original)

Similar to Blanchot's conclusion, Deleuze contends that thinking always circles around thinking, because thinking cannot think the unthinkable that thinks nevertheless through us. Engaging with the disruptive powers of thinking thus means breaking down the sensory-motor circuits of our thinking, behavior, and actions that hold us back from genuine thinking. In doing so, we are faced with intense but healthy forces that are intolerable and too great for us to conceive since they confront us with the untranslatability and the unthinkability of genuine thinking. Braidotti therefore rightly concludes that "[i]f thinking were pleasurable, more humans may be tempted to engage in this activity. Accelerations or increased intensities, however, are that which most humans prefer to avoid" (2012, 139). However painful and yet joyous the act of thinking is, Deleuze nevertheless asserts that we should "[b]elieve, not in a different world, but in a link between man and the world, in love or life, to believe in this as in the impossible, the unthinkable which none the less cannot be thought" (C2, 164). The force of thinking thus lies in its potency to think the unthinkable and therewith to engage with the intolerable and unbearable but vital and energetic forces of this world, of nature, and of "zoe."

Deleuze contends, however, that "[t]he modern fact is that we no longer believe in this world. We do not even believe in the events which happen to us, love, death, as if they only half concerned us" (C2, 166). The impossible link between man and this world is broken, because we do not seem to have the power and force to genuinely think, and therewith believe, anymore. The detachment from this world makes us megalomaniac but also passive, indifferent, and cynical. If we want to become happier and healthier Stoics and thus heal—in its etymological sense of "reconnecting"—the broken link between man and this world, we must devote ourselves to absolute immanence, dare thinking the unthinkable and, from there, believe in the vital forces of *this* world and *this* life. Following Artaud, Deleuze states that to believe simply means "believing in the body. It is giving discourse to the body, and, for this purpose, reaching the body before discourses, before words, before things are named [...]. Artaud said the same thing, believe in the *flesh* [...]. Give words back to the body, to the flesh" (C2, 167, emphasis in original). We must invent words that are the expression of the flesh, bring back expression to the body, and therewith find a corporal language that is not infected with a formalized system of signs that prevents us from genuine thinking. In this sense, Artaud's later works are written in the words of the flesh—the subtle and affective flesh of language. Believing in this flesh is a reengagement with the vital forces of this world, this body, and "zoe" and essentially reconnects with the "essence of being" from which thinking emerges. This zoology of language—a nonhuman, animal, *and* human language that perpetually vibrates and that resists any interpretation and that is, hence, an ongoing and open-ended performance—is a reengagement with the vitality of the expression of matter and is, in this sense, a religious practice that is fundamental to the natural contract of symbiosis.

A Postsecular Society of Immanence

Kristien Justaert describes Deleuze's urge to believe again in the broken link between man and this world as a "rhizomatic theology" and concludes that

> [d]ue to his metaphysics of univocity, one is already God. There is a univocal relation between creatures (beings) and creator (being). If there is some sort of aim within a rhizomatic theology, it would be the expansion of the rhizomatic network, making more connections—as many as possible—like the rampant growth of weeds. Then God is expressed (as a dynamic, creative force) in infinitely different ways, through an uncountable quantity of connections, though it is still God. (95)

Believing in *this* world, the flesh, and *this* life means reengaging with the incessant forces of thinking that indeed creatively make new connections. Engaging with the vitality of the expression of matter means speaking of nature, with nature, and as nature. To believe in *this* world is to heal the broken link between man and nature, matter, or God. Artaud engaged with the incessant fluxes that incited him to think the unthinkable forces that nevertheless could not be caught by his thinking. In doing so, he explored different ways to express these forces (poetry, drawings, cinema, and theater), searched for new ways to engage with this vitality in Mexico and eventually ended by developing a magical and materialist theosophy of immanence in a language of a genuine theology of "life" and "necessity," or "zoe" and "amor fati," which is cruelty. This language is religious, in the etymological sense of the word, because it expresses nature, matter, or God in a tangible way where the materiality of the medium is treated as a tactile and where words affectively interact with the reader. The question is however how serious one takes a new religion in our society—especially when it does not fit with the imposed logic of normativity and productivity.

Braidotti uses the term "postsecular" to describe our society that critically reconsiders belief systems (2011a, 174). Braidotti signals that "[s]ecular humanism has developed a strong connection to theism, and our current practice of secularism sits uncomfortably within this tense legacy" (2011a, 181). This postsecular turn within the practice of secularism does not necessarily lead to a revival of a Christianity—Charles Taylor's later works are exemplary within this logic—based on old models of thinking, but gives rather way to "a change of consciousness, which acknowledges not only the persistence of religious beliefs and practices but also their compatibility with processes of modernization" (2011a, 181). In her reading of Deleuze's works, Justaert also perceives a criticism of Taylor and claims that in our postsecular society, "the 'Taylorian' dualism between the secular and the non-secular (the sphere of believers) is overcome: the immanent ('secular') becomes divine!" (34). Following Justaert, postsecular societies are thus beyond the dualism of secular and non-secular because there is only one divine world from which anything is expressed. From the univocity of this world, everything belongs to matter, nature, or God and is, hence, divine.

Derrida suggests that the realization of this divine world is also the coming about of a posthuman world in which we see the realization of cruelty. He argues that

> [t]he divine has been ruined by God. That is to say, by man, who in permitting himself to be separated from Life by God, in permitting himself to be usurped from his own birth, became man by polluting the divinity of the divine. [...] The restoration of divine cruelty, hence, must traverse the murder of God, that is to say, primarily the murder of the man-God. (1978, 243)

In other words, man has perverted the divinity of the world by measuring himself against God supposing that God does not manifest himself in this life and this world. Restoring the divinity of the world thus implies the realization of a postsecular society in which cruelty, which is "life" and "necessity," or "zoe" and "amor fati," is revalued and in which man lives as a symbiotic host. In this postsecular society, religion is not concerned with a transcendental comprehension of the world but is rather devoted to the perpetual connection of man with this divine world. In order to do so, religion can be stimulated with rational arguments or with rather ontological reasons that incite us to believe again in *this* world. This religion, understood as a reconnection or a making whole again, is, essentially, a natural contract of symbiosis from which religo-ethico-aesthetic practices constantly combat the ever-increasing practices of overcodification, subjectification, and subjugation. In doing so, this religion is sustained by enterprises of language rethinking, rewriting, reconstructing, and therewith reappropriating the singularity of the body. These enterprises of language find their expression in a divine, which is a magical, materialist, and healing and hence a zoological language committed to the untranslatable forces of life. To believe in this world thus essentially means giving words to the impulsiveness of the flesh and crescively articulating an affective language of cruelty that is traversed by the vital forces of life whose meaning is an ongoing performance generated by its agential materiality. The postsecular society is thus stimulated by a religion of language that gives us reasons to believe again in *this* world.

Justaert interestingly speculates on the role of churches within these postsecular societies and contends that "[a] church assemblage is a non-hierarchical, temporary encounter of minorities, human and non-human, that function together in their resistance against the captivation of desire and the consequential forms of oppression and exploitation endemic to capitalist society" (130). A church is essentially a place where genuine believers gather—those, following Artaud, "few dozen/others who are like me" (CI, 751) who engage with the unthinkable forces that nevertheless incite them to think—resingularizing themselves in a zoological language expressed through practices of crescive writing. This idea of new church assemblages, guided or inspired by genuine intercessors, is interesting and relevant for our society of advanced capitalism and merits a more thorough analysis and discussion.

A Postsecular Religion of Language

In a notebook from April 1947, Artaud writes again at the speed of his thoughts and mainly reformulates his ideas on being, the body, the existence of evil and life. At the back of his notebook, he continues his writing by vertically writing in "I will now start again / this small operation"[14] (CI, 719). The small operation of which he speaks has to do with the automatism that he describes on the back of the fourteenth page—that he also writes vertically in the margins of his text: "what constitutes the automatism of beings is / that they imagine thinking by themselves / when it is their turn to think"[15] (CI, 718). In other words, the automatism—the mechanized anatomy of man and the sensory-motor circuit of our daily activities, habits, and customs that hold us back from genuine thinking—is sustained by the illusion that we think by ourselves. It is up to Artaud to engage with genuine thinking and thus repeating and therewith repairing this small operation that holds him back from thinking. His small operation turns out to be a struggle, because "on a day in a / great plain / I Antonin Artaud / I have / fought with / the automatism / of god"[16] (CI, 719). While Jacob fought with God in the night, Artaud fights with God (that he again minuscules as god)—in fact, he more precisely fights with the automatism of God—during the day, but the major difference is that Jacob asked God's blessing while Artaud wants to undo himself from a burden that God has allegedly imposed on him.

Artaud continues his story by claiming that he discovered that all beings, spirits, and other consciousnesses were only monkeys and "that I alone / Antonin Artaud / was a man because / only I had a body and / lived and that the rest / did not exist"[17] (CI, 719). Those final concluding lines echo an idea that he formulated on the back of the tenth page: "being is that which / only thinks / with a body // which needs / a body / to think / and which, without a body, / isn't even / there"[18] (CI, 716). Beings thus only think through and with their bodies and when they do not think like this—that is, when their thinking is but an illusionary thinking—they do not even exist. In other words, Artaud combats the automatisms that detach us from life and that break the link between man and *this* world. Through his writings, he fights with the automatism that a humanly constructed God has created and that needs to be combatted in order to re-enable us to genuinely think and hence to live. The strategy of a madman or a genius? Or an intelligent merging of the two? It is, again, up to the reader to draw a conclusion related to Artaud's logic. But before doing so, we however conclude by looking at the consequences and implications of Artaud's exploration, struggle, and play with language.

In combatting the automatisms, Artaud also wages a war against a language that is structured along theological (the discourse of reason, unity, and identity) and biological (the discourse of human and intelligent life) axes. This formalized system of signs that constitutes our daily language creates confusion and sickness by coding and overcoding the subjugated subjects it creates. In doing so, this language is accessory to our current passivity, indifference, and cynicism that outsources thinking and hence hinders an engagement with life and that is consequently an important fuel for the functioning of advanced capitalism. Artaud's later writings more actively and more bodily engage with this language in their practices of "crescive writing." This writing that encompasses the practices of creative, a rather critical performative and asemic writing, formulates, within a zoology of language, a magical and materialist theosophy along with the articulation of a theology of "zoe" and "amor fati," which is the writing of cruelty. The outcome of these practices of "crescive writing" is an affective flesh of language that gives us reasons to believe again in this world. Created from the necessity of a natural contract of symbiosis, these practices of "crescive writing" are materialist, healing, and religious practices that are most fully and effectively explored in Artaud's later writings. This religion of language incites us to reengage with the vitality of matter, to live healthier, happier, and more stoically in a postsecular society of divine and absolute immanence in which we must build new assemblages of churches, guided or inspired by intercessors, and in which we can, from there, express the singularity of our bodies in a divine, zoological, and religious, that is a healthy, materialist, and vital language of God, with God, and, finally, as God.

Notes

1 "La terre se peint et se décrit sous l'action d'une terrible danse à qui on n'a pas encore fait donner épidémiquement tous ses fruits" [my translation].

2 "j'en ai de plus en plus
   assez de souffrir
   et je sais
   que je peux
   1° me desintoxiquer sans
   souffrance
   2° en ayant le courage
   et « l'audace » (oh !)
   de m'<u>intoxiquer</u>
   plus profondément" [my translation].

3 l ineluctable vie est
   la
   force
   qui ne peut pas
   ne ~~peut~~/pas fuser
   jaillir/sortir
   or cette force
   <u>c est moi</u>
   il faut qu elle sorte à tout prix
   elle ne peut pas

>   ne pas
>   etre là
>   être partout
>   occuper tout
>   si l'on souffre
>   c est que des gens
>   l empêchent de
>   sortir
>   et la gardent
>   pour eux [my translation].

4. Le mal n est qu une
    invention imbecile
    et crapuleuse
    des êtres
    qui ont voulu

    signifier
    donner sens
    à une chose inventee,
    supposée
    supputée de toutes
    pieces et qui
    absolument n existait
    pas [my translation].
5. "forces informulées" (OCI*, 50).
6. "prompt comme la foudre" (OCI*, 51).
7. "ne doit pas lui permettre quitter le théâtre intact, mais, lui-même, épuisé, engagé, transformé peut-être !" [my translation].
8. "avance délibérément dans le mal. Il y plonge avec une sorte d'affreux courage, sur un rythme qui, au-dessus de la Danse, semble dessiner la Maladie" (OCIX, 45).
9. "S'ils me croient fou, mégalomane ou maniaque, tant pis pour eux. [...] Dis-leur que voilà des années que je les hais, eux et leurs idées politiques, sociales, morales, amorales et immorales" [my translation].
10. ce
    n est pas pour moi que je
    parle, ce n'est pas pour
    le bonheur de parler
    en mon nom et de
    m'elever au nom de mon
    nom mais pour quelques dizaines

      d'autres qui sont comme moi,
      et se trouvent dans le même cas
      que moi
      et quand je parle
      c'est eux
      ces inconnus sombres et
      cachés, mais bien vivants,
      et respirants et surtout
      souffrants, helas
      c'est eux donc qui parlent
      en moi [my translation].
11 "les possibilités perverses de l'esprit" (OCIV, 30).
12 "une véritable maladie et non à un phénomène d'époque, à une maladie qui touche à l'essence de l'être et à ses possibilités centrales d'expression, et qui s'applique à toute une vie. Une maladie qui affecte l'âme dans sa réalité la plus profonde, et qui en infecte les manifestations. Le poison de l'être. Un véritable *paralysie*. Une maladie qui vous enlève la parole, le souvenir, qui vous déracine la pensée" (OCI*, 40).
13 " je ne suis pas bête. Je sais qu'il y aurait à penser plus loin que je ne pense, et peut-être autrement. J'attends, moi, seulement que change mon cerveau, que s'en ouvrent les tiroirs supérieurs" (OCI*, 27).
14 je vais <u>maintenant</u> <u>recommencer</u>
      cette petite operation [my translation].
15 ce qui constitue l automatisme des etres est
      de s imaginer penser par eux-mêmes
      lorsque leur tour est venu de penser [my translation].
16 un jour dans une
      grande plaine
      moi Antonin Artaud
      je me suis
      battu avec
      l automatisme
      de dieu [my translation].
17 que moi seul
      Antonin Artaud
      etais un homme parce que
      seul j avais un corps
      et
      vivais et que le reste
      n existait pas [my translation].

18 l etre est ce qui
    ne pense
    qu avec un corps
    qui a besoin d un corps
    pour penser
    et qui sans corps
    n est même
    pas là [my translation].

Postscriptum:
Reading Artaud Today. Or, a Plea for a Language in Movement

Writing and rewriting a book on Antonin Artaud provoke an uncanny experience that ranges from a sense of complete misunderstanding to feelings of immense admiration, from nausea to passion, and from moments of hopelessness to waves of enthusiasm. Reading Artaud today sometimes feels like a victory over his psychiatrists. In an interview with Lotringer, the psychiatrist Latrémolière, who worked with Ferdière in Rodez, asserts that "Artaud is hardly taught in schools" (75) and later asserts that his works will soon "fade into oblivion, it's obvious. When you speak with people, nine out of ten … When I say nine, it's much more than that. Ninety-nine out of a hundred don't know who Artaud is" (106) and even predicts that "[i]n thirty or fifty years I'm sure no one will speak of him" (73).[i] Latrémolière knew Artaud during his internment in Rodez and seems mainly to be astonished by the publication of his later works of which he asserts that "[a]ll the words that he invented make no sense—they add nothing to civilization, nothing" (69) and contends of those students who still need to read Artaud's works in some very small and specialized fields of the university that "[t]his type of thing won't make them stronger. On the contrary, it will leave them crawling around in the dark" (76). Reading Artaud today, along with these criticisms, makes one doubt if the perceived activism at work in his writings, the discovery of a language that is brought back to its agential materiality, and the discussion of his writings that develop into practices of auto-detoxification, auto-immunization, and eventually healing practices is only illusionary, too far-fetched, or vague and abstract in such a way that it can be applied to any work of

---

[i] This interview was published in 1977 in *La Tour De Feu*. Latrémolière's words thus not seem to come true.

literature. Who knows? It is up to the reader to judge what terms can do justice to what this book has tried to conceptualize.

What is, however, certain is that this book cannot be the work of an Artaud Acolyte, because "the story of how they [Artaud Acolytes] came to understand this 'Artaud-Christ' is usually less than 15-minutes, because most Artaud Acolytes have short attention spans" (Jones, 68). Jones continues his logic by claiming that "[i]f Artaud Acolytes thought clearly, logically, and intelligently about their 'beliefs' on Artaud for more than 15 minutes, they'd probably be hit with how stupid most of it is" (68). This argument can be easily weakened by the reader who has read this book all the way through to this point (except if it took him or her less than fifteen minutes). And it can also be contested by my own experiences, because it took me several years to think about my "belief" on Artaud.

While writing these words, I come to doubt if I have a "belief" on Artaud and if this book is even genuinely *on* Artaud. To comment on the first doubt: I sometimes have had the feeling of reading the works of a madman or a patient and yet, at other times, I felt as if I discovered the writings of a genius, a true artist, and a genuine writer who has seen and experienced realms that I would never dare to explore. However, if a body of work can give way to such divergent responses, it makes me believe that something relevant, important, and necessary is going on in these writings that make me continue reading, studying, and trying to grasp these works. The second doubt concerns the research that is done for this book in general, because I think that, in the end, this book is not written *on* Artaud but rather *with* Artaud, because this study is essentially about the constitutive and liberating role that language plays for those who feel caged within the postulations of normativity of medical health care and the structures of productivity of advanced capitalism.

In his essay "The Intercessors," Deleuze contends that "[d]ifferent modes of expression may have different creative possibilities, but they're all related insofar as they must counter the introduction of a cultural space of markets and conformity—that is, a space of 'producing for the market'—together" (N, 131). In this resistance lies an important task for literature, and the arts in general, of which Deleuze asserts that "[y]our writing has to be liquid or gaseous simply because normal perception and opinion are solid, geometric" (N, 133) and also claims that "[y]ou have to open up words, break things open, to free earth's vectors" (N, 134). In an age where medical health care reinforces notions of normativity and advanced capitalism increases the logic of productivity through its structuring, language plays a key role to sustain their ideas of a good health and a happy life. Not anyone fits within these subjugating notions, and for those who feel oppressed by them, a creative play with the solidified language that causes their confusion, cynicism, and illness can bring about a sustainable and healing liberation of the imposed automatisms. In doing so, we need our intercessors—as discussed earlier, we consider Artaud as an intercessor—with whom we can breathe, plunge into a hitherto unexplored reality, and create other possibilities of life. We need these intercessors with whom we can more sustainably express our healthy and happy singular flexionality. I think that here lies a task not only for the arts, but also for the humanities in general, because Deleuze argues that "if we're so oppressed, it's because our movement's being restricted, not because our eternal values are being violated. In barren times philosophy retreats to reflecting 'on' things. If it's not itself creating anything, what can it do but reflect on something? So it reflects on eternal or historical things, but can itself no longer make any move" (N, 122). In terms of this book, I have not wanted to reflect *on* Artaud's works, but rather engage *with* Artaud's writings in order to plea for an immanent religion of language in which life matters, that is, a zoological language that healthily and happily engages with the vitality of the agential materiality of language through practices of "crescive writing." Putting it differently, I hope that this book contributes, *with* Artaud's writings, to a revalorization of a language in movement that critically reconsiders our solid notions of normativity and productivity. If the reader finally judges Artaud as a madman, a patient, or a genius, I think that this is also a question of taste. What genuinely matters, and I hope, again, which this book can make its contribution to this revaluation, is that the reading of Artaud today stimulates the relevance, importance, and necessity to revalue, recreate, and reengage with a language in movement.

References

Alizart, Mark. *Pop Théologie*. Paris: PUF, 2015.
Allier, Chantal. "Avatars du Nom Propre dans le Trajectoire d'Antonin Artaud." *Essaim. Revue de Psychanalyse*. no. 38 (2006): 7–53.
Alliez, Éric. "The BwO Condition or, The Politics of Sensation." Eds. Joost de Bloois, Sjef Houppermans and Frans-Willem Korsten. *Discern(e)ments. Deleuzian Aesthetics/ Esthétiques deleuziennes*. Amsterdam: Rodopi, 2004, pp. 93–112.
Ansell-Pearson, Keith. "Deleuze and New Materialism: Naturalism, Normativity, and Ethics." Eds. Sarah Ellenzweig and John Zammito. *The New Politics of Materialism*. London: Routledge, 2017, pp. 88–109.
Ansell-Pearson, Keith. "Naturalism as a Joyful Science: Nietzsche, Deleuze, and the Art of Life." *Journal of Nietzsche Studies*. vol. 47. no. 1 (2016): 119–41.
Artaud, Antonin. *Artaud Anthology*. Trans. Daisy Aldan, David Rattray and others. Eds. Jack Hirschman. San Francisco: City Lights Books, 1965.
Artaud, Antonin. *Cahiers d'Ivry*. Ed. Évelyne Grossman. Paris: Gallimard, 2011.
Artaud, Antonin. *Œuvres*. Ed. Évelyne Grossman. Paris: Quarto, 2004b.
Artaud, Antonin. *Œuvres Complètes. Tome I. Volume 1. Préambule—Adresse au Pape—Adresse au Dalaï-Lama—Correspondance avec Jacques Rivière—L'Ombilic des Limbes—Le Pèse-nerfs suivi des Fragments d'un Journal d'Enfer—L'Art et la mort— Premiers poèmes (1913-1923)—Premières proses—Tric Trac du ciel—Bilboquet— Poèmes (1924-1935) Textes surréalistes*. Ed. Paule Thévenin. Paris: Gallimard, 1976a.
Artaud, Antonin. *Œuvres Complètes. Tome I. Volume 2. Lettres. Appendice*. Ed. Paule Thévenin. Paris: Gallimard, 1970.
Artaud, Antonin. *Œuvres Complètes. Tome II. Théâtre Alfred Jarry—Une pantomime— Un argument pour la scène—Deux projets de mise en scène—Notes sur les tricheurs de Steve Passeur—Comptes rendus—À propos d'une pièce perdue—À propos de la littérature et des arts plastiques*. Ed. Paule Thévenin. Paris: Gallimard, 1961a.
Artaud, Antonin. *Œuvres Complètes. Tome III. Scenarii—À propos du cinéma—Lettres— Interviews*. Ed. Paule Thévenin. Paris: Gallimard, 1961b.
Artaud, Antonin. *Œuvres Complètes. Tome IV. Le théâtre et son double—Le théâtre de Séraphin—Les Cenci*. Ed. Paule Thévenin. Paris: Gallimard, 1964a.
Artaud, Antonin. *Œuvres Complètes. Tome V. Autour du Théâtre et son Double et des Cenci*. Ed. Paule Thévenin. Paris: Gallimard, 1964b.
Artaud, Antonin. *Œuvres Complètes. Tome VI. Le Moine de Lewis raconté par Antonin Artaud*. Ed. Paule Thévenin. Paris: Gallimard, 1966.
Artaud, Antonin. *Œuvres Complètes. Tome VII. Héliogabale ou l'Anarchiste couronné. Les Nouvelles Révélations de l'Être*. Ed. Paule Thévenin. Paris: Gallimard, 1982a.

Artaud, Antonin. Œuvres Complètes. Tome VIII. De Quelques Problèmes D'Actualité aux Messages Révolutionnaires. Lettres de Mexique. Ed. Paule Thévenin. Paris: Gallimard, 1971a.

Artaud, Antonin. Œuvres Complètes. Tome IX. Les Tarahumaras—Lettres de Rodez. Ed. Paule Thévenin. Paris: Gallimard, 1979.

Artaud, Antonin. Œuvres Complètes. Tome X. Lettres écrites de Rodez (1943–1944). Ed. Paule Thévenin. Paris: Gallimard, 1974a.

Artaud, Antonin. Œuvres Complètes. Tome XI. Lettres écrites de Rodez (1945–1946). Ed. Paule Thévenin. Paris: Gallimard, 1974b.

Artaud, Antonin. Œuvres Complètes. Tome XII. Artaud le Mômo. Ci-gît précédé de la Culture Indienne. Ed. Paule Thévenin. Paris: Gallimard, 1971b.

Artaud, Antonin. Œuvres Complètes. Tome XIII. Van Gogh le suicidé de la société. Pour en finir avec le jugement de dieu suivi de Le Théâtre de la cruauté. Lettres à propos de pour en finir avec le jugement de dieu. Ed. Paule Thévenin. Paris: Gallimard, 1974c.

Artaud, Antonin. Œuvres Complètes. Tome XIV. Volume 1. Suppôts et suppliciations. Ed. Paule Thévenin. Paris: Gallimard, 1978a.

Artaud, Antonin. Œuvres Complètes. Tome XIV. Volume 2. Suppôts et suppliciations. Ed. Paule Thévenin. Paris: Gallimard, 1978b.

Artaud, Antonin. Œuvres Complètes. Tome XV. Cahiers de Rodez (Février-Avril 1945). Ed. Paule Thévenin. Paris: Gallimard, 1981a.

Artaud, Antonin. Œuvres Complètes. Tome XVI. Cahiers de Rodez (Mai-Juin 1945). Ed. Paule Thévenin. Paris: Gallimard, 1981b.

Artaud, Antonin. Œuvres Complètes. Tome XVII. Cahiers de Rodez (Juillet-Août 1945). Ed. Paule Thévenin. Paris: Gallimard, 1982b.

Artaud, Antonin. Œuvres Complètes. Tome XVIII. Cahiers de Rodez (Septembre-Novembre 1945). Ed. Paule Thévenin. Paris: Gallimard, 1983.

Artaud, Antonin. Œuvres Complètes. Tome XIX. Cahiers de Rodez (Décembre 1945–Janvier 1946). Ed. Paule Thévenin. Paris: Gallimard, 1984a.

Artaud, Antonin. Œuvres Complètes. Tome XX. Cahiers de Rodez (Février-Mars 1946). Ed. Paule Thévenin. Paris: Gallimard, 1984b.

Artaud, Antonin. Œuvres Complètes. Tome XXI. Cahiers de Rodez (Avril-25 Mai 1946). Ed. Paule Thévenin. Paris: Gallimard, 1985.

Artaud, Antonin. Œuvres Complètes. Tome XXII. Cahiers du retour à Paris (26 Mai-Août 1946). Ed. Paule Thévenin. Paris: Gallimard, 1986.

Artaud, Antonin. Œuvres Complètes. Tome XXIII. Cahiers du retour à Paris (Août-Septembre 1946). Ed. Paule Thévenin. Paris: Gallimard, 1987.

Artaud, Antonin. Œuvres Complètes. Tome XXIV. Cahiers du retour à Paris (Octobre-Novembre 1946). Ed. Paule Thévenin. Paris: Gallimard, 1988.

Artaud, Antonin. Œuvres Complètes. Tome XXV. Cahiers du retour à Paris (Décembre 1946-Janvier 1947). Ed. Paule Thévenin. Paris: Gallimard, 1990.

Artaud, Antonin. Œuvres Complètes. Tome XXVI. Histoire vécue d'Artaud-Mômo. Tête à tête. Ed. Paule Thévenin. Paris: Gallimard, 1994.

Artaud, Antonin. *Collected Works*. Trans. Victor Corti. Vol. 1. Parchment: River Run Press, 1968.
Artaud, Antonin. *50 Dessins pour Assassiner la Magie*. Paris: Gallimard, 2004a.
Artaud, Antonin. *Le Théâtre et son Double*. 1938. Paris: Gallimard, 2008.
Artaud, Antonin. *Lettres. 1937–1943*. Ed. Serge Malaussena. Paris: Gallimard, 2015.
Artaud, Antonin. *Lettres à Génica Athanasiou*. Paris: Gallimard, 1969.
Artaud, Antonin. *Nouveaux Écrits de Rodez. Lettres au Docteur Ferdière 1943–1946 et Autres Textes Inédits*. Paris: Gallimard, 1977.
Artaud, Antonin. "Pour en Finir avec le Jugement de Dieu." 1947. *Antonin Artaud*, Andre Dimanche/INA, 1995a.
Artaud, Antonin. *Selected Writings*. Trans. Helen Weaver. Ed. Susan Sontag. California: University of California Press, 1976b.
Artaud, Antonin. *The Theatre and Its Double*. Trans. Mary Caroline Richards. New York: Grove Press, 1958.
Artaud, Antonin. *Watchfiends and Rack Screams: Works from the Final Period*. Trans. Clayton Eshleman. Boston: Exact Change, 1995b.
Austin, John. *How to Do Things with Words*. Oxford: Oxford University Press, 1962.
Bäckius, Per. "Other Work: A Dividual Enterprise." *Ephemera*. vol. 2. no. 4 (2002): 281–93.
Bailly, Jean-Christophe. *L'Infini Dehors de la Voix*. Marseille: André Dimanche, 1995.
Barad, Karen. "Posthumanist Performativity: Toward an Understanding of How Matter Comes to Matter." *Signs*. vol. 28. no. 3 (2003): 801–31.
Barber, Stephen. *Antonin Artaud: Blows and Bombs*. London: Faber and Faber, 1993.
Barber, Stephen. *Antonin Artaud: Terminal Curses*. Chicago: Solar Books, 2008.
Barber, Stephen. *The Screaming Body*. London: Creation Books, 1999.
Beaulieu, Alain. "L'Expérience Deleuzienne du Corps." *Revue Internationale de Philosophie*. vol. 4. no. 222 (2002): 511–22.
Beck, Heather. *Teaching Creative Writing*. Basingstoke: Macmillan, 2012.
Belhaj Kacem, Mehdi. *Artaud et la Théorie du Complot*. Auch: Tristram, 2015.
Belhaj Kacem, Mehdi and Philippe Nassif. *Pop Philosophie. Entretiens*. Paris: Denoël, 2005.
Bensmaïa, Réda. "From Kafka to Kateb Yacine: The Concept of Minor Literature." Eds. Constantin Boundas and Dorothea Olkowski. *Gilles Deleuze and the Theater of Philosophy*. London: Routledge, 1994, pp. 213–28.
Benveniste, Émile. *Problems in General Linguistics*. 1966. Trans. Mary Elizabeth Meek. Coral Gables: University of Miami Press, 1971.
Bermel, André. *Artaud's Theatre of Cruelty*. London: Bloomsbury, 2014.
Blanchot, Maurice. *L'Écriture du Désastre*. Paris: Gallimard, 1980.
Blanchot, Maurice. *L'Entretien Infini*. Paris: Gallimard, 1969.
Blanchot, Maurice. *Le Livre à Venir*. 1959. Paris: Gallimard, 1986.
Blanchot, Maurice. *The Book to Come*. Trans. Charlotte Mandell. Stanford: Stanford University Press, 2003.

Blanchot, Maurice. *The Infinite Conversation*. Trans. Susan Hanson. Minneapolis: University of Minnesota Press, 1993.
Blanchot, Maurice. *The Writing of the Disaster*. 1986. Trans. Ann Smock. Nebraska: University of Nebraska Press, 1995.
Boeri, Marcelo. "The Stoics on Bodies and Incorporeals." *The Review of Metaphysics*. vol. 54. no. 4 (2001): 723–52.
Bogue, Ronald. *Deleuze on Cinema*. London: Routledge, 2003a.
Bogue, Ronald. *Deleuze on Literature*. London: Routledge, 2003b.
Bogue, Ronald. *Deleuze on Music, Painting and the Arts*. London: Routledge, 2003c.
Bogue, Ronald. "Deleuze's Style." *Man and World*. vol. 29. no. 3 (1996): 251–68.
Bogue, Ronald. *Deleuze's Way. Essays in Transverse Ethics and Ethics*. London: Routledge, 2007.
Bogue, Ronald. "Gilles Deleuze: The Aesthetics of Force." *Journal of the British Society for Phenomenology*. vol. 24 (1994): 56–65.
Bogue, Ronald. "Nature, Law and Chaosmopolitanism." Eds. Rosi Braidotti and Patricia Pisters. *Revisiting Normativity with Deleuze*. London: Bloomsbury, 2012, pp. 98–112.
Bogue, Ronald. "To Choose to Choose—To Believe in This World." *CiNéMAS*. vol. 16. no. 2/3 (2006): 32–52.
Bogue, Ronald. "Word, Image and Sound." *Mimesis, Semiosis and Power*. vol. 2 (1991): 77–97.
Bousquet, Joë. *Le Meneur de Lune*. 1946. Paris: Albin Michel, 2006.
Bousseyroux, Nicole. "La Passion d'Antonin Artaud." *L'en-je lacanien*. vol. 2. no. 7 (2006): 125–33.
Bouthors-Paillart, Catherine. *Antonin Artaud. L'Énonciation ou l'Épreuve de la Cruauté*. Paris: Droz, 1977.
Braidotti, Rosi. "Animals, Anomalies, and Inorganic Others." *PMLA*. vol. 124. no. 2 (2009): 526–32.
Braidotti, Rosi. "Nomadic Ethics." Eds. Daniel Smith and Henry Somers-Hall. *The Cambridge Companion to Deleuze*. Cambridge: Cambridge University Press, 2012, pp. 170–97.
Braidotti, Rosi. *Nomadic Subjects. Embodiment and Sexual Difference in Contemporary Feminist Theory*. New York: Columbia University Press, 2011b.
Braidotti, Rosi. *Nomadic Theory*. New York: Columbia University Press, 2011a.
Braidotti, Rosi. "The Ethics of Becoming Imperceptible." Ed. Constantin Boundas. *Deleuze and Philosophy*. Edinburgh: Edinburgh University Press, 2006b, pp. 133–59.
Braidotti, Rosi. *The Posthuman*. Cambridge: Polity Press, 2013.
Braidotti, Rosi. *Transpositions: On Nomadic Ethics*. Cambridge: Polity Press, 2006a.
Braidotti, Rosi and Rick Dolphijn (eds). *This Deleuzian Century*. Leiden: Brill/Rodopi, 2015.
Brillenburg Wurth, Kiene. "Creation." Eds. Mercedes Bunz, Birgit Kaiser and Kathrin Thiele. *Symptoms of the Planetary Condition: A Critical Vocabulary*. Lüneberg: meson press, 2017b, pp. 37–42.

Brillenburg Wurth, Kiene. "Creative Writing." Eds. Mads Rosendahl Thomsen, Lasse Horne Kjældgaard, Lis Møller, Lilian Munk Rüsing, Peter Simonsen and Dan Ringgaard. *Literature: An Introduction to Theory and Analysis*. London: Bloomsbury, 2017a, pp. 373–84.

Brown, William. "Cognitive Deleuze." *Cinema. Journal for Philosophy and Moving Image*. vol. 1. no. 1 (2010): 134–41.

Brun, Anne. "Corps, Création et Psychose à Partir l'Œuvre d'Artaud." *Cliniques Méditerranéennes*. vol. 80 (2009): 143–58.

Buchanan, Ian and Adrian Parr (eds). *Deleuze and the Contemporary World*. Edinburgh: Edinburgh University Press, 2006.

Buchanan, Ian and Lorna Collins (eds). *Deleuze and the Schizoanalysis of Visual Art*. London: Bloomsbury, 2014.

Buchanan, Ian, Tim Matts and Aiden Tynan (eds). *Deleuze and the Schizoanalysis of Literature*. London: Bloomsbury, 2015.

Bunz, Mercedes. "Capital." Eds. Mercedes Bunz, Birgit Kaiser and Kathrin Thiele. *Symptoms of the Planetary Condition: A Critical Vocabulary*. Lüneberg: meson press, 2017, pp. 31–6.

Bunz, Mercedes, Birgit Kaiser and Kathrin Thiele (eds). *Symptoms of the Planetary Condition: A Critical Vocabulary*. Lüneberg: meson press, 2017.

Carroll, Lewis. *Alice's Adventures in Wonderland & through the Looking-Glass*. 1865/1872. London: Wordsworth, 2001.

Chalosse, Marc. "Artaud Remix." *Europe*. no. 873–874 (2002): 246–54.

Citton, Yves. *L'Avenir des Humanités. Économie de la Connaissance ou Cultures de l'Interprétation?* Paris: La Découverte, 2010.

Colebrook, Claire. *Gilles Deleuze*. 2002. London: Routledge, 2010.

Colebrook, Claire. *Irony*. London: Routledge, 2004.

Colebrook, Claire. *Understanding Deleuze*. Crows Nest: Allen & Unwin, 2002.

Dale, Catherine. "Cruel. Antonin Artaud and Gilles Deleuze." Ed. Brian Massumi. *A Shock to Thought: Expression after Deleuze and Guattari*. London: Routledge, 2002, pp. 85–100.

Dale, Catherine. "Knowing One's Enemy: Deleuze, Artaud, and the Problem of Judgement." Ed. Mary Bryden. *Deleuze and Religion*. London: Routledge, 2001, pp. 126–37.

Danchin, Laurent and André Roumieux. *Artaud et l'Asile*. Paris: Séguier, 2015.

De Mèredieu, Florence. *Antonin Artaud. Voyages*. Paris: Blusson, 1992.

De Mèredieu, Florence de. *Sur l'Électrochoc. Le Cas Antonin Artaud*. Paris: Blusson, 1996.

DeLacy, Phillip. "Stoics Views of Poetry." *The American Journal of Philology*. vol. 69. no. 3 (1948): 241–71.

DeLanda, Manuel. "Deleuze, Mathematics, and Realist Ontology." Ed. Constantin Boundas. *Deleuze and Philosophy*. Edinburgh: Edinburgh University Press, 2006b, pp. 220–38.

Delany, Samuel. *Longer Views: Extended Essays*. Hannover: Wesleyan University Press, 2012.

Deleuze, Gilles. *Critique et Clinique*. Paris: Minuit, 1993.

Deleuze, Gilles. *Essays Critical and Clinical*. Trans. Daniel Smith and Michael Greco. London: Verso, 1998.

Deleuze, Gilles. *Expressionism in Philosophy: Spinoza*. Trans. Martin Joughin. New York: Urzone, 1990a.

Deleuze, Gilles. *Francis Bacon. Logique de la Sensation*. 2002. Paris: Seuil, 1981a.

Deleuze, Gilles. *Francis Bacon: The Logic of Sensation*. Trans. Daniel Smith. London: Continuum, 2003.

Deleuze, Gilles. *L'Image-Temps*. Paris: Minuit, 1985.

Deleuze, Gilles. *Logique du Sens*. Paris: Minuit, 1969.

Deleuze, Gilles. *Negotiations. 1972–1990*. Trans. Martin Joughin. New York: Columbia University Press, 1995.

Deleuze, Gilles. *Nietzsche*. Paris: PUF, 1965.

Deleuze, Gilles. *Pourparlers. 1972–1990*. Paris: Minuit, 1990b.

Deleuze, Gilles. *Pure Immanence: Essays on a Life*. Trans. Anne Boyman. New York: Urzone, 2001.

Deleuze, Gilles. *Spinoza et le Problème de l'Expression*. Paris: Gallimard, 1968.

Deleuze, Gilles. *Spinoza. Philosophie Pratique*. Paris: Minuit, 1981b.

Deleuze, Gilles. *Spinoza: Practical Philosophy*. Trans. Robert Hurley. San Francisco: City Lights Books, 1988.

Deleuze, Gilles. *The Logic of Sense*. Trans. Mark Lester. London: Continuum, 1990c.

Deleuze, Gilles. *The Time-Image*. Trans. Hugh Tomlinson and Robert Galeta. London: Continuum, 1989.

Deleuze, Gilles and Claire Parnet. *Dialogues*. 1977. Paris: Champs, 1996.

Deleuze, Gilles and Claire Parnet. *Dialogues II*. 1987. Trans. Hugh Tomlinson and Barbara Habberjam. New York: Cambridge University Press, 2007.

Deleuze, Gilles and Félix Guattari. *A Thousand Plateaus*. 1987. Trans. Brian Massumi. London: Continuum, 1988.

Deleuze, Gilles and Félix Guattari. *Anti-Oedipus*. 1977. Trans. Robert Hurley, Mark Seem and Helen Lane. London: Continuum, 1984.

Deleuze, Gilles and Félix Guattari. *Kafka. Pour une Littérature Mineure*. Paris: Minuit, 1975.

Deleuze, Gilles and Félix Guattari. *Kafka. Toward a Minor Literature*. Trans. Dana Polan. Minneapolis: University of Minneapolis Press, 1986.

Deleuze, Gilles and Félix Guattari. *L'Anti-Œdipe*. Paris: Minuit, 1972.

Deleuze, Gilles and Félix Guattari. *Mille Plateaux*. Paris: Minuit, 1980.

Deleuze, Gilles and Félix Guattari. *Qu'est-ce que la Philosophie?* Paris: Minuit, 1991.

Deleuze, Gilles and Félix Guattari. *What Is Philosophy?* Trans. Graham Burchell and Hugh Tomlinson. London: Verso, 1994.

Derrida, Jacques. "Artaud, oui ...." *Europe*. no. 873–874 (2002): 23–38.

Derrida, Jacques. *Dissemination*. 1972. Trans. Barbara Johnson. London: The Athlone Press, 1981.

Derrida, Jacques. *L'Écriture et la Différence*. Paris: Seuil, 1967.

Derrida, Jacques. *La Dissémination*. Paris: Seuil, 1972.

Derrida, Jacques. *Writing and Difference*. 1967. Trans. Alan Bass. Chicago: Chicago University Press, 1978.

Dolphijn, Rick. "'Man Is Ill Because He Is Badly Constructed': Artaud, Klossowski and Deleuze in Search for the Earth Inside." *Deleuze Studies*. vol. 5. no. 1 (2011): 18–34.

Dolphijn, Rick and Iris van der Tuin. "A Thousand Tiny Intersections: Linguisticism, Feminism, Racism and Deleuzian Becomings." Eds. Arun Saldanha and Jason Adams. *Deleuze and Race*. Edinburgh: Edinburgh University Press, 2013, pp. 129–43.

Dolphijn, Rick and Iris van der Tuin. *New Materialism: Interviews and Cartographies*. Ann Arbor: Michigan University Press, 2012.

Dolphijn, Rick and Iris van der Tuin. "Pushing Dualism to an Extreme: On the Philosophical Impetus of a New Materialism." *Continental Philosophy Review*. vol. 44. no. 4 (2011): 383–400.

Dumoulié, Camille. "Artaud, la Vie." *Europe*. no. 873–874 (2002): 39–44.

Dumoulié, Camille. *Artaud, la Vie*. Paris: Éditions Desjonquères, 2003.

Eckerley, Andrea. "The Event of Painting." Eds. Ian Buchanan and Lorna Collins. *Deleuze and the Schizoanalysis of Visual Art*. London: Bloomsbury, 2014, pp. 205–26.

Esslin, Martin. *Antonin Artaud. The Man and His Work*. London: Calder Publications, 1999.

Fox, Nick. "Refracting 'Health:' Deleuze, Guattari and Body-Self." *Health. Journal for the Social Study of Health, Illness and Medicine*. vol. 6. no. 3 (2002): 347–63.

Galibert, Thierry (eds). *Antonin Artaud. Écrivain du Sud*. Saint-Rémy-de-Provence: Édisud, 2002.

Garner, Stanton. "Artaud, Germ Theory, and the Theatre of Contagion." *Theatre Journal*. vol. 58. no. 1 (2006): 1–14.

Gaze, Tim. "Asemic." http://www.asemic.net/. Last accessed August 15, 2017.

Gaze, Tim and Michael Jacobson. *An Anthology of Asemic Handwriting*. The Hague: Uitgeverij, 2013.

Genosko, Gary. *Félix Guattari. A Critical Introduction*. London: Pluto Press, 2009.

Goddard, Michael. "Felix and Alice in Wonderland: The Encounter between Guattari and Berardi and the Post-Media Era." Eds. Clemens Apprich, Josephine Slater, Anthony Iles and Oliver Schultz. *Provocative Alloys: A Post-Media Anthology*. Berlin: Mute Books, 2013, pp. 44–61.

Goodall, Jane. *Artaud and the Gnostic Drama*. Oxford: Clarendon Press, 1994.

Graham, Mort. "Transcultural Writing and Research." Eds. Jeri Kroll and Graeme Harper. *Research Methods in Creative Writing*. Basingstoke: Macmillan, 2012, pp. 201–22.

Grossman, Évelyne. *Antonin Artaud. "Aliéné Authentique."* Tours: Farrago/Scheer, 2003a.
Grossman, Évelyne. *Éloge de l'Hypersensible.* Paris: Minuit, 2017.
Grossman, Évelyne. *La Défiguration. Artaud, Beckett, Michaux.* Paris: Minuit, 2003b.
Grossman, Évelyne. *L'Angoisse de Penser.* Paris: Minuit, 2008.
Grossman, Évelyne and Jacob Rogozinski. "Deleuze Lecteur d'Artaud – Artaud Lecteur de Deleuze." *Rue Descartes.* no. 59 (2008): 78–91.
Guattari, Félix. *Chaosophy. Texts and Interviews 1972–1977.* Trans. David Sweet, Jarred Becker and Taylor Adkins. Los Angeles: Semiotext(e), 2009a.
Guattari, Félix. *Qu'est-ce que l'Écosophie?* Fécamp: lignes/imec, 2013.
Guattari, Félix. *Soft Subversions. Texts and Interviews 1977–1985.* Trans. Chet Wiener and Emily Wittman. Los Angeles: Semiotext(e), 2009b.
Guattari, Félix. *The Machinic Unconscious. Essays in Schizoanalysis.* 1979. Trans. Taylor Adkins. Los Angeles: Semiotext(e), 2011.
Guattari, Félix. *The Three Ecologies.* 1989. Trans. Ian Pindar and Paul Sutton. London: Continuum, 2008.
Halimi, Carole. "La 'Sensation Magique' du Tableau Vivant ou La Recherche d'une Image Active." Eds. Frank Kessler, Jean-Marc Larrue and Giusy Pisano. *Machines. Magie. Médias.* Villeneuve d'Asq: PU de Septentrion, 2018, pp. 383–98.
Holland, Eugene. *Baudelaire and Schizoanalysis. The Sociopoetics of Modernism.* Cambridge: Cambridge University Press, 1993.
Holland, Eugene. *Deleuze and Guattari's* Anti Oedipus. *An Introduction to Schizoanalysis.* London: Routledge, 1999.
Isou, Isidore. "Antonin Artaud Torturé par les Psychiatres." *Lettrisme.* no. 13 (1970): 5–130.
Jannarone, Kimberley. *Artaud and His Doubles.* Ann Arbor: Michigan University Press, 2012.
Jones, Andy. *Artaud and Strasberg. A Quest for Reality.* Los Angeles: L.P.I., 2008.
Jugnon, Alain. *Folie & Poésie Selon Deleuze et Guattari.* Fécamp: lignes, 2018.
Justaert, Kristien. *Theology after Deleuze.* London: Continuum, 2012.
Knapp, Bettina. "A New Type of Magic." *Yale French Studies.* no. 31 (1964): 87–98.
Kyriakou, Poulheria. "Aristotle's 'Poetics' and Stoic Literary Theory." *Rheinisches Museum für Philologie.* vol. 140. no. 3/4 (1997): 257–80.
Lambert, Gregg. *Who's Afraid of Deleuze and Guattari?* London: Continuum, 2006.
Le Clézio, Jean-Marie. *The Mexican Dream, or, The Interrupted Thought of Amerindian Civilizations.* 1988. Trans. Teresa Lavender Fagan. Chicago: University of Chicago Press, 1993.
Lefebvre, Thierry. "La Genèse Pharmacologique d'une Œuvre Antonin Artaud." *Revue d'Histoire de la Pharmacie.* no. 334 (2002): 271–84.
Lotringer, Sylvère. *Mad Like Artaud.* Trans. Joanna Spinks. Minneapolis: Univocal, 2015.

Madanes, Leiser. "How to Undo Things with Words: Spinoza's Criterion for Limiting Freedom of Expression." *History of Philosophy Quarterly*. vol. 9. no. 4 (1992): 401–8.

Marange, Valérie. "Écosophie ou Barbarie." 2006. *Ecorev' Revue Critique d'Écologie Politique*, http://ecorev.org/spip.php?article501. Last accessed August 15, 2017.

Massumi, Brian. *A Shock to Thought. Expression after Deleuze and Guattari*. London: Routledge, 2002a.

Massumi, Brian. *Parables for the Virtual. Movement, Affect, Sensation*. Durham/London: Duke University Press, 2002b.

Mayers, Tim. "One Simple Word: From Creative Writing to Creative Writing Studies." *College English*. vol. 71. no. 3 (2009): 217–28.

Memon, Arsalan. "Un-Marking and Re-Marking the Borders between Humanity and Animality: Towards Understanding Corporeal Differentiality." *The Society for the Study of Difference*. no. 45 (2006): 1–29.

Mengue, Philippe. *Faire l'Idiot. La Politique de Deleuze*. Paris: Germina, 2013.

Migone, Christof. *Sonic Somatic: Performance of the Unsound Body*. Los Angeles: Errant Bodies Press, 2012.

Milon, Alain. *L'Écriture de Soi, Ce Lointain Intérieur. Moments d'Hospitalité Littéraire Autour d'Antonin Artaud*. Fougères: Encre Marine, 2005.

Milon, Alain. *Sous La Langue. La Réalité en Folie*. Fougères: Encre Marine, 2016.

Murray, Ros. *Antonin Artaud. The Scum of the Soul*. London: Palgrave Macmillan, 2014.

Murray, Ros. "Des Corps Qui Agissent: Langage et Magie dans les Sorts d'Antonin Artaud." Eds. Pierre Zoberman, Anne Tomiche and William Spurlin. *Écritures du Corps: Nouvelles Perspectives*. Paris: Classiques Garnier, 2013, pp. 113–28.

Neyrat, Frédéric. *Instructions pour une Prise d'Âmes. Artaud et l'Envoûtement Occidental*. Strasbourg: La Phocide, 2009.

Nietzsche, Friedrich. *Götzen-Dämmerung, oder, Wie mann mit dem Hammer philosophiert*. 1889. Friedrich Nietzsche, *Werke in zwei Bänden (Band II)*. München: Carl Hanser Verlag, 1979, pp. 325–97.

Nietzsche, Friedrich. *Thus Spoke Zarathustra. A Book for All and None*. 1891. Trans. Adrian Del Caro. Cambridge: Cambridge University Press, 2006.

Nietzsche, Friedrich. *Twilight of Idols, or, How to Philosophize with a Hammer*. 1889. Trans. Duncan Large. Oxford: Oxford University Press, 1998.

O'Sullivan, Simon. "From Stuttering and Stammering to the Diagram: Deleuze, Bacon and Contemporary Art Practice." *Deleuze Studies*. vol. 3. no. 2 (2009): 247–58.

Oenen, Gijs van. *Nu even niet! Over de Interpassieve Samenleving*. Amsterdam: Van Gennep, 2011.

Oosterling, Henk and Arend Prins (eds). *La Chair. Het Vlees in Filosofie en Kunst*, special issue of *Rotterdamse Filosofische Studies*. vol. 8, 1988.

Pelias, Ronald. *Performative: An Alphabet of Performative Writing*. 2014. New York: Routledge, 2016.

Penot-Lacassagne, Olivier. "Singularité d'Antonin Artaud." *Europe*. no. 873–874 (2002): 104–14.

Penot-Lacassagne, Olivier. *Vies et Morts d'Antonin Artaud*. Paris: CNRS, 2007.
Pollock, Della. "Performing Writing." Eds. Peggy Phelan and Jill Lane. *The Ends of Performance*. New York: New York University Press, 1998, pp. 73–103.
Poulet, Elisabeth. "Les Filles de Cœur d'Antonin Artaud." 2008. *La Revue des Ressources*, http://www.larevuedesressources.org/les-filles-de-coeur-d-antonin-artaud,636.html. Last accessed August 15, 2017.
Prevel, Jacques. *En Compagnie d'Antonin Artaud*. 1974. Paris: Flammarion, 1993.
Protevi, John. "Deleuze and Life." Ed. Constantin Boundas. *Deleuze and Philosophy*. Edinburgh: Edinburgh University Press, 2006b, pp. 239–64.
Protevi, John. *Life, War, Earth: Deleuze and the Sciences*. Minneapolis: University of Minnesota Press, 2013.
Protevi, John. *Political Affect: Connecting the Social and the Somatic*. Minneapolis: University of Minnesota Press, 2009.
Protevi, John. *Political Physics: Deleuze, Derrida and the Body Politics*. London: The Athlone Press, 2001b.
Protevi, John. "The Organism as the Judgement of God: Aristotle, Kant and Deleuze on Nature (That Is, on Biology, Theology and Politics)." Ed. Mary Brydon. *Deleuze and Religion*. London: Routledge, 2001a, pp. 30–41.
Rey-Debove, Josette and Alain Rey. *Le Nouveau Petit Robert de la Langue Française*. Paris: Dictionnaires Le Robert, 2006.
Rahimy, Tina. "The Minor Philosopher: The Political-Philosophical Relevance of Incomprehension." Eds. Rosi Braidotti and Patricia Pisters. *Revisiting Normativity with Deleuze*. London: Bloomsbury, 2012, pp. 145–58.
Savan, David. "Spinoza and Language." *The Philosophical Review*. vol. 67. no. 2 (1958): 212–25.
Schafer, David. *Antonin Artaud*. London: Reaktion Books, 2016.
Serres, Michel. *Biogea*. 2010. Trans. Randolph Burks. Minneapolis: Univocal, 2012.
Serres, Michel. *Biogée*. 2010. Paris: Le Pommier, 2013.
Serres, Michel. "Information and Thinking." Trans. Joeri Visser. Eds. Rosi Braidotti and Rick Dolphijn. *Philosophy After Nature*. London: Rowman & Littlefield, 2017, pp. 13–20.
Serres, Michel. *La Légende des Anges*. Paris: Champs, 1999a.
Serres, Michel. *Le Contrat Naturel*. 1990. Paris: Champs, 2009.
Serres, Michel. *The Natural Contract*. 1990. Trans. Elizabeth MacArthur and William Paulson. Ann Arbor: Michigan University Press, 1995.
Serres, Michel. *Variations sur le Corps*. Paris: Le Pommier, 1999b.
Siccama, Wilma. *Het Waarnemend Lichaam. Zintuiglijkheid en Representatie bij Beckett en Artaud*. Nijmegen: Vantilt, 2000.
Simms, Karl (ed.). *Critical Studies. Ethics and the Subject*. Amsterdam: Rodopi, 1997.
Sollers, Philippe. *L'Écriture et l'Expérience des Limites*. Paris: Seuil, 1968.
Solomon, Eldra, Linda Berg and Diana Martin. *Biology*. 7th edition. Belmont: Brooks/Cole-Thomson Learning, 2005.

Spinoza, Baruch de. *Ethica*. 1677. Trans. Henri Krop. Amsterdam: Bert Bakker, 2006.
Spinoza, Baruch de. *The Ethics*. 1677. Trans. Robert Elwes. Vancouver: ISWB, 1883.
Stecopoulos, Eleni. *Visceral Poetics*. Berkeley: ON Contemporary Practice, 2016.
Stivale, Charles. *Gilles Deleuze's ABCs: The Folds of Friendship*. Baltimore: The Johns Hopkins University Press, 2008.
Taverniers, Miriam. "Hjelmslev's Semiotic Model of Language. An Exegesis." *Semiotica*. no. 171 (2008): 367–94.
Tedlow, Richard and Geoffrey Jones (eds). *The Rise and Fall of Mass Media*. New York: Routledge, 2014.
Thévenin, Paule. *Antonin Artaud, Ce Désespéré qui Vous Parle*. Paris: Seuil, 1993.
Thiher, Allen. "Jacques Derrida's Reading of Artaud: 'La Parole Soufflée' and 'La Clôture de la Représentation.'" *The French Review*. vol. 57. no. 4 (1984): 503–8.
Tinnell, John. "Transversalising the Ecological Turn: Four Components of Felix Guattari's Ecosophical Perspective." *The Fibreculture Journal*. no. 18 (2011): 35–64.
Tomiche, Anne. "Artaud et les Langues." *Europe*. no. 873–874 (2002): 141–53.
Tomiche, Anne. "Glossolalies: du Sacré au Poétique." *Revue de littérature comparée*. vol. 305. no. 1 (2003): 61–72.
Tomiche, Anne. "Glossopoïèses." *L'Esprit Créateur*. vol. 38. no. 4 (1998): 38–51.
Tomiche, Anne. *"L'Intraduisible Dont Je Suis Fait." Artaud et les Avant-Gardes Occidentales*. Paris: Le Manuscrit, 2012.
Tuin, Iris van der. "'A Different Starting Point, a Different Metaphysics': Reading Bergson and Barad Diffractively." *Hypatia*. vol. 26. no. 1 (2011): 22–42.
Tuin, Iris van der. *Generational Feminism: New Materialist Introduction to a Generative Approach*. Lanham: Lexington Books, 2015.
Valazza, Nicolas. "Antonin Artaud et l'Essouflement du Lógos." *Working Papers in Romance Languages*. vol. 1. no. 1 (2006): 1–11.
Veillard, Christelle. *Les Stoïciens. Une Philosophie de l'Exigence*. Paris: Ellipses, 2017.
Venet, Emmanuel. *Ferdière, Psychiatre d'Antonin Artaud*. Lagrasse: Verdier, 2014.
Virmaux, Alain. *Antonin Artaud et le Théâtre*. Paris: Seghers, 1970.
Virmaux, Alain and Odette Virmaux. *Antonin Artaud. Qui êtes-vous ?* Lyon: La Manufacture, 1996.
Visser, Joeri. "The Healing Practices of Language." Eds. Rosi Braidotti and Rick Dolphijn. *This Deleuzian Century*. Leiden: Brill/Rodopi, 2015, pp. 115–46.
Weiss, Allen. *Perverse Desire and the Ambiguous Icon*. New York: University of New York Press, 1994.
Yadin, Azzan. "A Web of Chaos: Bialik and Nietzsche on Language, Truth, and the Death of God." *Prooftexts*. vol. 21. no. 2 (2001): 179–203.
Zaoui, Pierre. *La Traversée des Catastrophes. Philosophie pour le Meilleur et pour le Pire*. 2010. Paris: Seuil, 2013.
Zepke, Stephen. "From Aesthetic Autonomy to Autonomist Aesthetics: Art and Life in Guattari." Eds. Éric Alliez and Andrew Goffrey. *The Guattari Effect*. London: Continuum, 2011, pp. 205–19.

Index

absolute immanence 3, 7, 19–20, 22, 31–2, 39, 60, 63, 152, 154, 159
advanced capitalism 3, 12, 18–19, 39, 74, 146, 150–1, 157–8, 164
advanced civilization (Europe) 5–8, 11, 74–5, 78, 84–5, 149
affective language/writing 129, 157
affirmative language 15, 55, 61, 64, 101
"Alienation and Black Magic" (Artaud) 149
Alliez, Éric 25
"amor fati," attitude 34, 36, 113–14, 125–6, 131–2, 134, 136, 147, 155–6, 159
animated words, creation 60–2
"anti-rule rule" 10
"Antonin Artaud, or the Mexican Dream" (Le Clezio) 71
Artaud, Antonin xv, 1, 25, 97, 163. *See also* works/writings (Artaud)
    as creative/crescive writer xvii, xviii (*see also* creative writings/language; crescive writing)
    electroshock therapy 33, 69, 90
    as "hyper-Christian" 87
    loss of life 27
    Mexican experiences 4–6, 70, 75, 92, 115, 119, 147–8
    notebooks 6, 7–8, 10, 47, 99, 100, 101–2, 106, 114–26, 135–6, 145–6, 149, 157
    premature death 135
    problem with language 47 (*see also* language)
    return to Paris 67–8, 97–100
    sufferings 1–2, 76, 83, 112
    in the Surrealist movements 2
    with Tarahumaras Indians 4, 71–3, 78, 90, 110
    treatment/internments 2, 6, 8, 17, 33, 67, 70, 81–2, 84, 90, 145–50, 153, 163
    voyage to Ireland 6, 77–8, 81, 86

articulated language 67, 112, 119, 132, 134, 148
art of caution 54, 86, 106
    destratification and 51–3
    violating 77–81
asemic writing 131–2
Athanasiou, Génica 2, 29
auto-detoxification, practices 11, 17, 20, 26, 39–40, 46, 55, 61, 101, 134, 145–50, 163

Bachelard, Gaston 132
Bacon, Francis 21, 23–4, 30
    Deleuze's analysis of paintings 21–3, 30, 39, 136
Bailly, Jean-Christophe 104
Barad, Karen 11
Barber, Stephen 104–5, 117, 123
Bataille, Georges 17, 114
Benveniste, Émile 129–30
Berne-Joffroy, André 97–8, 135
bestialization (becoming-animal) 122
bewitchment 85–6, 136
Biogea (Serres) 152
Blanchot, Maurice 57, 153–4
Blin, Roger 103–4
body and language 9, 12, 15–16, 27, 38, 78, 86, 111, 124
    articulation of a vital 22–4
    belief in this world 19–20, 24
    BwO (*see* body without organs (BwO))
    and flesh 18, 21–2, 124
    flexional singularity of 16–18
    infra-sense expression 25–6, 30, 36, 62
    primitive language 33
body without organs (BwO) 22–4, 25–6, 30, 39, 78, 105–8, 117
    articulation 49, 51
    as "pure language-affect" 25
Bogue, Ronald 25–6, 46, 86
Bousquet, Joë 36
Bouthors-Paillart, Catherine 108

Braidotti, Rosi 20, 23, 29, 32, 34, 53, 62, 122, 154
  "amor fati" 34, 36, 63, 113–14
  "postsecular" society 156
  thresholds of sustainability 51–2, 54
  "zoe" 50, 55, 61, 64–5, 113
Breton, André 78, 81–2

Camus, Albert 47–8
Casarès, Maria 103
Catholicism 72, 87, 89, 105
The Cenci 4–5, 7, 109–10, 114, 133, 147
Chéron, Germaine 91
Christ 68, 75, 83
  Artaud's understanding of 79
  Catholicism 72, 87, 89, 105
  nature, principle 72
  "The True Story of Jesus Christ" 120–3, 125
Ciguri 60, 85
  as God 72, 75, 88, 101, 152
  healing practices of 76–7, 83
  vitality of 76, 86
commitment to life 26, 29–31
Committee of Friends of Antonin Artaud 97–8
Corti, Victor 56
The Creative Mind (Bergson) 129
creative writings/language xvii–xviii, 4, 9–10, 12, 16, 36, 38, 63–4, 97, 103, 126–8, 133–4, 137, 148
crescive writing 103, 106, 132–4, 137, 148–9, 152, 158–9, 165
critical textual analysis 9–10, 148
cruelty 25, 103, 107. *See also* theater of cruelty
  affective language of 157
  as healing practice 109–11
  as necessity and life 107–8, 113, 147, 155–6
  philosophical determinism 107
  realization of 156
  writing of (*see* writing of cruelty)
culture and life 88

Dale, Catherine 79, 91, 107
Dance of the Peyote (Tarahumaras) 72–3, 77–8, 99, 110, 147

Danchin, Laurent 98
Dark Night of the Soul (John) 73
DeLacy, Phillip 111, 115
DeLanda, Manuel 16
Delany, Samuel 126–7
Deleuze, Gilles xvii–xviii, 10, 15–16, 19, 25–6, 30–1, 34–5, 38, 49, 51–3, 73, 78, 86, 122, 136, 156
  act of thinking 154
  belief in this world 18–21, 30, 36, 86, 154
  body and language (*see* body and language)
  Francis Bacon: The Logic of Sensation 21–4
  "The Intercessors" xvii, 164–5
  literature as enterprise of health 150
  The Logic of Sense 21, 25, 35–6, 62, 107–8
  "man's nonhuman becomings" 110
  minor literature 150
  Nietzsche and Philosophy 55–6
  performative utterances 129–30
  practice of literature, aspects 46–7, 102
  praise of Artaud 34–7
  schizoanalysis 10, 21, 107
  Spinoza: Practical Philosophy 50
  A Thousand Plateaus 54
  The Time-Image 19, 153
Delmas, Achille 98–9
depressionism, age as xvi, 18
Derrida, Jacques 26, 91, 106
  divine world, realization 156
  reading of Artaud 108, 128
Desnos, Robert 83
destratification 51–3
Dissemination (Derrida) 26
The Distant Interior (Michaux) 132
"50 Drawings to Murder Magic" (Artaud) 87, 148
Dubuffet, Jean 68
Dullin, Charles 2
Dumoulié, Camille 90

enterprise of health 37–40, 109, 150
"essence of being" 153, 155
The Ethics (Spinoza) 48, 50

"faciality" 136
Ferdière, Gaston 33, 57, 68, 83–4, 87, 89, 97–8, 134–5, 163
flesh, concept 123–4, 126
  belief in the 152–5
  body and 18, 21–2, 124
  mind, and expression 30, 38–9, 57, 147
  powers of the 31–4
  vitality of 26–9, 33, 38
formalized system of signs (language) 10, 16–18, 21, 28, 31, 34, 39, 45–7, 50, 55, 57, 63, 67, 119, 129, 133, 158
Fosse, Jean-Claude 57, 98
Francis Bacon: The Logic of Sensation (Deleuze) 21–4
"Further Letter about Myself" (Artaud) 56

The Gay Science (Nietzsche) 53
Gaze, Tim 131
generative language 26, 39, 101
genuine thinking 3, 23, 56, 88, 153–4, 157–8
Gide, André 109
glossolalia 32–3, 62–3, 99, 120, 135–6, 149
God 72, 79
  Artaud's understanding of 79
  automatism of 158
  Christ (*see* Christ)
  Ciguri as (Tarahumaras) 72, 75, 88, 101, 152
  hierarchy of 80
  judgment of 22, 29, 61
  Spinoza's understanding of 49–50, 56
grammar 100–1
  belief in 53–4, 61, 64–5
  disturbing of 63
  of organized languages 60
Grossman, Évelyn 3, 27, 32, 34–5, 87–8, 120, 124
Guattari, Félix xviii, 10, 15–16, 19, 31, 49, 51–3, 78, 122, 136
  minor literature 150
  performative utterances 129–30
  schizoanalysis 10
  A Thousand Plateaus 54

healing powers of magic 87–9
healing practices of language xvi, 15, 21, 35, 47, 61, 71, 88, 113
  auto-immunization xviii, 20, 26, 37, 39, 46, 64, 101, 134, 146, 163
  commitment to life 29–31
  flexional singularity of the body 16–18, 39
  infra-sense of the body 25–6, 30, 36, 62
  powers of the flesh 31–4
  vital body, articulation 22–4
  vitality of flesh 26–9, 33, 38
healthier culture 74, 92
Heliogabalus (Artaud) 58
"Here Lies" (Artaud) 64
Hjelmslev, Louis 51, 53, 115
"The Human Face" (Artaud) 115–16

immanence, philosophy of 15. *See also* absolute immanence
impossible theater 105–6
impure language 16, 18, 29, 39, 112
intercessors xvii, xviii, 8, 19–20, 31, 39, 92, 117, 126, 148, 157, 159, 165
"The Intercessors" (Deleuze) xvii, 164–5
Isou, Isidore 33, 131

Jannarone, Kimberley 4
John, Saint 73
Jones, Andy xv–xvi, 164
Joughin, Martin xvii
Jugnon, Alain 106
Justaert, Kristien 155–7

Klossowski, Pierre 16–18, 23, 29, 112. *See also* impure language
Knapp, Bettina 99
"Knowing One's Enemy" (Dale) 79

Lacan, Jacques 70
language xvi–xvii, 100. *See also* healing practices of language
  becoming-foreign 130, 133, 150
  belief in grammar 53–4, 61, 64–5
  bodily practices of 9, 12, 126, 132
  body and (*see* body and language)
  concrete and physical 111–14
  as deprivation of life 148

effect of literature on 46
formalized system of signs 10, 16–18, 21, 28, 31, 34, 39, 45–7, 50, 55, 57, 63, 67, 119, 129, 133, 158
immanent approach 10–11
of life 108, 133, 152
ossification/stratification 59
outside of 45–7
revalorization 165
role and use of 9–10, 11–12, 16, 99–100, 111, 113, 132
of space 5, 7
Stoic vision of 111–12
theater of cruelty and 103–5
underestimation 8–9
unity and autonomy of 10
untranslatable forces 4, 56–7, 63, 148, 157
zoology of 45, 47, 54–6, 63–4, 65, 67, 70, 75, 86, 90–2, 101, 113, 115, 119, 126, 130–1, 148–9, 155, 157, 159, 165
Latrémolière, Jacques 69, 83, 90, 163
Le Clezio, Jean-Marie 71
letter(s), Artaud 58
　to Albert Camus 47–8
　to ambassador of Ireland 77
　to André Breton 78–80, 82
　to Anne Manson 78, 147
　to Arthur Adamov 62–3
　to Bettina Knapp 99
　to Gaston Ferdière 89–90
　to Génica Athanasiou 2
　to Georges Le Breton 60
　to Henri Parisot 25, 72
　to Jacques Rivière 153
　to Jean Paulhan 4, 71, 104, 106–7, 110, 113
Levine, Don Eric 64
linguistic vampirism 83
Loeb, Pierre 69
The Logic of Sense (Deleuze) 21, 25, 35–6, 62, 107–8
Lotringer, Sylvère 69, 98–9, 163

magical and materialist theosophy 88, 89–90, 91–2, 97, 101, 115, 126, 131, 134, 149, 155, 159
"Manifesto in Clear Language" (Artaud) 15, 45, 64

Manson, Anne 78, 147
materialist linguistic model 16
materiality of language xvii, 11, 15–17, 21, 30–1, 52, 54, 61–2, 78, 86, 97, 112, 119, 124, 128, 132–3, 147, 149, 157, 163, 165
Mayers, Tim 127
megalomania, sense of persecution and 81–3
Memon, Arsalan 24
"Metaphysics and the Mise en Scène" (Artaud) 112
Mexico and Civilization 88
Michaux, Henri 132
Milon, Alain 132
minor literature 150
Mort, Graham 127
myth 59
　and true story of Christ 120
Mythomania 57–60

The Natural Contract (Serres) 84, 150–2
neologisms 9–10, 58, 59, 119
The Nerve-Meter (Artaud) 3–4, 30, 62
new human agony 62–4, 65
new materialism 20
new religion 84–7, 155
The New Revelations of Being 76, 80–1
Neyrat, Frédéric 84–5, 88, 105
Nietzsche, Friedrich 32, 47, 53–4, 61, 65, 73, 111
Nietzsche and Philosophy (Deleuze) 55–6

On a Voyage to the Land of the Tarahumaras (Artaud) 72
order-word assemblages 129–30
"organic culture" 5–6, 70, 78, 104
　search of 74–5, 92
　and Western civilization 88
O'Sullivan, Simon 30
overmedicalization xvi, 3, 39, 78, 146

paganism (Pagan Truth) 79–80
Parisot, Henri 25, 72
"The Patients and the Doctors" (Artaud) 20, 31–4, 59, 149
Paulhan, Jean 4, 71, 97, 104, 106–7, 110, 113
Penot-Lacassagne, Olivier 1–2

performative writing 128–31
Perverse Desire and the Ambiguous Icon (Weiss) 72
"pharmakon" 26, 35, 46, 52–3, 61, 63, 71, 78, 92
phonemes 136, 149
Plato 26, 80
poetic creation 127
Porché, Wladimir 104
"Portraits and Drawings by Antonin Artaud" (exposition) 115
"Posthumanist Performativity" (Barad) 11
postsecular religion of language 157–9
postsecular society of immanence 155–7
Pouey, Fernand 103
practices of writing
    asemic writing 131–2
    creative writing xvii–xviii, 4, 9–10, 12, 16, 36, 38, 63–4, 97, 103, 126–8, 133–4, 137, 148
    crescive writing 103, 106, 132–4, 137, 148–9, 152, 158–9, 165
    performative writing 128–31
Prevel, Jacques 67–9, 91–2, 98, 114
Protevi, John 19

Radiodiffusion française 103
Rahimy, Tina 17
rational language 100–1
reality xv, 6
    creation of 108, 119
    ego, concept of 129
    false ideas of 5
    forces of life and 5, 7–8, 146–7
religious language 101, 105, 126, 152, 155
"rhizomatic theology" 155
Richards, Mary Caroline 113
The Rite of Peyote at the Tarahumaras (Artaud) 73
Rivière, Jacques 38, 100, 126, 153
Robert, Marthe 68, 97–8
Rogozinski, Jacob 34

Savan, David 49
Schafer, David 52, 71, 79
schizoanalysis 103, 107, 133, 137, 148–9
    Artaud's writings 10–11, 31
    of Bacon's paintings 21

sense of life, belief 85
Serres, Michel 84, 150–2
Simms, Karl 111
"Situation of the Flesh" (Artaud) 26–9, 30
The Social Contract (Rousseau) 151
social language 53
Sontag, Susan 64
Spinoza, Baruch de 15, 18, 51–2, 56, 151
    Artaud's understanding of 47–8
    confusion for 48–50, 53, 61, 65
    The Ethics 48, 50
Spinoza: Practical Philosophy (Deleuze) 50
Stoicism 34, 36–7, 39, 115
    lexis and logos 115, 131
    "signifier" and "signified" 115
Such a Deathly Desire (Klossowski) 17–18
Supplement to the Voyage to the Land of the Tarahumaras (Artaud) 73
symbiosis, contract of 151–2, 155

Tarahumaras Indians, Artaud with 4, 71–3, 78, 90, 110
Taylor, Charles 156
the 'Taylorian' dualism 156
"The Theater and Culture" (Artaud) 85
The Theater And Its Double (Artaud) 110
"The Theater and the Gods" (Artaud) 1, 4, 74
theater of cruelty 4, 6, 12, 25, 69, 78, 90, 103, 106, 114, 124–7, 133, 147
    as healing practice 109–11
    and language 103–5, 112–13
    manifestation 108
    purpose of 147
"The Theater of Cruelty" (Artaud) 107, 117, 145
theater of impiety 114–15
theosophy 70, 83
    magical and materialist 88, 89–90, 91–2, 97, 101, 115, 126, 131, 134, 149, 155, 159
    zoological 75
Thévenin, Paule 97–9, 103–4, 134–5
    impossible theater 105–6
Thomas, Colette 68, 97, 103
Thomas, Henri 68, 98
A Thousand Plateaus (Deleuze and Guattari) 54

The Time-Image (Deleuze) 19, 153
Timaeus (Plato) 80
To Have Done with the Judgment of God (Artaud) 22, 79, 85, 104–6, 107, 114, 149
Tomiche, Anne 99, 102, 109, 119, 130
torsion 25
true ideas 48, 50
"true nature of evil" 2, 8, 20, 34, 38, 50, 71, 91, 101, 109, 119, 133, 147, 153
The True Story of Jesus Christ 120–3, 125
Tuin, Iris van der 129
Twilight of the Idols (Nietzsche) 53

Übermensch (Nietzsche) 32, 73, 77–8

vacuoles 25–6, 29–30, 35, 39, 119
Van Gogh, the Man Suicided by Society (Artaud) 47–8
violent loss of life 3–8
Virmaux, Alain 106
"The Voice of the Poets" 103

Weiss, Allen 72, 75
works/writings (Artaud)
  "Alienation and Black Magic" 149
  Anglo-Saxon literature, negligence xv, 8, 52, 69
  "50 Drawings to Murder Magic" 87, 148
  forces of life 12, 132
  "Further Letter about Myself" 56
  To Have Done with the Judgment of God 22, 79, 85, 104–6, 107, 114, 149
  Heliogabalus 58
  "Here Lies" 64
  "The Human Face" 115–16
  language (*see* language)
  letters (*see* letter(s), Artaud)
  "Manifesto in Clear Language" 15, 45, 64
  "Metaphysics and the Mise en Scène" 112
  mexican discoveries, expressing 75–7
  mystical and religious tone 70, 77
  The Nerve-Meter 3–4, 30, 62
  "The Patients and the Doctors" 20, 31–4, 59, 149
  responses 69–70
  revaluation 11–12, 39
  The Rite of Peyote at the Tarahumaras 73
  schizoanalysis 10–11, 31
  "Situation of the Flesh" 26–9, 30
  Supplement to the Voyage to the Land of the Tarahumaras 73
  "The Theater and Culture" 85
  The Theater And Its Double 110
  "The Theater and the Gods" 1, 4, 74
  "The Theater of Cruelty" 107, 117, 145
  Van Gogh, the Man Suicided by Society 47–8
  On a Voyage to the Land of the Tarahumaras 72
writing of cruelty 106
  laboratory of life 123–6
  mechanized to machinic anatomy 114–19
  "The True Story of Jesus Christ" 120–3
The Writing of the Disaster (Blanchot) 57
writing practices. *see* practices of writing

Yadin, Azzan 53

zoe 72, 75–6, 83, 103, 126, 133, 136, 147–8, 151–2, 154–6
  forces of 50, 61, 129
  generative power of 75
  theology of 131–2, 134, 159
  vitality of 83, 113, 130
zoological language 45, 47, 54–6, 63–4, 65, 67, 70, 75, 86, 90–2, 101, 113, 115, 119, 126, 130–1, 148–9, 155, 157, 159, 165